PUBLIC MANAGEMENT
OCCASIONAL PAPERS

1994 No. 6

NEW WAYS OF MANAGING
INFRASTRUCTURE PROVISION

MARKET-TYPE MECHANISMS SERIES N° 8

ORGANISATION FOR ECONOMIC CO-OPERATION AND DEVELOPMENT

Paris 1994

ORGANISATION FOR ECONOMIC CO-OPERATION AND DEVELOPMENT

Pursuant to Article 1 of the Convention signed in Paris on 14th December 1960, and which came into force on 30th September 1961, the Organisation for Economic Co-operation and Development (OECD) shall promote policies designed:

— to achieve the highest sustainable economic growth and employment and a rising standard of living in Member countries, while maintaining financial stability, and thus to contribute to the development of the world economy;

— to contribute to sound economic expansion in Member as well as non-member countries in the process of economic development; and

— to contribute to the expansion of world trade on a multilateral, non-discriminatory basis in accordance with international obligations.

The original Member countries of the OECD are Austria, Belgium, Canada, Denmark, France, Germany, Greece, Iceland, Ireland, Italy, Luxembourg, the Netherlands, Norway, Portugal, Spain, Sweden, Switzerland, Turkey, the United Kingdom and the United States. The following countries became Members subsequently through accession at the dates indicated hereafter: Japan (28th April 1964), Finland (28th January 1969), Australia (7th June 1971), New Zealand (29th May 1973) and Mexico (18th May 1994). The Commission of the European Communities takes part in the work of the OECD (Article 13 of the OECD Convention).

Publié en français sous le titre :
NOUVELLE GESTION
DE LA MISE EN PLACE DES INFRASTRUCTURES

© OECD 1994
Applications for permission to reproduce or translate all or part
of this publication should be made to:
Head of Publications Service, OECD
2, rue André-Pascal, 75775 PARIS CEDEX 16, France

FOREWORD

OECD countries, on average, devote nearly one-fifth of capital formation to infrastructure. The mechanisms established to decide on the aggregate level of infrastructure spending and to select individual projects, as well as the ways in which those decisions are implemented and managed, can have important implications for the quality of infrastructure spending. Faced with enduring tight fiscal constraints, strong demands for infrastructure extension and renewal, and ongoing pressure to improve public sector efficiency and cost effectiveness, the efficacy of conventional methods for the allocation and management of infrastructure spending are increasingly being questioned. A number of OECD countries are exploring possibilities for the more extensive use of the private sector and the discipline of markets in deciding whether and how to meet perceived infrastructure needs.

Private sector involvement in infrastructure provision is not new. Historically, most governments have contracted out the design and construction of major infrastructure projects to the private sector. What is different in the experiments currently underway is an attempt to engage the private sector in partnership with the public sector from the ground up and throughout the life of projects involving, to various degrees across sectors, the identification, design, finance, construction and operation of public infrastructure projects.

This Occasional Paper presents the results of eight separate sectoral studies drawn form the experiences of five OECD countries -- Australia, France, Germany, the United Kingdom, and the United States -- where experiments are underway or in prospect to provide public infrastructure by way of partnership arrangements with the private sector. The studies were undertaken under the guidance of Senior Budget Officials from OECD countries as part of the OECD Public Management Committee's ongoing analysis of the use of market-type mechanisms in the public sector. The results of PUMA's other work in this field are contained in the Market-type Mechanisms Series of Public Management Occasional Papers and in the publication *Managing with Market-type Mechanisms*, published in 1993.

The report is in two parts. Part I, prepared by Terry Wall and François Lacasse of the Public Management Service, consists of a synthesis of the main features and lessons emerging from the country studies of recent joint partnership approaches to infrastructure provision. Specific emphasis is placed on issues concerning both technological and economic risk, and the potential for equitable risk sharing between the public and private sectors. The public sector's responsibility for skilful bid preparation and well-prepared tender and project selection procedures is highlighted, as is its responsibility to ensure adequate in-house skills in contract evaluation and project management. These prerequisites are considered as crucial ingredients if potential efficiency gains accruing form any joint partnership arrangement are to be realised. The conditions necessary to ensure competitive behaviour on the part of the private sector are also discussed.

Part II contains the eight individual sectoral and country reports which formed the basis of the study. The paper prepared by Dale Raneberg reports on recent innovations in the provision of transport, prison and water treatment infrastructure in the Australian State of New South Wales.

Patricia Vornetti outlines the French experience of public/private partnerships in the construction and operation of tolled motorways. Sylvie Trosa and Martin Schreiner report on recent trends and current deliberations in Germany underlying considerations for more widespread use of private finance for public infrastructure investment. John Moore and Harry Havens present comprehensive overviews of the current status of private funding for roads and prisons in the United Kingdom and the United States. In addition, Mr. Havens contributes an extensive analysis of risk sharing and management in the area of military procurement, offering valuable insights for risk management in joint public/private undertakings in general.

The report is published on the responsibility of the Secretary General of the OECD. The views expressed are those of the authors and do not commit or necessarily reflect those of governments of OECD Member countries.

CONTENTS

Part I

Chapter One
**Public/private partnerships in infrastructure provision:
main issues and conclusions**
by François Lacasse and Terry Wall 7

Part II

Chapter Two
**Innovations in the public-private provision of infrastructure
in the Australian State of New South Wales**
by Dale Raneberg 27

Chapter Three
**The French experience of partnership between the public and private sector
in the construction and operation of motorways: Theory and practice**
by Patricia Vornetti 55

Chapter Four
Private financing of public infrastructure in Germany
by Sylvie Trosa and Martin Schreiner 73

Chapter Five
Private funding of prison operations in the United Kingdom
by John Moore 89

Chapter Six
Private funding for roads in the United Kingdom
by John Moore 111

Chapter Seven
**Private sector ownership and operation of prisons:
An overview of United States experience**
by Harry S. Havens 135

Chapter Eight

**Public and private sector roles in the construction of highways:
An overview of the United States experience**
by Harry S. Havens 153

Chapter Nine
**Sharing and managing risk in the acquisition of major weapons
systems from privately owned industrial firms:
An overview of United States experience**
by Harry S. Havens 169

Chapter One

**PUBLIC/PRIVATE PARTNERSHIPS IN INFRASTRUCTURE PROVISION:
MAIN ISSUES AND CONCLUSIONS**

by

François Lacasse and Terry Wall
OECD Public Management Service

INTRODUCTION

The involvement of the private sector in the provision of public infrastructure is not new. Governments rarely rely solely on the resources of the public sector for major infrastructure projects, but have generally tended to contract out design and construction to the private sector. This has been the case for all countries represented in this study and for all sectors.

In a "conventional" public sector project, a government decides what it wants to provide. In the case of a capital project, a government department or agency may use private sector designers and other specialists (architects, consulting engineers, quantity surveyors, etc.) to a greater or lesser extent in preparing schemes, and it is up to the commissioning department to ensure that the design takes proper account of, for example, ease of future maintenance. Governments use contractors and other suppliers (perhaps to a greater extent than they buy in design services) to construct the road, hospital office block or other structure. Forms of contract can be devised which specify in detail the nature and quality standards of the work; and terms of payment which may include penalties imposed on the contractor for time or cost overruns, to approximate the incentives that would have applied were the contractor the entrepreneur. The government finances the project and, once built, operates and maintains the asset.

What is new in the experiments currently underway is an attempt to involve the private sector more comprehensively in projects by way of partnerships or more complex forms of contracting. Private sector involvement in infrastructure provision is being explored from the ground up and throughout the life of projects involving, to varying degrees across sectors, the identification, design, finance, construction and operation/management of public projects.

This chapter identifies the main issues and conclusions arising out of the Secretariat's examination of country experience and innovations in the joint public/private provision of infrastructure. This chapter first suggests a framework for classifying the possible combinations of public/private involvement in infrastructure provision and discusses the rationale underlying developments. It then discusses the issues and conclusions arising from the programme of studies under the following broad headings:

- risk-sharing between the public and private sectors;
- economies and efficiencies from private participation;
- bid preparation and project selection;
- skills in contract evaluation and management;
- ensuring competitive disciplines; and,
- giving commitment to and gaining acceptance for arrangements.

THE PUBLIC/PRIVATE INTERFACE

The interface between public and private provision of infrastructure can be set out systematically according to the "essential" elements of any project: identifying the need; designing how to meet it; finance; construction; and operation/management.

Table 1. **The Public/Private Interface**

G signifies Government activity
PR signifies Private Sector activity

	Identify need	Design	Construct	Fund	Operate
1. Conventionally financed project	G/PR	PR	G	G	G
2. Leasing, etc. by government	PR	PR	PR	G	G
3. Private sector provides and operates asset	G/PR	PR	PR	PR	G
4. Private operation of government installation	G/PR	G/PR	G	PR	G
5. Private sector provision	PR	PR	PR	PR	PR

Additionally, for items 2 through 5 above, a further column could be added to reflect transfer of ownership of the infrastructure back to the government at some future period, which is a common feature of these arrangements.

In terms of the country experiences reflected in this study virtually all possible combinations are being experimented with. The US experience with defence procurement is an example of the conventionally financed project; German innovations in both road transport and waste water treatment include, in addition to other forms of delegated management, the exploration of leasing. By far the most common model being investigated and applied involves private sector provision and operation as, for instance, reflected in the Australian examples, and in the provision of new prisons and motorways in the United Kingdom. The UK market testing initiative, as applied to public prisons, provides an example of a strategy to introduce competition into the provision of existing services by making possible the private operation of existing government installations. Similarly, the United Kingdom is the only country reflected in the study which has formerly introduced arrangement -- the Private Finance Initiative -- which, as part of a policy designed to bring the private sector into the provision of services and facilities, encourages the private sector to participate in identifying the need for infrastructure and submitting proposals accordingly.

RATIONALE FOR MORE EXTENSIVE PRIVATE INVOLVEMENT

Proposals to extend "conventional" methods for the provision of infrastructure to encompass the use of private finance and/or management to provide services customarily provided by the State are prompted by two main motives:

-- to find ways to accommodate pent-up and/or emerging infrastructure needs within tight and continuing fiscal constraints;

-- to improve productive, dynamic and allocative efficiency in determining and meeting infrastructure needs and improving the cost effectiveness of resulting service provision.

The first seems to be an important concern in Germany where the magnitude of the costs involved in rejuvenating infrastructure in the east following re-unification cannot be met through the public budget. Similarly, in the United States, debt and tax limitations at the state and local government level which have sought to constrain the size of government by limiting government revenues, have severely restricted the ability of governments to undertake infrastructure expansion both for prisons and for additional highway capacity. While in Australia ongoing budgetary restraint forced at the federal level through, *inter alia*, limits on states' borrowing capacities have encouraged an examination of the scope for private solutions to public infrastructure needs.

Perhaps of greater significance in the willingness or desire of governments to consider a wider role for the private sector in infrastructure provision has been the vigorous climate for reform in the management of government itself, in part driven by the need for fiscal restraint. Such reforms have focused on achieving an optimal allocation of scarce public sector resources, greater efficiency and cost effectiveness in the delivery of public programmes, better service and accountability for performance in terms of results. A key strategy in this process has been to introduce, where possible and appropriate, a greater reliance on competitive market disciplines in determining the nature, extent and manner of service provision. In this sense the search for models to encourage the greater involvement of the private sector in infrastructure provision can be seen as a subset of wider developments to improve the efficiency and outcome performance of the public sector and resource allocation in the economy as a whole.

While debate continues over the question of whether or not infrastructure spending has borne a disproportionate share of the burden of budget restraint over the last decade, it is clear that infrastructure spending is significant with estimates that OECD economies are, on average, devoting nearly a fifth of capital formation to infrastructure. Against this background, it is to be expected that issues of efficiency and value for money in infrastructure provision should be of concern. Simply to expand infrastructure in ways that respond to the strongest pressures is not efficient. In this context, the conventional approach to the provision and management of infrastructure are characterised by two related problems: governance structures which shield suppliers of infrastructure services from the disciplines of competition , and hence reduce the pressure to innovate and cut costs; and, prices which do not adequately reflect costs, and which therefore give rise to distorted consumption and investment decisions.

Virtually all countries cite explicitly anticipated gains in productive allocative and dynamic efficiency arising from the introduction of private finance and management in the provision of infrastructure as a major reason justifying its adoption. Private sector involvement is seen to bring a greater ability and willingness to monitor performance via governance structures with simpler, clearer and more efficiency oriented objectives than those which characterise public ownership and provision, and with effective means to assess the extent to which those objectives are being met. These derive where a core group of owners exercise fairly close control, equity is widely traded leading to the diffusion of information about private firms in equity markets. Private sector involvement also shifts the risk associated with firms' performance away from taxpayers as a whole. Ideally risks should fall on those best placed to bear them (equity owners) who can insure against risk by both monitoring performance and diversifying their portfolio. How far this transfer of risk actually takes place depends to a significant extent on the associated regulatory and oversight mechanisms put in place with respect to individual projects. These are discussed more fully below.

Additionally, (notably in the case of transport infrastructure, but also in the case of water treatment and other instances where elements of user charging apply) failure to charge users of infrastructure full costs reduces efficiency by artificially increasing infrastructure demand and skewing investment decisions. Putting infrastructure prices on to a more rational basis such that prices more closely reflect costs is seen as potentially effective in shifting demand onto a basis which better reflects consumers' value of the services. Using road transport as an example, evidence suggests that traditional forms of charging for road use through fuel and vehicle taxes -- which raise revenues on the basis of average cost of usage rather than the marginal system costs (i.e. congestion, wear and tear and pollution) which the user's transport decision gives rise to -- generates excess demands on the transport system and concomitant demands for greater investment in roads (OECD, 1994, Annex 3, pp. 121-124).

Greater recourse to pricing on a commercial basis is seen to provide benefits in a number of areas. Bringing prices into line with costs may trim investment programmes, and raise the rate of return on investment, as consumers who valued the resources they had previously consumed at less than the cost of providing them shifted their consumption to other goods and services, and increases in capacity for which proven willingness to pay could not be established were therefore no longer made.

The experiences reflected in the many country studies accompanying this report are of relatively recent origin. Countries are only beginning to experiment with alternative ways of organising and managing infrastructure provision with greater involvement of the private sector and it will require a greater passage of time before a full assessment of the value of these arrangements is possible. Nevertheless some modest early successes are evident across countries. Two take a couple of examples, the Raneberg paper notes that in Australia, the technical innovations contained in private sector proposals for construction of the Sydney Harbour Tunnel overcame concerns over location and the environmental impact which had stalled the proposal. Efficiencies have been achieved from private sector involvement in the design, construction and operation of the Junee Prison. Moore notes that in the United Kingdom the private Thames bridge crossing at Dartford has alleviated congestion on the existing crossing with only minor costs on the public purse and involving relatively short time scales. Market testing of all aspects of the management of existing prisons in the United Kingdom is leading to reductions in costs and improvements in service delivery, even where contracts are awarded to the in-house management team.

Yet the clear message to emerge from a consideration of these and other projects, whether they be examples of success or cases where the anticipated benefits from wider private sector involvement have failed to match expectations, is that simply obtaining private equity is not a sufficient condition to ensure potential efficiency gains are optimised or achieved. Rather, success depends crucially on the involvement of government particularly with respect to the quality of the procedures established to attract and manage private sector participation and in bearing some of the risks associated with projects.

RISK-SHARING BETWEEN THE PRIVATE AND THE PUBLIC SECTOR

Innovations contemplated or implemented in the joint public-private provision of infrastructures (JPPPI) are partly aimed at having the private sector share the risks involved in infrastructure investments. While this intent seems widespread, country experience suggests that the issue of risk-sharing has rarely been specified in detail, and that some confusion remains. The issues related to risk-sharing in joint investments focus on three questions:

1. Which risks are present and are the target of innovations in the field of joint projects?

2. How do possibilities and techniques for risk sharing differ according to the types of risks involved?

3. What principles do and should govern risk sharing between the private and public sector, given the comparative advantages of each partner?

Adapting the traditional categorizations of risks incurred in transactions or joint endeavours to the specific case of joint infrastructures provision leads to the identification of three types of risk: moral hazard, technological risks, economic risks.

Moral hazard

This is the most well known category of risks and the one about which a long tradition of public administration has devised quite strong systems to eliminate or reduce it. Moral hazard refers to the possibility that one party, such as the private sector supplier of infrastructure, may be tempted not to fully carry out their contractual obligations. An abundant literature has shown that this type of risk increases with the complexity of contracts; lack of clarity in defining the outputs to be supplied and the respective obligations of the parties; the costs of detecting non-performance; the absence of effective sanctions; and, the weaknesses in or costs of mechanisms for mediation and enforcement.

Notwithstanding the burgeoning literature of recent years in this field, efforts to address this type of risks have for a long time been prominent features of laws, regulations and procedures framing transactions between the private and public sector. For instance, exacting specifications for products purchased from the private sector have been a familiar feature of governments' procurement systems. The same can be said about rigid competitive tendering procedures and the alertness of systems to the possibilities of collusion. Finally, the well developed auditing functions within the public sector have aimed at, and have generally achieved, a high degree of integrity in operating systems within government and in transactions between government and the private sector.

This suggests that control of moral hazard in traditional transactions with the private sector has been achieved in most situations. Consequently, the questions raised by the JPPPI are restricted to assessing whether and to what extent recent innovations differ from more traditional procurement arrangements.

In the cases of roads, bridges, tunnels, etc., the present system is based on government owned and operated facilities with most of the design, building and heavy maintenance let out to private contractors. Going a few steps further and having the individual facilities financed, owned and operated by the private sector does not appear to change much in terms of the moral risks involved: controls over design and implementation remain essentially in the hands of the public sector; major disasters (toxic spills for instance) will inevitably remain a risk to be borne by the only party big enough to self-insure (i.e. government); and, such risks are probably only very tenuously, if at all, linked to regulated roads' owners performance. In these circumstances the only possibility for the government to reduce moral risk may lie in ensuring construction and operation of infrastructure are vested with the same company. Gains from such arrangements are said to flow from incentives placed on the private entrepreneur to optimize the overall investment, i.e. build in such a way as to minimize the joint building and operating costs. However, with well known technology and decades of outside procurement by governments in this field, this advantage in reality is probably likely to be small.

The same limited advantage vis-à-vis moral risk seems equally to apply in the case of private prisons, albeit for different reasons. Taking the traditional situation as a benchmark, the main moral risks identified with respect to prisons do not relate to adherence to design specifications or training of private prison staff (i.e. the inputs which again are subjected to tight regulations). Rather the perceived risks arise from possible inadequate care for inmates and perverse incentives for private owners to seek the easiest-to-manage prisoners. In both cases these risks are likely already to exist in the public sector. Moreover, the government will continue to bear the burden of redress if, on these scores, the private sector does not perform. With present information, it is simply impossible to know if any reduction in this type of risk has occurred for the government.

Technological risks

This risk refers to situations where uncertainty (e.g. as to technical feasibility) is inherent in the activity, difficult to assess beforehand, and difficult to insure against. The paper on US weapons systems procurement (Chapter Nine) attempts to draw some lessons in matters of public-private sharing of technological risks. It describes experience in the largest weapons procurement system based on quasi-total reliance on private suppliers. This situation is extreme in terms of the levels of risks incurred: for instance, many weapons systems developed may never see the light of day. Decades of trying different techniques and different systems, of having operations scrutinised by evaluators and auditors have meant that the whole set of relations between the private and the public sector have been "reformed" a number of times. In these attempts, improved risk sharing was a prominent target.

The results are meagre in terms of techniques which can be expanded to other areas. The lessons are exceedingly simple: when very large technological risks are present (e.g. a failure of *one* weapon system might bankrupt a major supplier) the partner in the transaction which is most able to diversify and bear risks, does. This has meant that the State has essentially born the risks.

The arrangements which are available to the private sector -- such as cross ownership of shares and other means to spread this type of risk -- are not available to public-private dealings. This has meant that the most efficient solutions to joint undertakings in such matters has been some form or other of long-term partnership between the public and private sector, where it has been in the interest of both parties to minimize the moral risk which could be associated with the technological one. For large investments however, this has meant a reduction in competition over the years.

These observations, even though they were deliberately drawn from a case where technological risks were maximum, seem to fit other situations observed on the more mundane level of roads, systems development in informatics and prisons. The French experience with joint road provisions (Chapter Three) has seen the government compensate owners who become the victim of circumstances like the oil shocks. Road, tunnel and bridge contracts drawn or planned in the United Kingdom or Australia leave to the government the obligation to meet the additional costs of unforeseen soil conditions or accidents involving large quantities of toxic pollutants. Analogously, major incidents (riots) at private prisons are routinely assumed to involve government interventions. It seems also to be assumed that as the state is the only supplier of inmates, some guarantees have to be offered against possible changes in sentencing practices or political shifts which would change the basic environment assumed in the contract. The same can be observed in roads with respect to changes in petrol tax or other important policy shifts. These dispositions confirm those that have been observed in other fields such contracting-out of systems development or contracts for pipelines (OECD, 1992).

All in all, the JPPPI in roads and prisons does not offer promises for substantial shifting of this type of risk to the private sector, nor does it offer necessarily an avenue of global reduction in risks over existing procedures in planning and assessing technical conditions. However, it may be that, as in the case of informatics contracting-out, the very necessity of providing for risky occurrences in formal contracts acts as an impetus for more careful planning and assessment of technological risks.

Economic risks

This is the field where it seems that most of the expectations for risk reduction on the part of the state have been concentrated. The rationale for JPPPI from this angle appears to be that, if private firms are willing to shoulder part of the risks involved not only will the state be better protected but also the total risk to the economy as a result of poor investment decision making may be reduced. The conditions for this outcome to materialise are quite clear in principle, but subject to important qualifications in practice.

The commercial risks involved are quite well known: for a road or bridge, they amount to the possibility for error in traffic forecasts and/or in the elasticity of demand of motorists to the level or structure of tolls levied. The reasoning also extends to the case of shadow tolling since the private partner continues to bear the consequences of inaccurate forecasting or assessment of "needs".

Commercial risks arising from bad estimation of the cost of construction or maintenance do not seem to play a substantial role; they may however be more important in the case of prisons. There, the very fact that private prisons are an institutional novelty entails risks that costs are underestimated either because of misjudgments about the quality or quantity of resources needed, or simply because economies of scale are not yet available to private owners and operators. The provision for public assistance in the case of major incidents mentioned above can be interpreted in that light; the same applies, in part, for the United Kingdom government's plans to ensure a substantial minimum size for the private sector in prison ownership and operation.

Risk sharing and overall risk reduction will occur if market disciplines are used in the selection of infrastructures projects and if there are no implicit or explicit governmental guarantees to private investors. Going private in roads will reduce risks to government essentially by ensuring that only those projects which are economically justified will be realised and that the government will not compensate private investors when they misjudge demand and overinvest.

These propositions are perfectly congruent with those arrived at in the earlier section of this paper, chiefly on the necessity for pricing and demand led results if the advantages of JPPPI are to be realised. On the risk side however, these propositions need to be qualified.

First, where a free of charge network already exists (the situation in virtually all cases) the capability of investors, be they private or public, to estimate the returns to a specific (tolled) addition to the network raises substantial difficulties whose resolution might have to await the development of system-wide pricing. This situation may explain why, in the Australian and British cases (Chapters Two and Six), it has been much easier to get serious proposals from the private sector for bridges and tunnels i.e. for investments where these network effects are minimal and where traffic forecasts and the capacity to charge are much easier.

Second, the advantages of commercial risk sharing from the point of view of *total* public expenditures will occur only if the privately authorised projects do not come as net additions to roads construction which would have taken place in their absence. Were this to be the case, it would result in the public sector simply contracting out the economically justified projects while investing greater of its own resources on those which were not. This special kind of "cream skimming" on the risk side converges with the concerns voiced in some country studies that ear-marking of road charges for additional spending on roads should not be used as a means of insulating expenditures from restrictions imposed on public finances and the economy generally. Whether or not this condition of non-additionality is actually met is very difficult to ascertain in practice, as is usually the case with additionality questions in fields such as grants to industry or agriculture.

Third, if investments are of sufficient magnitude or occur in sensitive areas, questions of externality cannot be ignored. This is particularly the case for example where projects run up against environmental concerns. In terms of the examples described in the background papers, these seem best handled through the establishment, in advance, of appropriate consultative procedures whose results are integrated into final project specifications. However, where externalities concern road congestion, and insofar as charging takes place under minimal restrictions and alternative routes exist, a market solution to congestion is provided. This is a key rationale for research into and investment in ways to introduce charges which would vary according to usage of road networks.

Fourth, implicit guarantees are notoriously difficult to identify and control, depending -- as they do in other sectors such as public enterprises, banking, fisheries etc. -- on specific national circumstances and attitudes. Of course, if such guarantees do exist, the very notion of risk sharing becomes rather meaningless and only the appearance of the system will change.

Conclusions on risk sharing

No important advantages over the present situation seems likely to arise from JPPPI concerning moral or technological risks, unless through indirect means whereby contracting out places increased pressure on administrations to better plan, specify and control infrastructure investments.

The key possibilities for risk sharing occur with respect to economic risks, when private suppliers are able and willing to undertake some risks. However, the size of advantages thereby accruing to the public sector depends on whether the market disciplines introduced are allowed to influence the total quantity and priorities of investments, i.e. if JPPPI is used as a tool to ensure that the projects undertaken are the economically justified ones and if commercial risk sharing or shifting leads to an increase in the quality of investment choices by the public sector. This would involve a clearer trade-off between political and economic justifications in this field.

There are good reasons to believe that JPPPI can make such a contribution. They can do so even for projects which may be uneconomic but socially justified. For instance, a joint private-public undertaking where part of the project is commercially justified while another is not can serve the aims of increasing efficiency of investment choice by forcing a clear identification of what is economically justified and what is not. The conditions that private sector bidders would then require in terms of government financial participation provide good benchmarks in separating the two parts of the projects if a modicum of real competition can be achieved.

These very real potential advantages amount to economic counter-veils to temptations on the part of governments to indulge in infrastructure spending which are not justified on the demand side, have a low rate of return from the point of view of the overall economy, or which exhibit commercial risks beyond what the private sector would be willing to incur. As seen above, the conditions for these advantages to materialise are rather demanding. The main vehicle to secure the full benefits from private sector involvement in the provision of infrastructures could be the added transparency in decision making that the search for risk sharing imposes on the public sector in terms of the costs and benefits of projects, and as to who pays and who benefits.

ECONOMIES AND EFFICIENCIES FROM PRIVATE PARTICIPATION

From this overall perspective the JPPPI, as with many other market type mechanisms, offers some very interesting potential benefits, but virtually none of them can be considered an automatic consequence of the increased involvement of the private sector in the provision of infrastructures. To secure them requires efforts, rigour and innovations on the part of the public sector, as well accepting that implementing JPPPI requires time, patience and risks taking. As with all other substantial changes in public management, the transition is most realistically seen as an investment. One important factor will be the extent to which arguments in favour of JPPPI on the grounds of economic efficiency can counter resistance to change traditional procurement practices

The main parameters of possible gains in efficiency thrown up by our examination of the question and the limited experience to date can be summarised as follows.

Gains in efficiency in running prisons or managing roads are probable. They can be established only by rather difficult empirical studies. This is probably best exemplified by the data comparability problems which arose in trying to assess the cost savings associated with private prisons in the United States and the fact that little comparative costs data has emerged from the roads experiences which could be documented. Nevertheless, fragmentary evidence points to modest savings. It should be noted however that, given existing and newly devised controls, it is difficult to imagine that increased private sector involvement could lead to higher costs unless the moral risks questions are not dealt with in the traditional manner. The gains under present circumstances are however limited by the fact that, certainly in roads and probably in prisons, the base case (i.e. the traditional methods of procurement), already ensure most of the savings associated with competition are captured.

The efficiency gains to be derived from innovation in private sector design and operation remain largely speculative at this point, although some indication of these benefits can be read into the

US and UK prisons experiences and Australian roads experience, where some latitude was left to private entrepreneurs on this score.

The use of JPPPI in order to circumvent rules and regulations (or even constitutional provisions as in some US states) and thereby to reduce delays in design, financing and construction raise some thorny questions. The efficiency gains that might theoretically be available simply from changes in existing regulations could very well be greater than pursuing JPPPI. For instance in the German cases of pre-financing and leasing, such a solution may economise on the additional financing costs which private sector projects must bear. However, if such changes are not really feasible, the political/regulatory environment should be considered as given and the savings from JPPPI as genuine.

Before being able to draw such conclusions, however, gains need to meet three conditions. First, the gains obtained by cutting through red-tape must not compromise processes designed to ensure honesty and integrity in public/private dealings. Second, the rules circumvented must only reflect the consequences of the sheer size and complexity of the public sector. In this case, if it is possible to escape from these rigidities in a particular sector, the gains are real. Finally the gains will be real where JPPPI is used not as a means to circumvent the budget but as a way of compensating for its technical imperfections. For instance if JPPPI arrangements were to act as a proxy for accrual accounting (by allocating project costs across more evenly across the life of the assets created), it would compensate for the shortcomings of present public accounting conventions which treat investments as current expenditures on a cash basis similar to current expenditures and which, as a result, create psychological barriers to investment spending.

However, in the absence of accrual accounting arrangements it may be difficult to distinguish between those arrangements which seek to allocate costs more realistically to accounting periods and those which simply seek to insulate a particular sector from budgetary restrictions via resort to off-budget financing. One possible way of dealing with this very genuine problem (which may undermine the legitimacy of JPPPI and impede access to its potential advantages) could be to treat all joint projects within the budget process as if they were public sector projects by controlling aggregate spending through either notionally counting project costs as part of public spending totals, or establishing aggregate borrowing limits for JPPPI projects as a whole. Thus the issue of democratic and political control of the budgetary process could be tackled, and the inclinations to use private finance to expand off-budget financing could be contained. Alternatively, long range planning of transportation networks and other infrastructures, as debated in and approved by Parliament in some countries may provide adequate safeguards against the use of JPPPI to weaken the budget process.

From the standpoint of its contribution to economic growth, the key potential of JPPPI rests with its possible role in improving and rationalising investment choices. This is where large sums are probably at stake. However, realising this potential calls for other conditions to be realised. The experience to date does not support any firm judgement on whether or not JPPPI can really be used in this fashion and to what extent. These conditions were examined above, in a nutshell they are:

a) substantial increase in user charging which in turn necessitate technical innovations;

b) no perverse use of JPPPI simply to circumvent budget discipline and/or "cream-skim" economically justified projects out of the public sector as a way of increasing total resources allotted to the sector;

c) stimulating better quality infrastructure investments by allowing market disciplines to influence which projects are carried out, or by a better rationing of public funds in infrastructures via the increased transparency facilitated by JPPPI projects. This in turn makes substantial savings contingent upon the use of JPPPI on a much wider scale than appears to have occurred to date.

BID PREPARATION AND PROJECT SELECTION

Problems observed in public sector procedures have the potential to undercut potential efficiency gains from JPPPI if not addressed. The basis of project selection and procedures developed in the public sector for the management of bid preparation and the tender process seem relatively poorly developed at this stage.

On one score, various legislative and procedural limitations in existence in countries (e.g. limitations on States borrowing capacity in Australia and the United States; requirements for consultation and agreement by the German Lander for certain wholly public projects) while encouraging the pursuit of alternative private sector solutions may result in situations where the *de facto* priority for projects becomes the availability of funding rather than the fundamental need for the infrastructure or the economic attractiveness of the project. Ideally decisions on the nature and extent of private participation should be based on an objective assessment of the relative costs and benefits of private versus public provision, including the additional transaction costs incurred in managing private involvement. Yet there appears to be surprisingly little *ex ante* cost benefit analysis being undertaken which clearly demonstrate anticipated gains.

Government has an important role to play through improving and facilitating statutory and administrative arrangements, particularly in ensuring complete preparation for bids and tender processes. Lack of preparation can lead to significant delay, major changes to specifications, and in some cases can lead to abandonment of projects. The private sector may thus be exposed to significant risks, including excessive planning costs which add to overall project costs (and thus reduce potential efficiency gains) and may even result in project failure. Delays in obtaining planning approval and in fulfilling necessary public consultation requirements have been a source of delay in effecting new motorway developments in the United Kingdom resulting in new legislation and rules for public enquiries aimed at speeding up the planning and approval process. Similar issues are cited in the study of Australian experiences. They reflect a growing acceptance of the need for governments to where possible undertake all necessary preliminary work, including bearing relevant costs, prior to calling for bids.

In a similar vein to the above, governments also need to guard against seeking bids for which technical feasibility has not been established. Bidding is expensive and serious bidders will only commit themselves if schemes are viable and the risks reasonable. While it may seem desirable or efficient from the governments perspective to avoid detailed specification in order to keep open options which the private sector may propose, such arrangements run the risk of adding to eventual project costs as a result of the private sector demanding greater returns in accordance with the additional risks they must bear; may result in projects which do not accord with real needs; or, may indeed alienate or dissuade private sector bidders from participating, calling into question the overall strategy for private involvement which further add to delays and increase costs.

Nevertheless a delicate balance must be sought. Preparation should be complete without being overly prescriptive. The purpose of preparation is to reduce risk but it will be most efficient if project specifications leave latitude for innovation. Too narrow a brief may reduce the efficiency gains anticipated from private sector innovation. The approach recommended by the New South Wales Roads and Traffic Authority in Australia probably best sums up the approach required:

> *...the technical description of the project needs to be sufficiently detailed to leave no doubt as to the objectives of the project so that the innovations which will be embodied in responses are within an envelope of government expectations. Similarly, technical specifications should be of the performance type and not prescriptive. It is often in the delivery of a conforming product that consortia are able to bring real efficiencies, make savings and achieve the commercial viability of the project.*

(Public Accounts Committee, 1993, p. 78)

SKILLS IN CONTRACT EVALUATION AND PROJECT MANAGEMENT

Consistent with findings of earlier Secretariat work on complex contracting out in information technology, it is also the case that to the extent that skill deficiencies and lack of experience exist in the public sector in relation to JPPPI this will limit the extent to which allocative efficiency gains may be achieved from private sector involvement. Given the considerable experience gained in the public sector in managing conventional construction projects involving the specification and subsequent conservative application and monitoring of proven technologies under contract to the private sector, it should be the case that a core set of skills already exist within the public sector. However the wider role envisaged for the private sector in developing more complex proposals involving project finance, operation/management and innovation require additional skills in the public sector to identify appropriate opportunities for private sector involvement, to identify marginal advantages between proposals, as well as developing skills in financial matters such as project analysis, finance structuring and risk analysis.

Independent enquiry in Australia into infrastructure management and financing in New South Wales identified skill deficiencies and lack of experience in complex contracting with the private sector as a significant reason why some projects had languished and why others which had been identified as suitable for private sector involvement had not been pursued. Similarly, US experience in defence procurement outlined in Chapter Nine highlights a significant imbalance in technical and managerial expertise as between the government and defence contractors.

Countering these problems will require concentrated efforts in the public sector to build up the necessary skills. A successful strategy applied by the Roads Traffic Authority in Australia has been to establish composite review teams combining expertise from throughout the public service, and private sector financial advisers. While individual initiatives of this sort have been of benefit, most developments to date are concentrated within a small number of ministries and agencies. The benefits for the public sector as a whole will depend on both embedding these skills more extensively throughout the public sector thus ensuring the transfer of knowledge gained in individual departments and agencies. This suggests an important role for central agencies in establishing mechanisms for ready exchange of information and identification of best practice or methodological alternatives.

ENSURING COMPETITIVE DISCIPLINES

Gains in productive efficiency from private involvement in infrastructure projects are seen to flow in all countries from arrangements whereby bids are obtained from a sufficient number of alternative possible suppliers, in competition with each other, and in accordance with broad project specifications provided by the Government. Efficiencies are expected as a result of competition on price, but also from the technical and managerial innovations which are contained within proposals. There is no evidence which would question the premises underlying this strategy.

Experience suggests however, that the extent to which anticipated efficiency gains will eventuate, and the magnitude of those gains, may be affected by the efficiency of the tendering process itself and by the quality of the procedures for assessing bids. Issues raised earlier concerning poor preliminary planning by the public sector and project specifications which provide little latitude for innovation are relevant here. Additionally however, rigid, risk averse procedural adherence within the public sector which extend the time taken for tender evaluation and approval is costly and may also threaten the success of projects. Additional costs are incurred in the elapsed time for tenders to be considered and in the cost of tender preparation . These costs, reflected in project bids, will eventually be passed on to end users or to tax payers.

In seeking both competition between tenders and a desire to be fair, the public sector may also approve too many bids for tender which, in a perverse way, may limit possible efficiency gains. Approving too many tenders incurs unnecessary costs for many tender parties which may dissuade initial bidders from progressing through the tender. When bidders are short listed only to find themselves in competition with a large number of others they may simply withdraw. This may say nothing about the quality of the bidders or their chance of success, but reflects an entirely rational response to the risks and thus costs involved. Rather, the process reflects the risk averse nature of public sector institutions manifested in an inability to effectively cull the bids for fear of excluding technically superior or highly competitive proposals. Experience in the United Kingdom and Australia suggests that given appropriate skills and incentives to bear risk within the public sector, the benefits of competition can be achieved from as little as three or four well chosen tenders.

Ensuring productive efficiency gains are actually achieved in implementation can principally be achieved through careful project selection and the establishment of fixed price contracts between the government and the eventual contractor. Such arrangements have been a common feature of virtually all the experiences outlined in the accompanying studies (either for total construction costs or in terms of the basis of remuneration in situations where the private sector also operates the service). However, as noted in Chapter Nine in the discussion of risks above, the extent to which fixed price contracts actually limit the costs to government depend on the extent to which the government can effectively quarantine itself from unforeseen costs subsequently incurred by contractors.

Nevertheless, there appear to be some mechanisms available to place pressure on contractors to continue to seek efficiency gains in construction and operation. These include the incorporation of financial incentives in contracts and mechanisms to ensure competition in supply. On the first, limits on tariffs (where charges are levied on users) or caps on the rate of return which the private sector can earn are features of some projects in Australia, the United Kingdom and the United States. The suggestion raised in Chapter Five for the establishment of two-part tariffs (one part relating to fixed costs and another related to variable costs with some scope for incentive payments on the basis of qualitative independent opinion as to performance) may also spur greater efficiency and effectiveness.

Ensuring competition in supply is more difficult given the nature of infrastructure provision which, in the case of roads for example, can involve the creation of monopoly rights for the private sector. A useful approach regarded as being an important element in the success of the French motorway system have been requirements to preserve a toll-free minor road in parallel to a for-profit motorway. In the case of prisons, the UK approach in ensuring that contracts are, at least initially, awarded to a number of different contractors; that contracts contain detailed performance criteria; and, that there is an ongoing process of market testing existing public prison operations, provides a useful range of continuing competitive pressures on the private and public sectors alike.

GIVING COMMITMENT TO AND GAINING ACCEPTANCE FOR ARRANGEMENTS

An important element in attracting private sector interest and in determining the success of projects appears to be government's willingness to give a commitment to a global strategy involving a wider role for the private sector and clear commitment to individual projects. While a number of governments have sought to articulate their objectives through public statements (Germany), guidelines (Australia) or through the establishment of global initiatives (United Kingdom), much of the experience to date appears to have developed on a largely ad-hoc project basis.

Most countries included in this study do not appear to have developed an integrated strategic plan by which global infrastructure needs can be identified. Without this guidance, the ability to determine relative priorities across government departments or agencies may be hampered. Integrated plans could allow appraisal of alternative methods of meeting infrastructure needs between agencies and therefore determination of the most efficient infrastructure options. Moreover, the lack of clear identification of forecast project activity may leave private investors with little ability to plan their involvement. Uncertainty about future activity can create a risk for potential investors, can prevent efficient business planning, and may fail to attract an efficient level of competitive presence.

The more extensive use of private resources and expertise in infrastructure provision has raised issues for a number of countries in gaining public acceptance for the innovations proposed. For the most part concerns raised relate to perceptions about what are inherent government functions and involve overcoming notions that public responsibility for infrastructure provision necessarily means public ownership and management.

Nowhere is this issue probably more evident than in Germany where the constitution stipulates that the bulk of public utilities are the responsibility of the public authorities. Moreover, the courts have traditionally taken the view that government responsibility was equivalent to public provision and management, the underlying concern being that a private contractor might not fulfil the requirements of continuity and equality of service.

The cultural change involved in gaining a greater acceptance of the distinction between the responsibility and ownership/management is delicate and will probably only be fully recognised after considerably more experimentation and experience with private sector participation. In particular, it will depend upon the evidence of success based on assessment against objective performance information on the benefits (efficiency, effectiveness and quality of service) which result from private sector involvement. The development of and systematic reporting against performance standards should thus be a priority.

A further difficulty in the area of road transport concerns gaining acceptance for the perceived distributional impacts of levying user charges on new infrastructure when existing infrastructure has historically been provided "free" (or at least perceived to have been paid for through existing taxes and charges). This is clearly less of an issue in the case of tolled bridges and tunnels where the charges levied can clearly be associated with savings in time and fuel, but remains important in the case of roads. In the end, the perceived redistributive effects of introducing economically efficient pricing may depend on the use made of the extra revenues thus generated. The distributional impact of introducing road charges might be addressed by earmarking some funds for new road construction; additionally some of the additional revenue could be used to reduce motor vehicle registration taxes, or to lower effective tax rates on low income groups as a whole.

CONCLUSIONS

The conclusions arising out of our consideration of country experiences in the joint public/private provision of infrastructures can be summarised as follows:

- Gains are possible in productive, allocative and dynamic efficiency from the wider involvement of the private sector in infrastructure provision.

- They can be expected to result from the application of greater market disciplines to individual project selection and to aggregate investment choices for the public sector as a whole; from innovation by the private sector in project design and implementation; and from the rationalisation (or circumvention) of burdensome public sector procurement regulations which have historically imposed delays in design, finance and construction (and thus increased costs) of projects.

- Consistent with findings of earlier Secretariat studies on the use of market type mechanisms in the public sector, the potential benefits of JPPPI will not flow automatically from more extensive private involvement. Securing them will require rigour, innovation and above all good management on the part of the public sector, as well as an acceptance that implementing JPPPI effectively is an investment which will require time, patience and risk taking.

- Capturing potential efficiency gains will require, inter alia, complete and sound preparation by the public sector for bids and tender selection, including obtaining necessary planning approvals and fulfilling public consultation requirements more quickly; tender requirements that allow for innovation; and the development (and dissemination) of skills within the public sector in contract evaluation and management. In particular, the evolution of skills in negotiating complex contracts must be stressed.

- Maximising gains will require: procedures which ensure that budget disciplines are not circumvented and where only the most economically justified proposals proceed; the wider use of user charging/congestion pricing; and adequate incentives within contracts which place pressure on private sector suppliers to continue to seek efficiencies throughout project implementation. Additionally, the establishment within the public sector of integrated infrastructure plans may better guide the development of infrastructure priorities and the most efficient infrastructure options. However, care needs to be exercised to ensure that strategies for the establishment of integrated infrastructure plans do not become an additional procedural impediment which would delay or exclude consideration of cost-effective private sector proposals.

- It is unrealistic for the public sector to expect JPPPI to result in the private sector bearing all the risks associated with projects. Moral and technological risks will almost certainly remain with the public sector. The key possibility for ensuring the private sector bears its share of risk will be in ensuring that market disciplines are used in the selection of infrastructure projects and that no (or only limited) government guarantees are provided to the private sector.

Finally, one very important aspect of JPPPI experiences to date is to show that 1) such arrangements are possible, and 2) that traditional boundaries between the private and the public sector are not sacred. For instance, the whole debate on private prisons has advanced immensely by virtue of the fact that they now do exist; that the bulk of the problems to be solved are adjustment ones; and that no significant erosion of the public interest has occurred, contrary to some dire predictions of a decade ago. The message is clear: real experimenting with the use of markets in and by public administrations provides an irreplaceable way of testing how the public sector can be better managed. This dynamic has already shown itself to be quite powerful in promoting greater efficiency by expanding perspectives on what can be tried. This has been exemplified in the past in many sectors where market type mechanisms have been introduced: fishing and emission rights market creation; the introduction of competition in postal, telephone and telecommunications services; the design and implementation of internal competition within hospital and school systems; airline and airports privatisation and deregulation. Given time and careful management similar benefits should be obtainable from public/private partnerships in infrastructure provision.

BIBLIOGRAPHY

OECD (1992), *Complex Contracting out for Information Technology*, Public Management Occasional Paper, Market-type Mechanisms Series No. 5, OECD, Paris [OCDE/GD(92)134].

OECD (1994), *Assessing Structural Reform: Lessons for the Future*, OECD, Paris.

Public Accounts Committee (1993): *Infrastructure Management and Financing in New South Wales, Report No. 73, Volume 1*, NSW Parliament, Sydney, NSW, Australia.

Chapter Two

**INNOVATIONS IN THE PUBLIC-PRIVATE PROVISION OF INFRASTRUCTURE
IN THE AUSTRALIAN STATE OF NEW SOUTH WALES**

by

Dale Raneberg
Australian Consulting Partners
Sydney, New South Wales, Australia

INTRODUCTION

Infrastructure projects in New South Wales (NSW) involving the private sector are of world scale. These projects are increasingly sophisticated, creative, and well-managed. Several significant issues (including many revolving around risk) have finally been resolved and approaches are becoming more innovative. However, many innovations have been occurring in isolation and processes are not well developed. Central agencies should do more to remove impediments and assist departments, while effective leadership and demonstrated commitment would do more to build confidence in potential investors.

A strong tension persists between the different attitudes to risk-bearing held by the public and private sectors. Resolution of this tension is only possible if the public sector is prepared to accept some risk. Risk aversion is actually creating risk for the private sector and unnecessary costs for the public.

BACKGROUND

NSW is facing increasing demand for infrastructure of all types. This demand has been especially difficult to meet in recent years as, consistent with all other states, NSW has undergone considerable budgetary restraint.

Australia's policy of promoting immigration has added 850 000 people to the state in the past 10 years. Most of this increase has been concentrated on Sydney as the capital of NSW. At 3.5 million and growing, Sydney's low density expansion multiplies the need for basic infrastructure. At the same time existing infrastructure no longer adequately serves the new volume needs nor is it sufficiently matched to the changing patterns of demand of a demographically different population.

With existing public assets of over A$ 115 billion, the annual maintenance bill alone is sizeable. Furthermore, past political priorities for establishing new projects have created a need for extensive upgrading, refurbishment, and even replacement of some assets.

Economic conditions have compounded the problem. The Federal government's fiscal response to a recent period of recession has forced restraint in spending by the states. From 5.8 per cent of gross state product in 1987/88 the NSW capital program has been trimmed to 5.2 per cent in the 1993/94 budget. In 1993/94 capital expenditure of A$ 5.5 billion is planned.

This vigorous fiscal restraint has driven an equally vigorous climate of reform in the management of government. These reforms have been embraced by all tiers of government and by governments of different political majorities.

The NSW government gives four key objectives for reform:

-- optimal allocation of scarce public sector resources;
-- efficiency;
-- better service;
-- accountability for performance.

A range of market-oriented initiatives have been employed to secure these objectives. While the central initiative has been competition, other changes have sought better management.

Pricing reforms have been used to encourage more efficient allocation of resources where increased competition has not been possible. These changes have primarily sought to manage demand by removing cross-subsidies and making the user pay:

-- The Hunter Water Corporation has switched from set rates based on land value to charging for water used. Together with the elimination of cross subsidies between users this has resulted in a fall in water demand sufficient to defer planned construction of a major new dam.

-- The Sydney Water Board has also started to introduce usage based charges and, under direction from the Government Pricing Tribunal, will now modify expenditure to meet environmental standards that are consistent with consumers tolerance.

-- A *de facto* road usage charge has been introduced through a special additional tax on petrol. This tax is dedicated to future expenditure on road maintenance.

Where possible, complete competition has been introduced while corporatisation has opened other agencies to effective competition. Importantly, competition here is recognition of the government's role as a service provider with the responsibility of ensuring the delivery of those services in the most efficient manner -- regardless of who actually delivers the service.

Various competitive mechanisms have been used which have increased the involvement of the private sector (and transferred risk for service delivery). This involvement ranges from wholesale privatisation to contracting out in house service needs, and includes private sector participation in infrastructure projects.

Eight government corporations have been privatised in the last five years while another four are planned to be privatised during 1994.[1] Contracting out services from road maintenance to hospital catering has achieved average savings of 20 per cent on previous costs (NSW Government, 1993, p. 10.19). The A$100 million saved each year has been retained by agencies for reallocation, while the shedding of some activities has brought focus and clarity to agency activities. Contracting itself has allowed greater flexibility in choosing between appropriate methods of service delivery.

Since 1988, well before privatisations had been considered, and while contracting out was still new, guidelines have been in place for private sector involvement in infrastructure. These guidelines were subsequently rewritten and published again in 1990 (Department of State Development, 1990). Similar guidelines for contracting were not published until 1991.

At least 34 major projects of privately provided infrastructure have either been completed or are planned. The total cost of these amounts to over A$ 13 billion. Virtually all these projects broadly follow the build/own/operate (BOO) or build/own/operate/transfer (BOOT) models. An exception is the new correctional facility at Junee. The Junee Prison is a build/operate/transfer (BOT) project. Ownership transferred to the government on completion while the facility operates under private management.

In some agencies it is now regarded as commonplace to consider using the private sector. For some others it is still untried. Of experience to date almost half the major projects completed or under development were from a transport portfolio (rail, road, ports). Add to this the projects in Health (30 per cent) and Water (12 per cent) and these portfolios account for 90 per cent of projects.

Furthermore, private transport projects alone comprised 90 per cent of the combined cost for all private projects (see Figure 1). With the consequent accrued skills and experience inside these departments some of these projects have been regarded as the most successful to date. These agencies dominate the list of forthcoming proposals.

However, many departments are still struggling with their understanding of involving the private sector and projects are floundering. Some structural issues also hinder progress. This strains relationships between the public and private sectors, reduces allocation efficiencies, and retards capital investment.

The government is aware of these issues and many have been confronted, while others are currently under review. Most notably two initiatives have focused directly on these problems. A Task Force was set up in 1989 to reconsider existing guidelines. These guidelines were reissued in 1990. Second, the Public Accounts Committee of the Parliament of NSW (PAC) held an inquiry into current problems and potential solutions. The PAC has since issued four separate reports over the past three years of its now concluded inquiry.

Some of these recommendations are too recent for any response, but where relevant the discussion of current problems and solutions draws on these recent recommendations.

EXPERIENCE OF PRIVATE-PUBLIC INFRASTRUCTURE IN NSW

Experience in NSW reveals several significant areas of difficulty. In some areas innovation has brought success, in others problems persist. The key features of this experience are how risks have been managed and why risks remain.

The process of devising risk management techniques and processes has not always been smooth. An understanding of the causes of dispute is informative of how the process could be managed for speedier resolution. From these experiences lessons may be drawn of the key elements of success.

Experiences can be grouped in sequence:

a) *Structural problems and consequent risks.* Problems have arisen from inter governmental relations, taxation, and financial markets which generate additional costs, and create uncertainty and risk.

b) *Project selection and reaping efficiency gains.* Planning and skill deficiencies have reduced achievable efficiency gains.

c) *Problems of Procedure.* Poor preparation of bid specifications and risk aversion in evaluating tenders is costly and inefficient for both parties. Lack of information about future proposals creates uncertainty.

d) *Recent NSW projects.* Six projects illustrate the nature of current work and some successful innovations.

e) *Key elements of success.* From experience in NSW, four key elements are identified for the success of individual projects. Some efficiencies have resulted from specific projects but an integrated infrastructure plan is needed for the government to achieve efficient allocation.

I. STRUCTURAL PROBLEMS AND CONSEQUENT RISKS

Several problems have emerged in the formal relationship between levels of government, and between the government and the private sector. These structural problems involve the transfer of risk and the problems that emerge from procedures to deal with risk as it is borne in private sector infrastructure projects. The structural relationships and associated risks are:

-- intergovernmental relations and avoidance of moral hazards;
-- taxation arrangements and recognition of risk assumed; and
-- the impact of financial markets on project operating risk and finance risk.

Considerable time has been spent on the appropriate mechanism to *avoid moral hazards* in the relationship between the federal and the state governments. This can be an issue wherever there are administrative tiers of government.

As a state government in a federation, the overall budget position of NSW is subordinated to that of the Commonwealth of Australia. The amount available to NSW for capital expenditure is limited by the country's aggregate need to borrow to support this expenditure. This restriction occurs because of the implicit support given the states by the Commonwealth (who is the prime collector of taxation revenues). Without some mechanism to monitor and control outstanding liabilities the Commonwealth will face a moral hazard of exposure to state's spending.

The mechanism for avoiding this moral hazard is called the Loan Council. The Loan Council has twice reviewed the manner in which it deals with private sector infrastructure spending in the past two years. New guidelines have now been approved which overcome unintended consequences of previous guidelines.

Under the old terms the Loan Council would assess projects to be either completely within the purvey of government or completely private ventures. This toggle of "all on, or all off" was based on who in balance controlled the project and whether the private sector carried most of the risk. If a project was regarded as being within the Loan Council it would only proceed if the state had not already exceeded its rationed spending limit (and therefore borrowing constraint). But if a project was regarded as being outside the Loan Council, because in balance it was controlled by the private sector, then rationed spending limits do not apply.

This meant governments were inclined to expend significant energy to contrive as much outside Loan Council as possible. The private sector had a similar incentive, to ensure a project would proceed. This led to wasted effort and inefficient outcomes.

> *As a result, all sorts of structures and arrangements have been developed, not to improve outcomes, but to serve the needs of the various processes, including Loan Council evaluation -- invariably to the detriment of projects and increasingly the ultimate cost to the people of the state concerned.*
>
> (Pidcock, 1993, p. 61)

Furthermore, while risk may be inefficiently transferred merely to get outside Loan Council guidelines real liabilities may still remain with the government. These liabilities will not be accounted.

At least one more flaw existed under the old approach. By considering gross exposure to liabilities the method overlooked the natural hedge against these liabilities provided by the underlying assets of the project. That is, "if the assets are a perfect hedge there is no requirement for a government guarantee and the debt is risk free" (Dodd, 1993, p. 111). Such a complete hedge may be highly unlikely but indicates that the gross liability position is the wrong level of assessment.

These technical matters were addressed only as recently as February 1994. As deliberations of liability were essentially about risk assessment the conclusions provide a general answer to risk sharing.

New guidelines will introduce a risk adjusted weighting system under which projects will be evaluated. This recognises that where it is optimal for government to accept some risk it should do so. But relative risk bearing should equate to relative apportionment of liability and projects should not be jeopardised by some arbitrary cut off for total inclusion or exclusion from the government's balance sheet.

Under the new guidelines liability to be apportioned is net of the realisable value of the project in the market. Realisable value is calculated after applying an average variability weight depending on the project type and duration. So the liability assumed to reside with the government is based on risk borne and the ratio of assets to liabilities for the project.

Of course, the extent of government exposure to debt will depend on the nature of any arrangement with the private sector. If the government bears no risk and has no residual liability then there is no exposure. And this leaves one remaining problem for BOT and BOOT schemes: What is the appropriate value at which the asset should transfer back to the government?

The Loan Council's view is that if the asset transfers at a nil value then the government had a vested interest all along, and this interest should be acknowledged (along with a share of project liabilities). However, the structure of most BOT and BOOT schemes accept that while the asset may have a life beyond the term of the period of private ownership, the return to the investors will be reaped during the ownership period. Indeed it will be necessary for financial arrangements that the project is able to generate sufficient income to cover its debt while privately owned.

Transfer at nil value does not involve risk to the government but merely reflects the financial arrangements of the project during private operation. Depending on the duration of private ownership and the magnitude of residual value these arrangements may affect efficiency (as an acknowledged residual value would lower required charges). However, where transfer would be at nil value the Loan Council's position imposes an extra cost on the community as it means that "consumers must pay for the assets twice -- once through the capital component of the user pays revenues, and a second time at the end of the concession" (Pidcock, 1993, p. 64).

This problem has not been addressed by recent changes to Loan Council guidelines which insists on transfer at market value. After two attempts the guidelines still pose institutional problems to investors, the NSW government, and consumers.

Taxation arrangements have been slow to adapt to the new relationships between governments and the private sector. Despite positive moves by the federal government problems still exist. These problems breed uncertainty and increase risk for projects.

The federal government has introduced some tax concessions to encourage infrastructure investment by the private sector. In the "One Nation" national strategic package released in 1992, three important measures were introduced: Generous depreciation allowance; Streamlining of special rulings by the Tax Office on treatment of different proposals; and, a new non-deductible/non-assessable bond for project financing.

While all measures were valuable, and the expedited rulings were recognition of the difficulties of uncertainty that would otherwise exist, it was the investment bonds that were the most innovative. The bonds recognised that the tax benefits of the usual start-up losses were often deferred for some time. By not allowing a deduction for financing cost and not assessing the interest received the benefit passed immediately to the lender. This meant financing costs could be priced lower to reflect total investor benefit. With lower financing costs the project would reap some benefit earlier.

However, as it is the responsibility of the investor to seek rulings on tax effects, and the bond provision is automatic, it is open for some investors and sponsors to enter arrangements while unaware of these changes. This would bring about distortions in payoffs and unanticipated tax consequences.

In other ways the Taxation Office is struggling to find the correct mechanisms for evaluating projects. Like the early deliberations of the Loan Council, the difficulty arises in naive categorical assessment. Hence some tax arrangements continue to treat infrastructure projects dichotomously: as either all public or all private.

This leads to extreme outcomes for the private investor. If the project is either funded by non-recourse debt[2], or if the end activity itself is not considered to be producing taxable income then the arrangement between the government and the private sector is regarded as financial only. This means that while the taxpayer will be denied deductions for depreciation, interest on funds borrowed, repairs, as well as any investment allowances, tax will apply to income received.

The Sydney Water Board now seeks rulings on draft contracts before arrangements are entered. If the ruling is unfavourable the Board redrafts the contracts, seeks preliminary acceptance from the private party and resubmits the draft contract for ruling. This eliminates uncertainty and guarantees the tax effects of contracted arrangements (albeit at some cost in time and legal expense for drafting iterations).

What the Tax Office is struggling with is the true form of these arrangements. The Tax Office should adapt to the actual risk share arrangements in much the same way as the Loan Council. Evaluating projects on actual risk borne by each party would be much fairer than the non-specific thresholds of "predominant" share.

The lack of appropriate project financing has imposed additional risks on infrastructure projects in NSW. These risks include operating risk, and financial risk.

The undeveloped long term capital market in Australia has led to problems for NSW projects attracting appropriate long term finance or institutional equity investment.[3] The market has been characterised by an inverted yield curve which dissuades long term investment, a thin market which creates pricing problems, and risk aversion among institutions and superannuation funds who are the ideal investors for long term projects.

This structural constraint has impeded project development and imposed additional costs which have increased the operating risk of projects. This situation has been amplified in recent years as a succession of privatisations by governments throughout the country has absorbed much of what finance was available.

To date, banks have been the main providers of finance, but the investment term for banks is short compared to the life of infrastructure projects. It is most efficient for the debt profile to match that of the life of the asset. In this way, the financing cost can be spread more evenly over the years the facility is operating. This results in lower charges to users. Having a shorter term, bank finance imposes high costs on projects in early years and, therefore, higher charges. This increases operating risk, as the artificially high charges may dissuade demand.

Infrastructure funds have been suggested as a means of developing the long term capital market. The fund would be attractive to investors because as a large fund it could take some share in a range of projects. This diversification would quarantine the fund investors from many of the operating risks faced by individual projects.

The first of these funds has been set up. A joint venture between superannuation funds and the Infrastructure Development Corporation, the fund plans to pool A$ 200 million for investment. A significant amount but not sufficient on its own to cover those projects already planned for NSW.

Some proponents of the fund, including the Public Accounts Committee (PAC) of the NSW Parliament, have suggested that the government be involved. This involvement would provide additional appeal to those who see some risk in dealing with the government. To them this risk is managed when the government is itself an investor.[4]

The Commonwealth Bank of Australia has suggested the government could play a more important role by issuing long term government bonds (Talbot, 1993, p. 88). Long term government bonds would provide valuable information to the market by indicating the local risk free investment return over extended maturities. This information would allow others to make similar issues, with an identifiable risk premium against the risk free benchmark.

More important is the ability of project investors to hedge their exposure to risk. With the risk free rate established, and instruments available, financial risk management derivatives could be generated. Given the greater exposure of long term investments to financial risk these instruments would encourage long term investment.

Risk management is seen as especially important given the two antagonistic features of the long term market: the fact that long-term investments carry more risk, and the risk-adverse nature of the superannuation funds and others who have investment profiles most suited to longer-term investments.

Recent developments have occurred which indicate the market situation may change. For the first time in decades the yield curve has assumed an upward sweep that recognises the extra risk of longer investments. This will be more attractive to investors.

Two large institutions have signalled an interest in direct equity participation. These institutions recognise that the extra risks borne by projects will give better return to equity.

The Sydney Harbour tunnel project successfully pioneered direct use of the bond market for debt finance. That project raised part of its own debt through a bond issue. The 30-year bonds, which raised A$ 394 million, give a return of 6 per cent, and are indexed to inflation.

II. PROJECT SELECTION AND ALLOCATION EFFICIENCY

Potential gains from allocation efficiencies are frustrated by planning and skill deficiencies. In NSW there is no integrated planning and few agencies have skills in the complexities of private sector investment issues. Two main problems have been observed which prevent potential efficiency gains from better allocation.

-- poor prioritisation from lack of integrated planning;
-- difficulty identifying appropriate projects because of skill deficiencies.

NSW does not have an integrated infrastructure plan nor even an integrated strategic plan by which infrastructure needs can be determined. Without this guidance priorities across agencies can not be established. An integrated plan also allows appraisal of alternative methods of meeting infrastructure needs between agencies, and therefore, determination of the most efficient infrastructure options.

Efforts have been made to develop strategic plans covering several departments and the Metropolitan Strategy, and the Integrated Transport Strategy for Greater Sydney are two examples. However, these strategic documents do not prescribe methods for infrastructure provision nor are there mechanisms to review proposals in accordance with these strategic directions.

There are also problems of co-ordination between the several committees of cabinet who have a role in infrastructure planning. Hence, the Urban Development Committee, who review infrastructure needs, operates in relative isolation from the Capital Works Committee (CWC), who reviews specific proposals. So the priorities that emerge from the committees charged with planning fail to translate into a prescription for allocation.

The Department of Planning raised these problems in a submission to the PAC's inquiry.

> *... the level of co-ordination being attained is limited by the absence of a mechanism for collectively considering capital works programs of individual agencies ... there is currently no co-ordination of agencies' separate budget*

> *proposals. This has implications for the effectiveness and efficiency of funds allocated to urban development.*
>
> (Public Accounts Committee, 1993a, p. 59)

The consequence of this is that there is no overall prioritisation or co-ordination of projects. Without prioritisation the ability to achieve allocation efficiencies from private sector involvement is limited.

It is also inevitable that without proper co-ordination clashes in planning will occur. At the extreme the lack of co-ordination is best illustrated with recent experiences in transport. During 1993 both the Roads and Traffic Authority (RTA) and the Department of Transport separately advertised for formal expressions-of-interest for different projects which provided the same service.

The RTA had in mind a freeway which would improve transport between eastern Sydney and Sydney's north. The Department of Transport, looking also to improve transport between these eastern and northern suburbs, had decided that a mass transit link should be built. Both projects were deemed suitable for private sector involvement; both had advertised for expressions-of-interest; and both projects addressed the same need.

These problems are currently being addressed by Treasury. Treasury has chosen to develop a link between the two processes of planning and review of proposals. This work has absorbed considerable resources without a solution yet emerging.

There are at least two alternatives to that adopted by Treasury. First, the number of committees could be reduced with the roles consolidated in fewer, perhaps larger committees. Second, an integrated infrastructure plan could inform proposals and decisions. The PAC favours an integrated plan informing decision making within the CWC. An alternative is for the integrated plan to guide agencies in the proposals they present to the CWC -- effectively undertaking some rationing of proposals before they emerge for approval.

In the face of this lack of planning departments have exhibited a propensity to look for interest and ideas in a way which expresses a lack of prioritisation -- indeed, the guidelines encourage unsolicited approaches. The *de facto* priority becomes the availability of funding rather than the fundamental need for the infrastructure, or the economic attractiveness of the project.

The extent to which these proposals are efficient for the government will depend on how consistent these projects are with government objectives and immediate priorities, and the extent to which the government is involved and carries risk.

Of all projects completed in NSW only two arrangements gave rise to an additional funding source. In all others expenditure was required by the "traditional 6 public sector sources under various take or pay contracts" (Talbot, 1993, p. 84). For this expenditure to be efficient for the government it must promote the provision of appropriate infrastructure to meet priority needs or replace existing inefficient services.

Skill deficiencies and lack of experience in the public sector severely limit achieving gains from allocation efficiencies. While some of the detail of complex negotiations may have been successfully covered by hired expertise, skill is required in a more fundamental way to identify appropriate opportunities for private sector involvement.

Recognising opportunities for the private sector requires much of the skill and experience needed to manage and process the arrangements. When suitable projects are identified the opportunities then need to be exploited. The PAC reported that the private sector believed that lack of experience meant some projects languished.

> *... unfamiliarity makes public servants reluctant to try anything new. The private sector believes that this is one reason why the numerous projects shown in agencies' capital works plans as suitable for private sector involvement are not emerging into the intrays of the public servants. The private sector believes that public servants are unfamiliar with ways of protecting the public interest; that they are even unfamiliar with what exactly constitutes the public interest in public-private deals; that they know little about finance matters like project analysis, finance structuring, risk analysis,...*

(Public Accounts Committee, 1994, p. 170)

This view was largely shared by senior public servants appearing before the inquiry to give evidence, including the Director-General of the Cabinet Office.

Lack of specific skills in the public sector also make it difficult to identify marginal advantages between proposals. Proposals must be evaluated and the mechanics of various arrangements must be understood for efficient allocation decisions to be made. Several departments have countered these problems with composite review teams combining expertise from throughout the public service, and private sector financial advisers. The Roads and Traffic Authority (RTA) is the best example having continued with this approach through three successful large scale freeway projects.

Several methods have been suggested to embed these skills within the public sector. These proposals variously support a central pool of internal expertise from which departments can draw, short term establishment of a specialist unit drawn from the private and public sectors to work with agencies, and mechanisms for transfer of the skills which have already developed within the more experienced agencies such as the RTA.

All of these proposals rest with central agencies as the vehicle for promoting skill development and knowledge transfer. To date the Premier's Department has produced useful guidelines on capital planning and private sector participation but the high level financial skills to match the complexities of negotiated contracts require more detailed training.

III. PROBLEMS OF PROCEDURE

Problems with procedure have generated the biggest and most heated response from the private sector. Poor management of the bid preparation and the tender process has led to excessive risk, borne of long delays, and significant uncertainty. This adds to project cost.

At the recent PAC inquiry, procedural problems and the associated risks were cited by many giving evidence as their single biggest concern. These problems are:

- poor preparation for project bids;
- tendering problems from risk aversion;
- uncertainty.

Incomplete preparation has been a common cause of problems. Lack of preparation can lead to significant delay, major changes to specifications, and in some instances deficient planning has led to the abandonment of projects. The private sector is therefore exposed to significant risks, including excessive planning cost and project failure.

The extent of these problems is indicated by a survey in which the Infrastructure Development Corporation sampled projects initiated throughout the country (Perry, 1993, p. 96). This sample of 50 projects comprised 66 per cent from NSW. The survey found:

- only 22 per cent of projects proceeded as proposed;
- 25 per cent were cancelled;
- major changes occurred to 11 per cent;
- 3 per cent faced attempts for change from new governments.

The extent of these problems is only just being understood. The inquiry by the PAC received considerable representations and evidence on this subject. Recently, in acknowledgment of responsibility for some cancellations, the Premier of NSW announced that compensation was being considered.

Previously, some attempts had been made to remedy this exposure with detailed guidelines and refinement to "requirements" from agencies issuing a call for expressions of interest. However, poor procedural discipline, skill deficiencies, and lack of experience have contaminated the implementation of these guidelines. Examples abound.

Evidence before the parliamentary inquiry suggested several steps in preparation were ignored. Agencies had called for bids before undertaking basic preliminary work and that this threatened project success. The inquiry found that at least three projects had even bypassed cabinet approval (Public Accounts Committee, 1993a, p. 73).

One industry representative cited a A$ 400 million rail project for which basic preparatory work had not been undertaken (Public Accounts Committee, 1993a, p. 71). This representative claimed the entire project and the investment of potentially hundreds of thousands of dollars by both the public and private sectors was at risk because of the absence of basic preparation work worth A$ 20 000-40 000.

The inquiry recommended that in order to minimise the risks to the private sector, departments should before seeking bids "determine as definitely as possible:

- what the acceptable funding arrangements are likely to be;
- what the market's response is likely to be;
- what they envisage will be the broad allocation of risks in the project;
- the costs and benefits of the project;
- the project's technical feasibility."

(Public Accounts Committee, 1993a, p. 72)

A further, more specific recommendation was that the government finance the Environmental Impact Statement (EIS) and that this also be completed before seeking bids.

Some of these steps had been omitted purely in error from poor administrative practice, or a lack of diligence borne from no appreciation of the commercial consequences. The PAC recommendation sought compliance with a base level of preparation in order to prevent these omissions. However, the PAC's requirement of detailed appraisals and the EIS addressed important issues about the role of private sector involvement and efficient risk bearing.

In some cases the government had avoided detailed appraisal to keep open options the private sector may propose. In these instances, the government was seeking suggestions on matters of detail for projects it had not yet established as feasible. By leaving open matters of detail, the government effectively relied on the private sector to refine the proposal itself.

Agencies have also floated projects to register the level of interest. This practice reveals a lack of priorities and an inefficient process of selection, which unnecessarily exposed the private sector to significant risk of project delay and possible failure.

Deficiencies in preparation and unassessed environmental impacts prevented the government from committing fully to a project. If the government can not commit fully, the private sector bidders will all carry the risk and potential cost of a stalled or abandoned project. If however, the government absorbed these steps into its planning phases it could eliminate risks of delay and eventual project failure. The risk would most efficiently remain with the government who should undertake the necessary analysis and bear those costs.

Several risks currently faced can be aligned to preparation required to avoid unnecessary exposure. For example proper examination of environmental issues will avoid any potential for environmental issues stopping the project. This relationship between planning and private sector risk exposure is illustrated in Figure B.

Preparation should be complete without being overly prescriptive. The purpose of preparation is to reduce risk but it will be most efficient if the project has latitude for innovation. Too narrow a brief could reduce gains from innovative proposals. The RTA has noted that the appropriate level of preparation need only be sufficient to cover contingencies:

> ...the technical description of the project needs to be sufficiently detailed to leave no doubt as to the objectives of the project so that the innovations which will be embodied in responses are within an envelope of government expectations. Similarly technical specifications should be of the performance type and not prescriptive. It is often in the delivery of a conforming product that consortia are able to bring real efficiencies, make savings and achieve the commercial viability of the project.
>
> (Public Accounts Committee, 1993a, p. 78)

During the tendering process the private sector bears the cost of the public sector's risk aversion. Risk aversion leads to dysfunctional orientation to the process of approval rather than the outcome and also generates approval of too many tenders.

Under current public sector arrangements the trade off between efficiency and risk is intractable. The accountability dicta of the public sector has come to mean accountability for procedural integrity, and perhaps, albeit subordinate, the final project (or service), but not the efficiency of the process. This accountability has bred a complete aversion to risk which is extremely inefficient.

The PAC has commented on the inefficiencies of rigid procedural adherence:

> *In a number of cases discussed informally with the Committee, the problem of the public sector's preoccupation with process to the detriment of outcome was raised, often with some heat by the private sector. This preoccupation has led to long delays in implementing projects, sometimes of several years, to the worsening of the original problem while the "process" was being slowly followed, and to the ultimate expenditure of much larger sums than would have been necessary otherwise.*
>
> *(Public Accounts Committee, 1994, pp. 170-171)*

The risk avoided by the government is merely passed to all tenderers, as they churn through the process. Not only is this extremely costly, but it also threatens the actual success of many projects. Costs are incurred in two ways: In the elapsed time for tenders to be considered, and in the cost of tender preparation. These costs, factored in to project bids, will eventually be passed to end users or to tax payers.

Furthermore, in seeking competition among tenders, and a desire to be fair the public service approves too many bids for subsequent tendering. Typically there will be a "short list" of more than six. This list reflects more the inability of the public service to effectively cull the bids, a fear of excluding technically superior or highly competitive proposals, and possibly public scrutiny from those "unfairly" excluded.

Approving too many tenders incurs unnecessary costs for many tender parties. It also displays a process which is rational only for the individual public servant as the benefits of competition could be reaped from as little as two or three well chosen tenders. Given the costs involved "(m)any prospective tenderers are not prepared to accept these odds" (Lattimore, 1993, p. 60).

It is clear that this dissuades initial bidders from progressing through the tender. In many instances when bidders are short listed, only to find themselves pitched against a long list of other hopefuls, they simply withdraw. In some cases alternative bids have teamed up in a consortium in an exercise in risk management.

This self de-selection process says nothing at all about the quality of the bidders and their chance in reasonable circumstance of success. Their action demonstrates a lack of faith in the process itself and in the capabilities of decision makers who continue to defer decisions. Indeed, it may be precisely those who do fall away that best understand the risks involved.

A number of measures are being developed to counter the perverse incentives that determine how public servants handle tendering. The government's guidelines now limit the number of short listed tenders to four, while some departments have already imposed an internal restriction of three, and in some cases only two.

Expert teams have played a key role in managing risk in evaluation of proposals. In several projects these review teams comprised merchant bankers, management consultants, accounting firms, as well as representatives from central agencies and other departments. These teams have introduced a high degree of expertise and taken on the decision risk involved in selecting a preferred tender.

The PAC have suggested as a third method, vesting responsibility for the efficiency of the entire process of project proposal bidding and tendering with a central agency. The agency would monitor and report on efficiencies achieved by departments.

Unfortunately none of these measures actually change the incentives themselves. A system of meaningful assessment, and reward for efficiency for those involved in the tendering process would encourage some risk to be borne within the public sector. This requires a reasonably fundamental shift in current understanding and practice, but would provide the right motivation for change.

Apart from the uncertainty, already discussed, around various outstanding taxation, (until recently) Loan Council matters, and that can follow from poor preparation there are some medium to long term issues for private sector investors. The patchy experience to date along with no clear identification of forecast project activity leaves investors with little ability to plan their involvement.

Uncertainty about future activity creates a risk for potential investors, can prevent efficient business planning, and fail to attract an efficient level of competitive presence. To counter this there have been calls for better forecasting and available information. The government has responded with a promise to publish the forward capital program.

The forward program would signal, but not assure, the market of forthcoming projects planned for the medium term. This indicates priority areas of infrastructure development and allows the private sector to position for future work and investment activity. The forward programs will not be a guarantee but will nonetheless better inform the market and by reducing uncertainty will relieve the private sector of considerable business risk.

This innovation has been warmly welcomed by the market, who see great merit in even indicative forecasts. The government has emphasised that the forward program would not guarantee any project but this is still regarded by the private sector as providing better information that at present.

Leadership is another important element in encouraging confidence. The determination of government has assured investors and promoted projects which had faced some controversy. Infrastructure industry bodies cite leadership and the personal capacities of the relevant minister as one of the main factors guaranteeing a project's success.

Other related mechanisms have been used to encourage confidence and protect projects. The Sydney Harbour Tunnel was a contentious project which survived a change of government and outlived three state Premiers. All through the project enjoyed the protection of an Act of parliament vesting specific authority in the venture.

IV. FEATURES OF RECENT PROJECTS

Examples of recent projects illustrate the practical consequences of problems and the mechanisms which have been used for resolution. This exposes key elements of success, some significant errors, and innovative arrangements.

Six projects are discussed:

-- Sydney Harbour Tunnel;
-- Sydney Opera House car park;
-- M4 Motorway;
-- M5 Motorway;
-- Blue Mountains Sewerage Transfer Scheme;
-- Junee Prison.

Sydney Harbour Tunnel

Before the construction of the A$ 550 million Harbour Tunnel, successive price increases failed to stem congestion on the Harbour Bridge which serves the same route. These increases had taken the price from A$ 0.20 to A$ 2.00 per southbound crossing in just over two years, to little effect.

But the tunnel project was originally set aside because of difficulties with route location and environmental issues. The final project is regarded as a significant success because the private sector proposal overcame these difficulties with technical innovations which eliminated the need for land acquisition and reduced environmental risk. These innovations made the project possible.

An Act of Parliament further protected the project and overcame statutes which may have hindered construction or operation. The project then easily withstood occasional resistance and political challenges.

Under the BOOT agreement, the project will transfer to the government after 30 years of private operation. The private sector party assumed design, construction, finance, and operating costs risks but was protected by renegotiation provisions in its contract. These provisions being triggered by either unexpected inflation, Taxation Office disallowance of deductions for depreciation or losses, or acts of government detrimental to tunnel operation.

Toll rates for the tunnel are set by the government at a 1986 A$ 1 equivalent, but the government also accepts market risk. Market risk is covered by an Ensured Revenue Agreement under which the government provides a top up payment if toll revenues fall below forecast.

The tunnel project employed a combination of financial arrangements. Unusually for NSW, the tunnel used a special bond issue to raise A$ 350 million. These bonds currently provide a 6 per cent return but are indexed for inflation. A loan from the government provided another A$ 220 million. This loan is interest free.

The Sydney Opera House car park

This project was an early success. Much of the success was due to good planning and management. Preparatory work was finalised before progress to subsequent stages, a single minister was given responsibility and vested with adequate authority. Furthermore, the project emerged from the competitive capital approval process, and as a programmed item resulted in resource allocation efficiencies.

The project was chosen as an appropriate project for private sector involvement. A special Act passed through parliament to provide the Minister for Public Works with the authority to manage the entire project approval process. This included any necessary assumption of land and final details of eventual operation.

The government passed all risk for the project to the developer/operator. This included risks associated with construction and eventual operation. To contain any exposure to developer failure during construction, the government required a bond to safeguard completion. This included any clean-up needed in surrounding areas.

The government also expected a return from the project and chose the developer on the basis of technical merits, feasibility, capability and the return it would receive. A special evaluation panel, comprising inter agency representatives and outside consultants was used to make that choice. The panel was aided by separate contracted advice on the financial elements of the tenders, the business positions of the tendering parties, and relevant legal issues.

The developer, who was appointed early in 1990, completed the project by early 1993. This was seven months ahead of schedule.

The M4 motorway

The M4 Motorway project in western Sydney added 10 kilometres of road and substantially improved and widened another 12 kilometres at a cost of A$ 230 million. A BOOT scheme, the toll road will transfer to the government at no cost after 20 years of operation.

The private sector has assumed all risk from design development, construction, and operation but is protected from political risk. Damages provisions give protection from adverse government action while special legislation was passed to remove the need for approval from local area governments for construction work.

Toll arrangements were negotiated between the government and the private sector. The toll is indexed to inflation but can only increase in increments of A$ 0.50. Toll increases then only occur when indexation adds A$ 0.26 and rounding lifts the toll the next increment.

This project is particularly novel for NSW because it is one of only two projects to receive ongoing funding from a source other than government. Indeed the government actually leases land to the project from which it collects A$ 46 million over the period of private operation. As such, it stands as an example of the efficiency gains possible from private sector involvement.

Another feature of the M4 is the method adopted to assess both preliminary submissions and final proposals. In both assessments the RTA employed composite review teams. These teams comprised engineers, legal staff, and finance staff from within the RTA, and external financial advisers.

Tendering for the M4 progressed quickly and the project was competed well ahead of schedule.

M5 motorway

The 15-kilometre M5 motorway was built in southern Sydney. Costing A$ 250 million, the BOOT project will transfer to government ownership in 30 years. Risk share arrangements are similar to the M4. The M4 was also a model for the use of a team composed of various public and private sector advisers in the review process.

The M5 received some support from the RTA via several loans. In total A$ 85 million was provided in land and construction finance for which no interest will be paid.

The toll has been negotiated by the government and indexed to rise in increments of A$ 0.50 in the same way as the M4, but return to the private sector is capped at 19 per cent. Any return above this level is split 5 per cent to the operating party, and 95 per cent of the increment to the government.

This project finished over 18 months ahead of schedule. A A$ 65 million extension of 6 kilometres to the M5 is already underway.

Blue Mountains Sewerage Transfer Scheme

The Sewerage Transfer Scheme is designed to connect Sydney's outlying mountain districts to a modern sewer system. The scheme, initiated in 1990, reached finalisation of contract arrangements in 1993 and is now due for completion in 1997.

The project will cost A$ 80 million and involves a number of parties in a novel, and potentially valuable, ownership arrangement. In this scheme the role of the project "vehicle" is limited to setup and construction only. Unlike most other ventures, the financier, a superannuation fund, will assume actual ownership of the project assets upon completion. The financier will then engage a third party under a management contract to operate the project.

As owner the SASFIT will receive regular payments for provision of the infrastructure. These payments, to be made quarterly, were negotiated before construction and are indexed to Average Weekly Earnings. Therefore, under these arrangements the financier has direct access to both the asset and the income stream the project generates.

The status of the Sydney Water Board as a corporatised utility left its own guarantees at arms length from government backing. While this support still existed the mechanics of any claim, for special appropriations from the parliament itself, made the arrangements unattractive. A discretionary statutory guarantee solved these issues and assured the operator of future payments with simpler recourse.

Contractual arrangements protect the government from project failure with provisions for default.

The Scheme was hampered by significant problems in the tendering period. These problems stemmed from an attempt by the Water Board to avoid being subject to rationing priorities. In advertising for interest the Board required proposals to be arranged to be outside guidelines that would review funding against competing projects. Subsequently, the Board was unable to meet Loan Council criteria to remain outside its guidelines and the project stalled. The project finally proceeded in a form quite different to that originally advertised.

The Junee Prison

The PAC referred to the Junee Prison as an example of "Best Practice" for private sector participation. The project was processed quickly, construction was ahead of schedule, and significant savings were achieved in both the cost of construction and operation.

The A$ 57 million 600-bed medium security prison was assisted from the beginning by clear specification, use of an evaluation committee comprising both public and private sector advisers, and separate assessments of the capacities of those who expressed interest. A short list of four were nominated to tender, and tender requirements were clear but flexible enough to allow innovation in proposals.

The resulting innovations led to savings in design, construction, and operation. The proposal of the preferred tenderer providing significantly better value. Tight construction deadlines and early payment saved almost A$ 5 million in construction costs. Design and management reduced operating costs by almost A$ 3 million per annum.

Political resistance to private ownership of a correctional facility meant the prison transferred to the government on completion as a BOT project. However, a management contract was let, along with the contract for design, construction, and commissioning, to the same consortium. Upon completion the management contract took effect and the facility was turned over to the consortium for operation.

V. KEY ISSUES AND ELEMENTS OF SUCCESS

The success of individual private sector infrastructure projects in NSW depends on several key factors which counter potential problems and promote efficiency. Some efficiency advantages are already apparent from private sector projects, but efficient allocation will not result from the involvement of the private sector alone. Clear specification of government goals and better planning from which private sector projects can emerge as part of an integrated infrastructure plan will add significantly to allocation efficiencies. Central agencies need to take responsibility for developing this plan.

From experience in NSW, we can identify at least four elements of success for a project. These elements have added noticeably to the success of projects to date:

- *Commitment from the government.* The government must be willing to give a commitment to the private sector to proceed with projects, and one minister should accept responsibility for its success. Both the public and private sector have nominated this as an important element for success. Without commitment and identifiable responsibility the project is at risk of failure.

- *Complete preparation for bids.* Complete preparation for bids avoids risk and reduces costs. Incomplete preparation leads to a high potential for project delay or failure. The private sector faces significant risk when submitting a bid for a project that has no guarantee of continuing. These risks translate into higher costs.

- *Tender requirements that allow for innovation.* Innovations can bring important efficiency gains and are a valuable reason for using competitive bids. Tender requirements that are too narrowly specified limit innovation and can reduce efficiency gains.

- *Use of relevant expertise to review tenders.* A range of expertise may be needed to review tenders. Without enlisting the necessary skills evaluation of complex arrangements, or even the marginal benefits of each proposal is not possible. These arrangements and benefits are at the core of the rationale for private sector participation.

Where projects have been successful, efficiency gains are evident. The involvement of the private sector has a strong efficiency advantage in the inclusion of capital costs in cost and pricing calculations. While some government agencies do include the cost of capital in project (and service method) evaluations this practice is not yet common.

Gains also flow from efficiencies in design, construction, and operation. Operation savings have been made in projects like the Junee Prison, while most private sector projects finish within schedule and within budget. The M5 was completed over 18 months earlier than planned. This delivers construction cost savings and provides facilities sooner. These efficiencies and the innovations that drive them add to public sector knowledge and are transferable to other projects.

The advantage of competition among tenderers is now apparent. Competition has variously resulted in design innovation, construction and operating efficiencies, and creative financing. This has been most obvious where consortia have drawn on experience from overseas or elsewhere in Australia. As local experience is now growing, the benefits of competition should increase further.

The NSW government needs to address three key issues that will maximise the efficiency gains possible from individual projects:

- *Comprehensive integrated planning and prioritisation of projects.* Prioritisation of projects can only follow from a proper planning process. Without adequate planning within and across departments priorities can not be established. Planning should begin with service needs and from this can emerge those solutions (including infrastructure projects) which most efficiently meet those needs. The government can then select priorities from among these competing proposals. Only in this way can allocation efficiencies be maximised.

- *Transfer experience and develop skills within all agencies.* Most successful projects have been from a small number of agencies. Not all agencies have either the necessary skills or the understanding of how to acquire them. Even the experienced agencies can gain from understanding innovations in other portfolios. A mechanism for ready exchange of information and identification of best practice or methodological alternatives would be valuable to all departments.

-- *Incentives for efficient risk bearing in the public service.* The right incentives will encourage efficiency in the processing of bids and tenders. There is presently no incentive for efficiency, as behaviour is distorted by procedural accountability and complete risk aversion on the part of the public sector. This is inefficient for the government and for those who tender, adding considerable cost to the process.

To address the first two of these issues it will be necessary for the central government agencies to play a greater role. Central agencies need to generate core objectives by which departments can plan, and integrate the planning effort across government. Treasury and the Premier's Department are also well placed to act as a conduit for skill transfer and dissemination of new experience and ideas.

The third issue requires a fundamental shift in current attitudes, and different methods of performance evaluation. This can not occur without the mandate from a suitably high level, but would rest with each department to implement. This change, although very difficult to introduce, would have payoffs in efficiency for all projects.

In NSW, transport projects account for half the major private projects, and almost 90 per cent of these projects' cost.

Figure 1. **Profile of major private infrastructure projects in NSW**[1]
(%)

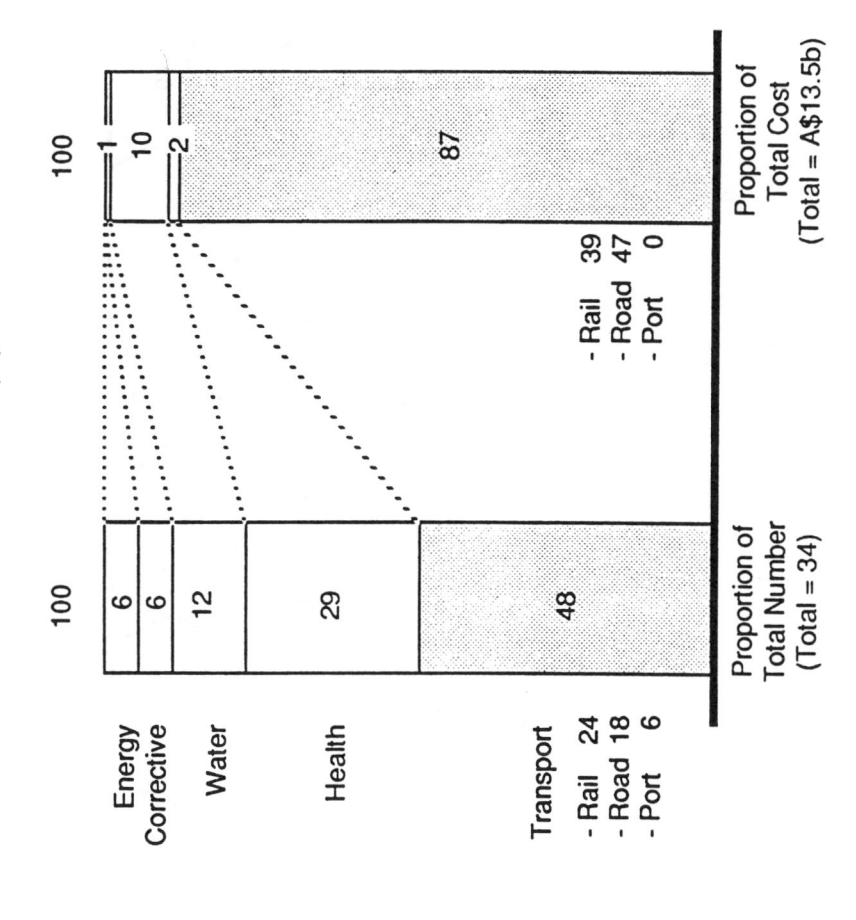

Category	Proportion of Total Number (Total = 34)	Proportion of Total Cost (Total = A$13.5b)
Energy	6	1
Corrective	6	10
Water	12	2
Health	29	—
Transport	48	87
- Rail	24	39
- Road	18	47
- Port	6	0

Note:
1. Includes those projects completed or under development.

Source: Public Accounts Committee, Interdata, Estimates.

Preparation by the government reduces risk for the private sector.

Figure 2. **Reduction in private sector risk exposure in bid preparation**

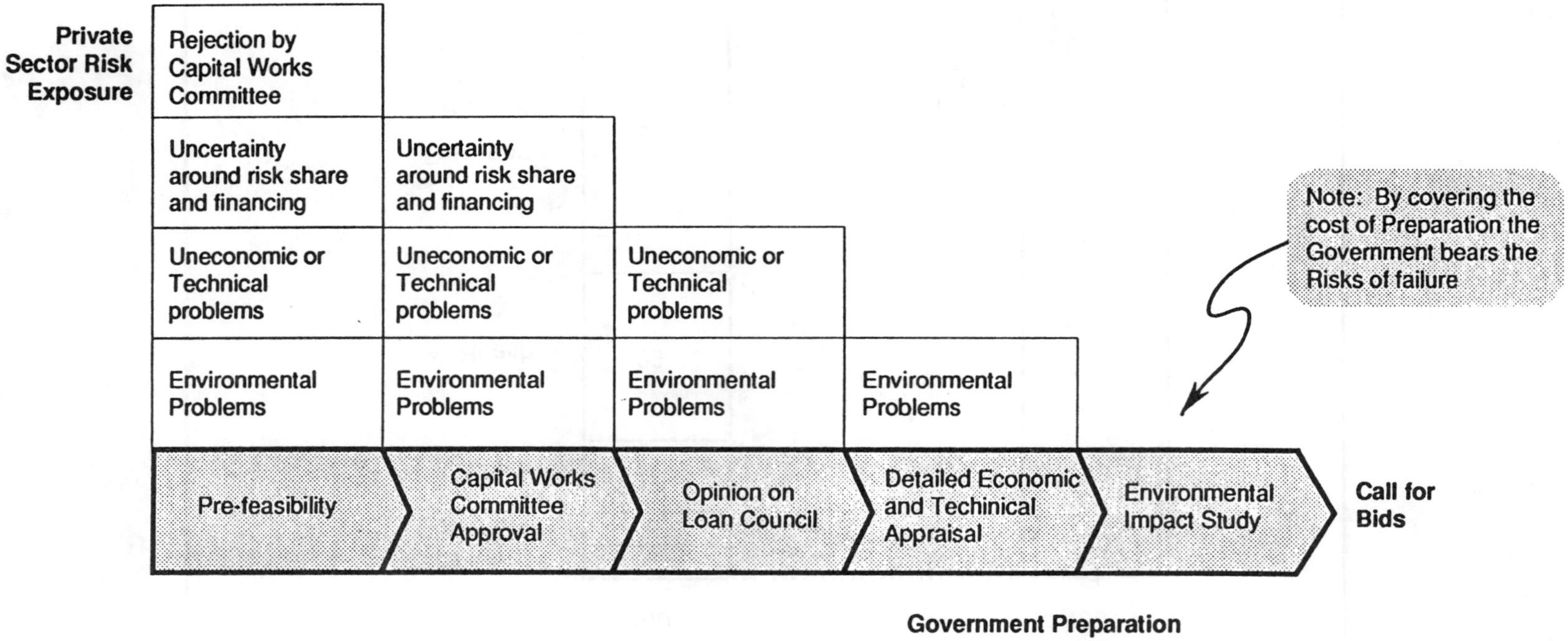

Private Sector Risk Exposure	Rejection by Capital Works Committee				
	Uncertainty around risk share and financing	Uncertainty around risk share and financing			
	Uneconomic or Technical problems	Uneconomic or Technical problems	Uneconomic or Technical problems		
	Environmental Problems	Environmental Problems	Environmental Problems	Environmental Problems	
	Pre-feasibility	Capital Works Committee Approval	Opinion on Loan Council	Detailed Economic and Technical Appraisal	Environmental Impact Study	Call for Bids

Note: By covering the cost of Preparation the Government bears the Risks of failure

Government Preparation

NOTES

1. Privatisations include the NSW Investment Corporation; NSW Egg Corporation; State Brickworks; Government Clothing Factory; MSB Coal Loaders; First State Computing; NSW Grain Corporation; and the Government Insurance Office (GIO). Corporations planned for privatisation are the Government Cleaning Service; School Furniture Complex; MSB Waterways Authority Navaids, Waterfront Services and Signs businesses; and Hunter Valley Coal Freight.

2. Non-recourse debt instruments preclude the lender from seizing any other assets of the borrower (party to the infrastructure development). This lessens the risk exposure of the borrower.

3. For a detailed discussion see Industry Commission, 1991.

4. From experience in California with transport projects, the Assistant Director of Caltrans commented, "We are convinced that even modest and direct government involvement (even perceived participation) will assuage most of the doubt harboured in the hearts of lenders", Williams, 1993, p. 13.

REFERENCES

Bureau of Industry Economics (1992), *Occasional paper 7, Private Provision of Economic Infrastructure*, AGPS, Canberra, ACT.

Department of State Development (1990), *Guidelines for Private Sector Participation in Infrastructure Provision*, Sydney, NSW.

DODD, P. (1993), "The New Loan Council Guidelines", in Public Accounts Committee (1993b), *Proceedings of the Conference on Risk and Projects*, Report No. 77, NSW Parliament, Sydney, NSW.

Industry Commission (1991), *Availability of Capital*, Report No. 18, AGPS, Canberra, ACT.

Interdata (1993), *The Interdata Infrastructure Handbook*, I.D.P. Interdata PL, Sydney, NSW.

LATTIMORE, N. (1993), "Financing Private Sector Participation in Public Infrastructure", in Interdata (1993), *The Interdata Infrastructure Handbook*, I.D.P. Interdata PL, Sydney, NSW.

NSW Government (1993), *Budget Paper No. 2*, Treasury, Sydney, NSW.

PERRY, M. (1993), "Private Infrastructure -- Myth or Reality", in Interdata (1993), *The Interdata Infrastructure Handbook*, I.D.P. Interdata PL, Sydney, NSW.

PIDOCK, D. (1993), "Public-Private Co-operation in Infrastructure Financing", in Public Accounts Committee (1993b), *Proceedings of the Conference on Risk and Return -- Traditional and Innovate Financing for Infrastructure Projects*, Report No. 77, NSW Parliament, Sydney, NSW.

Public Accounts Committee (1993a), *Infrastructure Management and Financing in New South Wales*, Report No. 73, Volume 1, NSW Parliament, Sydney, NSW.

Public Accounts Committee (1993b), *Proceedings of the Conference on Risk and Return -- Traditional and Innovative Financing for Infrastructure Projects*, Report No. 77, NSW Parliament, Sydney, NSW.

Public Accounts Committee (1994), *Infrastructure Management and Financing in New South Wales*, Report No. 73, Volume 2, NSW Parliament, Sydney, NSW.

TALBOT, J. (1993), "Developing Long Term Capital Markets", in Public Accounts Committee (1993b): *Proceedings of the Conference on Risk and Return -- Traditional and Innovative Financing for Infrastructure Projects*, Report No. 77, NSW Parliament, Sydney, NSW.

WILLIAMS, C. (1993): *Proceedings of the Conference on Risk and Return -- Traditional and Innovative Financing for Infrastructure Projects*, Report No. 77, NSW Parliament, Sydney, NSW.

Chapter Three

**THE FRENCH EXPERIENCE OF PARTNERSHIP
BETWEEN THE PUBLIC AND PRIVATE SECTOR
IN THE CONSTRUCTION AND OPERATION OF MOTORWAYS:
THEORY AND PRACTICE**

by

Patricia Vornetti
Laboratoire d'économie publique
de l'Université de Paris I et
Maître de Conférence à l'Université de Tours

INTRODUCTION

France today has the third-longest motorway network in the world. According to 1989 figures, the United States had by far the largest network (85 000 km), followed by West Germany (8 600 km); France, with 6 560 km, was placed ahead of Italy (6 100 km) and had almost twice as much motorway as fifth-ranked Japan (3 500 km) (Merlin, 1991, p. 164.).

Motorway construction in France has been relatively recent. Whereas in Germany and Italy several thousand kilometres of motorway were built between the two world wars, in 1955 France had less than 100 km.

A catching-up programme was launched in that year, but the government funding earmarked for the programme was patently insufficient. The introduction of a concession system to make up the shortfall meant that the necessary investment could be financed through borrowing and that contributions from users could be collected in the form of tolls. As a result, France was able to acquire a vast and modern motorway network which grew at an average rate of 180 km a year over thirty years.

France has often been cited as an illustration of successful partnership between the public and private sector in the construction and operation of motorways. However, although the principle of private sector involvement in the concession system was clearly stated, the management of the motorway network, though delegated, has remained largely in public hands. The system in France at present includes only one private company and six mixed-economy companies (*sociétés d'économie mixte* - SEM) with limited autonomy from the State, which, through two public corporations, is a majority shareholder.

The legal framework for the French motorway concession system was introduced in two stages:

- The law of 18 April 1955 authorised the use of concessions for the construction and operation of motorways and the collection of tolls by the concession holder. However, concessions could only be awarded to public bodies.

- A reform in 1970 allowed the State to award concessions for new motorways to entirely private companies and extended the responsibilities of concession holders.

In practice, a third phase followed these first two "legislative" phases. In the early 1980s, three of the four private concession-holding companies experienced severe cash-flow problems and were ultimately taken into the public sector.

Thus, of the nine companies (seven motorway companies and two tunnel companies) that currently operate the 5 700 km of French motorway covered by concessions[1], only one (COFIROUTE) is entirely privately-owned, public bodies being the majority shareholders of the others.

To avoid ambiguity, the meaning of the terms used to refer to the French public authorities "State" and "public sector" should be made explicit. The State is generally defined in two different ways. Strictly speaking, the State consists of central administrative departments whose operations are outlined in the finance law voted annually by Parliament (i.e. the State budget). More broadly, it corresponds to all public administrations, including central administrations (the State in the strict sense and various bodies such as universities, specialist institutions of higher education, the National Centre for Scientific Research), local administrations (local authorities at regional, departmental and commune level and various bodies such as lower and higher secondary schools) and social security departments. This paper uses the term State in its first, strict definition. The term "public sector" means all public administrations (the State in the broad sense), together with bodies controlled directly or indirectly by them (such as public credit institutions and public corporations).

PHASE 1: INTRODUCTION OF A PUBLIC SYSTEM OF MOTORWAY CONCESSIONS (1955-1970)

With economic recovery in the mid-1950s and the expectation of increased trade as a result of the creation of the EEC, the expansion of transport capacity and the modernisation of the national network became a matter of urgency. As the State budget alone was unable to provide the necessary resources, given the amount of investment required, it seemed essential to raise funds on the financial markets. However, the use of spending ministry budgets for debt service and the collection of tolls by State administrations were precluded under French budget rules.

The solution, introduced in the law of April 18, 1955, consisted in allowing "a concession for the construction and operation of a motorway [to be] awarded by the State to a public authority, grouping of public authorities, chamber of commerce or mixed economy company in which public authorities are the majority shareholder". The latter option was adopted. Concession-holding bodies were incorporated as mixed economy companies (*sociétés d'économie mixte* - SEM), authorised to contract long-term loans to finance the construction of the sections of motorway covered by the concession and to collect tolls "to ensure service of the interest and redemption of the capital invested [...] and the maintenance and possible extension of the motorway".

The first concession holder, ESCOTA[2], was created in 1956 with capital of FF 15 million and an initial concession of 48 km. Subsequent SEM were formed with much less capital or even, in the case of the last three, purely symbolic amounts in relation to the cost of building one kilometer of motorway (approximately FF 4.3 million in the early 1960s): SAVR (initial concession of 71 km) was created in 1957 with capital of FF 2 million, SAPL (158 km) in 1961 with FF 850 000, SAPN (69 km) and SANEF (132 km) in 1963 with 500 000 F (Fayard, 1980).

The SEM's equity was held by local authorities and by the *Caisse des Dépôts et Consignations*, a public credit institution, either directly or through one of its subsidiaries, SCET. As there were no private shareholders, these companies were "mixed" in name only.

Furthermore, although the State had no direct stake in any of the SEM, it nevertheless played an essential role in both the financial and technical aspects of the enterprise.

Financial assistance from the State, in the form of repayable advances from the Road Investment Special Fund (*Fonds spécial d'investissement routier* -- FSIR), represented 30 to 40 per cent of the amounts invested. The remainder was provided from loans guaranteed by the State and contracted by the *Caisse nationale des autoroutes* (CNA), an institution managed by the *Caisse des Dépôts* responsible for "issuing loans earmarked for financing the construction or development of toll motorways and dividing the proceeds of such loans between the authorities or companies holding the concession" (decree creating the CNA).

On the technical side, the State was responsible for design and acted as general contractor for construction and maintenance work.

Organised in this way, the system showed the motorway concession-holding SEM to be a "disguise" for the State, an expression used by the Minister for Public Works in 1969. The SEM served merely to provide a legal framework for the earmarking of loans and the collection and allocation of tolls.

By circumventing the budget restrictions which were hampering the development of the French motorway network, the system paved the way for the construction of some 1 000 km of motorway in 15 years, the rate of construction rising gradually from 50 to 150 km a year between 1960 and 1970 (see Figure 1). However, although construction was progressing apace, it was not sufficient to meet sharply rising demand resulting from the rapid increase in traffic. Fresh impetus was required.

PHASE 2: BRINGING IN THE PRIVATE SECTOR -- THE 1970 REFORM

Under the 1970 finance law and the decree of May 12, 1970, the concession system was extended to private companies.

The purpose of these new measures was to diversify the sources of funding by making it possible to raise private capital and contract loans not guaranteed by the State.

They were also intended to improve the efficiency of existing concession holders (through lower costs and the greater discipline of having to return profit and loss accounts) by giving the SEM greater independence from the State in technical, financial and pricing matters. However, the system applied to the SEM was not the same as the one applied to private concession holders.

New responsibilities for the SEM

From a technical standpoint, concession-holding companies acquired a certain degree of control over construction projects and full responsibility for carrying them out.

Design

Once the planning aspects had been settled, the Ministry of Public Works (*ministère de l'Équipement*) defined the principal characteristics of the future motorway (route, technical conditions for construction and operation, etc.).

In particular, the State decided whether the motorway should operate as a closed system (users are given a ticket at their point of entry onto the motorway and pay on leaving it; the amount of the toll thus depends on the number of kilometres travelled) or as an open system (users pay a single toll on entry, the preferred system for motorways with a large number of interchanges).

Local authorities were consulted through the Prefect, a representative of the State. The resulting motorway project, called a "summary draft project" (*Avant-projet sommaire* - APS), was submitted to public inquiry, a procedure which enabled the inhabitants of the municipalities concerned to make comments and suggestions. The draft project was then declared to be of public utility. Up to this point, the State alone was responsible for the project.

The concession-holding company then took over and was responsible for carrying out more detailed studies, including work on refining traffic and cost forecasts. These studies resulted in a "draft motorway project" (*Avant-projet d'autoroute* - APA), submitted for approval to the Ministry for Public Works which ensured that it complied with the technical characteristics and route defined by the State.

In Spring 1970, the SEM created a common design company, Scetautoroute (a subsidiary of the SEM and the *Caisse des Dépôts*), to act as general contractor for construction work.

Construction

The concession holders were entirely responsible for contracting, which had to be carried out on the basis of competitive tendering, except with authorisation to the contrary from the minister responsible for Public Works.

The concession holders were also responsible for acquiring land on the State's behalf.

- From a financial standpoint, the general thrust of the 1970 reform was to give the SEM greater independence from the State. Whereas under the previous system all their loans were contracted by the *Caisse nationale des autoroutes* and guaranteed by the State, under the new system the SEM were able to contract loans directly, without State guarantees.

- As regards pricing, the 1970 measures entitled the SEM to set tolls up to an index-linked ceiling.

This relative freedom was curtailed by an order of March 1975 by which the State (or more accurately, the Ministry of the Economy and Finance) took back control over motorway tolls.

The changes to the initial rules regarding toll-setting also applied to private concession-holding companies, despite the fact that under the 1970 legislation they had been granted considerably more freedom to set tolls than the SEM.

The principles of private concessions

In technical matters, the only difference between the rules for private concession holders and the SEM concerned tendering procedures. While the SEM were required to award contracts on the basis of competitive tendering, private companies were free to engage the companies of their choice.

Otherwise, the principles governing the private concession system under the 1970 reform reflected the particular nature of motorway investments.

The trend over time of the investment in and return on a motorway project is described in Figure 2 (which is typical of the construction and operation of most infrastructures).

Structurally, a company holding a motorway concession experiences heavy operating losses during the first few years of operation and only moves into profit after a fairly long period (the "normal" duration of the loss-making period is around 15 years). However, the company is assured of making large profits for many years thereafter.

The principles of private concessions took the following features into account.

1. Given the trend of expenditure and receipts in the construction and operation of a motorway, the concession had to be granted for a long period. So as to allow the concession holder to achieve "suitable profitability", the duration was set at 35 years following completion of half the section covered by the concession.

2. Because the investment does not become profitable for many years, State participation in the financing risk seemed necessary in order to interest private investors in motorway concessions. The State thus agreed to guarantee some of the loans contracted (the initial limit was 60 per cent). From 1977 onwards the State guarantee, originally accorded free of charge, was charged at a rate of 0.5 per cent of the amount of the loan.

   Under the 1970 reform, private shareholders were required to provide at least 10 per cent of the amount of the investment (excluding State contributions). The risk initially assumed by the State thus concerned 54 per cent of the cost (60 per cent of 90 per cent).

3. The trend over time of toll receipts, which depends on traffic and tariff trends, is a decisive factor in the concession holders' assessment of acceptable risk. The rules for private companies, under which they were responsible for traffic forecasts, also allowed them a certain degree of latitude in setting tolls. They were entirely free to set tolls during 10 years following the opening of half the section of motorway covered by the concession. This freedom was subsequently restricted by an index-linked ceiling; the private concession holders were thus subject, after 10 years' operation, to the same system as the SEM.

It was assumed that competition from parallel routes would limit the temptation for private companies to set their tolls too high during the first 10 years.

(By virtue of the French principle of access to the national network free of charge, set out in 1789 and intermingled with that of the equality of the citizen before public services, to which the law of 1955 concerning the status of motorways created an exception, the State is required to maintain alternative toll-free routes, i.e. to maintain trunk roads, accessible free of charge, parallel to the motorways.)

As the Minister for Public Works said at the time, "the best sanction in this respect [is] the law of the marketplace. The existence of tolls will have a dissuasive effect on some traffic. It is in the interest of the concession holder, who operates in order to make a profit, to calculate the toll in such a way as to dissuade as little traffic as possible". The imposition of a ceiling after 10 years was justified by the fact that competition from parallel routes decreases as total traffic increases (the price elasticity of motorway traffic, which varies between -2 and -0.3 and also depends, for a given section, on the quality of the alternative route, is a decreasing function of the level of traffic).

However, as mentioned above, the government reneged on the principle of the freedom to set tariffs. An order of March 1975 signed by the Finance Minister and the Minister for Public Works required concession holders to submit their revised tariffs prior to any change; tolls could thus be examined and if necessary vetoed by the Finance Minister. This change was reflected by a reduction in the existing differential between the average tolls charged by private concession holders and those charged by SEM, and by a harmonisation of their rate of increase. On January 1, 1975 the average toll in F/km for a saloon car charged by private companies was more than double the toll charged by SEM; the ratio settled at around 1.63 from 1977 and the average tolls of both private companies and SEM increased at an annual rate of around 5 per cent over the period 1977-1979.[3]

4. Because of the considerable time lag between the initial investment and the time when toll receipts come one stream, specific accounting rules were defined for concession holders (both private companies and SEM). The chart of accounts for concession holders allows them to include deferred charges as balance sheet assets (i.e. to treat what in conventional accounting would be losses in the same way as charges to be carried over to subsequent years). The only restriction on this system of deferred charges[4] is that concession holders are not allowed to distribute dividends until the charges have been absorbed.

The results

Between 1970 and 1973, four private companies[5] joined the existing five mixed economy companies.

Most of their equity was owned by civil engineering companies, with banks holding around 10 per cent. They were in essence groupings of entrepreneurs with the backing of their banks, and the private concession system in fact proved to be just a system for awarding contracts: as private concession holders were free to engage the companies of their choice to carry out the work, they awarded contracts to their shareholders.

The rate of motorway construction surged ahead as a result of the legal and financial changes introduced in 1970, averaging 350 km a year during the 1970s. In 10 years, almost 3 000 km of additional motorway were brought into service (see Figure 1).

However, this outcome required more State participation than the 1970 reform had foreseen. In 1976 and 1977 the State granted substantial (repayable) advances to the concession holders. When COFIROUTE, a private company, wished to extend its concession it was granted advances under highly favourable conditions (unlike the practice for the SEM at the time, the advances were not index-linked).

Motorway investment is a very long-term business, financed over 15 to 20 years; as the return is deferred for many years, the investment is highly sensitive to changes in economic circumstances during the early years.

The first few years of the private concession system coincided with the first oil crisis, reflected in:

- *a considerable increase in the cost of works* (the price of bitumen increased by 3.1 between 1973 and 1976, while the overall civil engineering index increased by 18 per cent in 1974 and around 24 per cent in 1975 compared with 8 to 9 per cent in the preceding years), in operating costs (higher payroll costs) and in financing costs (long-term interest rates doubled between 1970 and 1974, from 6 to 12 per cent)[6];

- *a slower rate of increase in receipts*, less because of slower traffic growth (after little or no growth in 1974, from 1975 motorway traffic grew at a rate close to the rate recorded before the oil crisis) than because tolls did not rise fast enough.

In the early 1980s, three of the existing four companies[7] were experiencing such severe cash flow problems that they had to call in the State guarantee in order to repay some of their loans.

The State's response to this crisis in the private concession system was to buy out the loss-making companies.

PHASE 3 : A MAINLY PUBLIC SYSTEM (SINCE THE EARLY 1980S)

The State, whose guarantee had been called in by private companies in difficulty, negotiated a buy-out with their shareholders and "repaid their stake (at current values), ultimately [covering] the risks for which their contribution had been requested" (*Cour des Comptes*, 1992, p. 32). The companies were either taken over by an existing SEM (as with APEL, taken over by SANEF) or transformed into mixed economy companies.

The State's takeover of the system was consolidated in 1988 by the acquisition by public bodies (*Autoroutes de France* and the *Caisse des Dépôts*) of majority shareholdings in all the SEM holding motorway concessions.

Tighter public control has been reflected in the centralised management of the cash balances of the concession holders and a clarification and redefinition of pricing policy.

Management of cash balances

In 1982 it was decided to introduce a mechanism for equalising cash balances with the aim of protecting the SEM against the likelihood of cash flow problems suggested by 10-year forecasts. Implementation of this policy was entrusted to *Autoroutes de France* (ADF), a public body created for the purpose in 1983 and managed by the *Caisse des Dépôts*. The State transferred all its claims on the SEM (advances and contributions in kind) to ADF, which became responsible for ensuring that they were repaid. As ADF now held the State's claims on the SEM, it was able to carry out the desired equalisation.

This equalisation involved lending the cash surpluses from profitable SEM to loss-making SEM. If the aggregate cash balances of the various SEM proved to be negative, ADF was authorised to raise loans in order to bring the system back into balance. This was the case in 1984 and 1986.

The mechanism allowed profitable SEM which had repaid all their debts to ADF to leave the equalisation system. However, the inevitable question arose of how to use the revenue thus raised, ie, the cash surplus of SEM that had left the equalisation system. On the one hand, the rules governing SEM prohibited them from distributing dividends in excess of 7 per cent of their paid-up non-amortised capital. On the other hand, returning this type of cash surplus to the State budget would require legislative changes that have never been contemplated in earnest. The solution adopted consisted in recycling such "motorway revenues" internally: concessions for planned new sections of motorway were awarded as a priority to the SEM with the largest surpluses, thus allowing them to finance some of the necessary investment from their own resources.

The present system is currently being reorganised. The ADF is due to be scrapped and the SEM are to be regrouped as subsidiaries, the system being restructured around a small number of central cores. Regroupings are likely to be carried out along both geographical and financial lines, with the most profitable SEM acting as nuclei and being linked to loss-making SEM. A system for equalising cash balances, identical in principle to the one introduced by ADF for the network as a whole, is likely to be used within each of the cores formed in this way.

This development should also ensure that the structure of the system corresponds to its network-oriented, rather than project-oriented, approach, which calls for a certain degree of solidarity between regions. The probable profitability of certain sections of motorway is very low or even zero. Although they are regarded as essential to a coherent national development policy, they could only be constructed by companies operating highly profitable sections.

According to the *Cour des Comptes*, this is the case for one third of the new sections of motorway included in the national master plan adopted in 1988.

In its 1990 report (Vol. I, p. 232), the *Cour des Comptes* notes that "traffic of 1 500 vehicles/day is generally regarded as necessary to cover the costs of toll collection alone; 4 500-5 000 vehicles/day make it possible to cover operating costs; 15 000-20 000 vehicles/day make it possible to cover all costs, including the repayment of loans. [...] the forecast traffic on one third of the planned sections of motorway is less than 6 000 vehicles/day, making it uncertain whether operating costs can be covered. [...] The immediate rate of return, corresponding to operating profits in the first year, excluding interest, depreciation and repairs, in relation to total investment costs, is negative or zero for 5 of the 32 projects included, equal to or less than 1 per cent for 13 projects and is not more than 3.6 per cent for any project. The internal rate of return, corresponding to the real interest rate required to finance a project over 35 years without any imbalance in the accounts, never exceeds 3.5 per cent. For 22 projects it actually ranges between 0 and - 10 per cent".

Pricing policy

ADF, the public corporation responsible for implementing the cash balance equalisation mechanism outlined above, was also asked to help to homogenise tolls across the network as a whole. As a result of its efforts, the difference between tolls at opposite extremes was reduced from a ratio of 1 to 3 in 1980 to 1 to 2 in 1990. According to the Finance Ministry, "the harmonisation of tolls between old sections and new sections has a dual aim: the pursuit of national development objectives and the setting of tolls in an economically rational way. It would be paradoxical to set very low tolls for old motorways, which are well travelled and well on the way to being amortised, while setting high tolls for new sections, which are both expensive and as yet relatively little travelled" (*Cour des*

Comptes, 1990, p. 243). Price equalisation thus institutes a kind of solidarity in time and place between motorway users.

Except between 1970 and 1974, the Finance Ministry consistently maintained tight control over motorway tolls[8] although there was no basis for this position in law. Following the acquisition by ADF and the *Caisse des Dépôts* of majority shareholdings in the SEM (34 per cent and 17 per cent respectively), its control over motorway tolls was confirmed by a decree of December 30, 1988 which provides for tolls to be set by the Finance Minister after consulting the Minister for Public Works. The decree further states that "the amount of tolls shall vary, as an average and for each company, according to developments in the structure of the network and variations in financial charges, the cost of works and maintenance, wages, taxes and traffic".

A relaxation of the system set up under the 1988 decree has been announced, with annual authorisations being replaced by five-year price brackets set by each company and, in some cases, for individual motorways.

Since 1988, pricing policy has to a certain extent been oriented towards the use of tolls as a means for managing traffic.

Geographical variations in tolls are beginning to be introduced, a trend that coincides with the changing shape of the motorway network. Under the new national master plan drawn up in 1988 the network, hitherto star-shaped, is being transformed into a close-mesh structure; in other words, existing motorway routes are being supplemented by alternative motorway routes. Tolls are then varied in order to channel traffic towards these new routes.

Since 1992, time-based pricing has been used as well as geographical toll variations, with the aim of reducing peak traffic levels by ensuring that the external costs caused by congestion are charged more fairly. On some sections of motorway, different tolls are charged at week-ends and during the summer.

The trend at present is towards a better distribution of costs between different user categories. The rate at which expenditure is covered by receipts [tolls + domestic tax on oil products + axle tax for Heavy Goods Vehicles (HGVs)] is currently 52 per cent for HGVs and 232 per cent for light vehicles, given that the maximum ratio between tolls for light vehicles and tolls for HGVs is set at 2.5. This maximum ratio is likely to rise to 3 or even 4. However, a cautious approach must be taken to policy in this area because of the possible displacement of road haulage traffic onto parallel routes for which there is no charge.

However, these changes in pricing policy remain marginal. Tolls are still primarily regarded not as a means for managing traffic flows but as a source of funding, the purpose of which is to ensure the financial equilibrium of concessions.

The national master plan, revised upwards in 1990, provides for a French motorway network with a total length of 12 120 km, including 9 540 km covered by concessions and 2 540 km of links ensuring the continuity of the motorway network, very similar to motorways but without tolls.

With the additional 3 500 km of motorway in the plan covered by concessions being shared out between the various companies, and given that the term of a company's concession is extended with each new section[9], concessions are likely to end between 2010 and 2012. By that time, the total financing capacity is likely to be almost zero. From 2010-2012 the motorway network as a whole, operated under conditions similar to those pertaining at present, should thus generate net revenues.

There are in theory two possible options for future operation.

The system could be changed into one of operating concessions, under which tolls would be used solely to cover maintenance costs, in which case they would need to be only about one third of their present level. However, it is difficult to see the State giving up such an important source of revenue.

The second, and much more likely, solution would be the creation of a State-owned company (*régie*) to operate the motorways. This option, which would not require any change in current pricing, would make it possible for toll revenues to be included in the State budget. The question arises, however, of whether it would be socially acceptable for tolls paid by motorway users only to be used for any purpose other than improving the motorway network.

* * *

Overall, although the French experience demonstrates the budgetary disengagement of the State from the extension and modernisation of the national network, it has been achieved more by the steady removal of interest charges from the State budget and their transfer to mixed economy companies and local authorities than by developing genuine partnership between the private and public sector.

In the early 1950s the State financed almost all capital expenditure on the national road system (trunk roads and motorways) from budget credits. By 1980, borrowings and internal financing by concession-holding companies (a little over 45 per cent of investment capacity) exceeded funding from budget credits (around 42 per cent), the remainder being assumed by local authorities (ie, around 13 per cent). The share of local authority funding rose to almost 29 per cent in 1990, with that of concession-holding companies remaining stable at around 44 per cent, while the State contributed only 27 per cent. "A situation was thus created in which the State, while retaining legal control over the entire national road system, funded only one third or one quarter of capital expenditure on it" (Report of the *Cour des Comptes*, May 1992, p. 22).

It is true that private investors were brought into the system at the worst possible moment, that of the first oil shock. However, although the oil crisis was the main reason for the failure of private companies, the nature of the companies interested in motorway concessions was also a contributory factor. Motorway concessions held little attraction for financial groups because any return on investment was delayed for many years; thus, they were of genuine interest only to civil engineering companies. It may be supposed that some companies of this type embarked on motorway concessions with an eye not so much on the profitability of the operation as on the assurance of a certain volume of work.

The network-oriented, as opposed to project-oriented, approach of the system considerably limits the options for future private sector involvement. Only a few motorways are still to be built and their profitability is hypothetical, to say the least. Urban motorways are the only conceivable area for private sector involvement at present. In the Ile-de-France region, for example, a private company, Ville Express, has recently been created and there are plans for an underground motorway (the "Muse" project) involving both private and public investment.

It should also be pointed out that the concession system in itself causes certain perverse effects. Because of the favourable financing terms on offer, the concession system means that motorways may be preferred to dual carriageways even where the latter are more appropriate. (Because of annual budgeting procedures, the time lag between deciding to build a dual carriageway and bringing it into service is around 20 years; the construction time for a motorway under the concession system is around 6 years.) The preference for building motorways from scratch rather than upgrading existing trunk roads to dual carriageway also engenders excess costs of a different type. First, the cost of building a motorway is around 30 per cent higher than that of upgrading a trunk road to dual carriageway. Second, the principal of access free of charge to the national network means that a route for which there is no charge has to be maintained parallel to a motorway for which tolls can be charged. Thus the cost has to be borne of maintaining and improving an existing trunk road covering the same route as a newly built motorway. Third, the fact that a charge is made for using the motorway and that tolls are expensive to collect (collection costs represent approximately 10 per cent of turnover) means that the number of access points to the motorway is limited (there are half as many motorway access points in France as in Germany). The area served by a toll motorway is therefore not as extensive as that served by a dual carriageway for which there is no charge.

However, in terms of the speed with which the motorway network has been built the concession system has been an undisputed success. The French example is not in any sense an illustration of successful partnership between the public and private sector in the construction and operation of motorways. However, it is undeniably an example of a country which has taken the necessary steps to catch up with other comparable European countries and build a vast and modern motorway network in record time.

ACRONYMS AND ABBREVIATIONS

ACOBA	Société de l'autoroute de la Côte Basque	Former private company
ADF	Autoroutes de France	Public corporation
APA	Avant-projet d'autoroute	Draft motorway project
APEL	Société des autoroutes Paris-Est-Lorraine	Former private company
APS	Avant-projet sommaire	Summary draft project
AREA	Société des autoroutes Rhône-Alpes	Former private company
ASF	Société des autoroutes du sud de la France	SEM (formerly SAVR)
CNA	Caisse nationale des autoroutes	Public corporation
COFIROUTE	Compagnie financière et industrielle des autoroutes	Private company
ESCOTA	Société de l'autoroute Estérel-Côte d'Azur	SEM
FSIR	Fonds spécial d'investissement routier	Road investment special fund
SANEF	Société des autoroutes du nord et de l'est de la France	SEM
SAPL	Société de l'autoroute Paris-Lyon	SEM (subsequently SAPRR)
SAPN	Société de l'autoroute Paris-Normandie	SEM
SAPRR	Société des autoroutes Paris-Rhin-Rhône	SEM (formerly SAPL)
SAVR	Société des autoroutes de la Vallée du Rhône	SEM (subsequently ASF)
SCET	Société Centrale pour l'Equipement du Territoire	Public corporation
SEM	Société d'économie mixte	Mixed economy company

Figure 1. **Highways construction rate (1960-1979)**

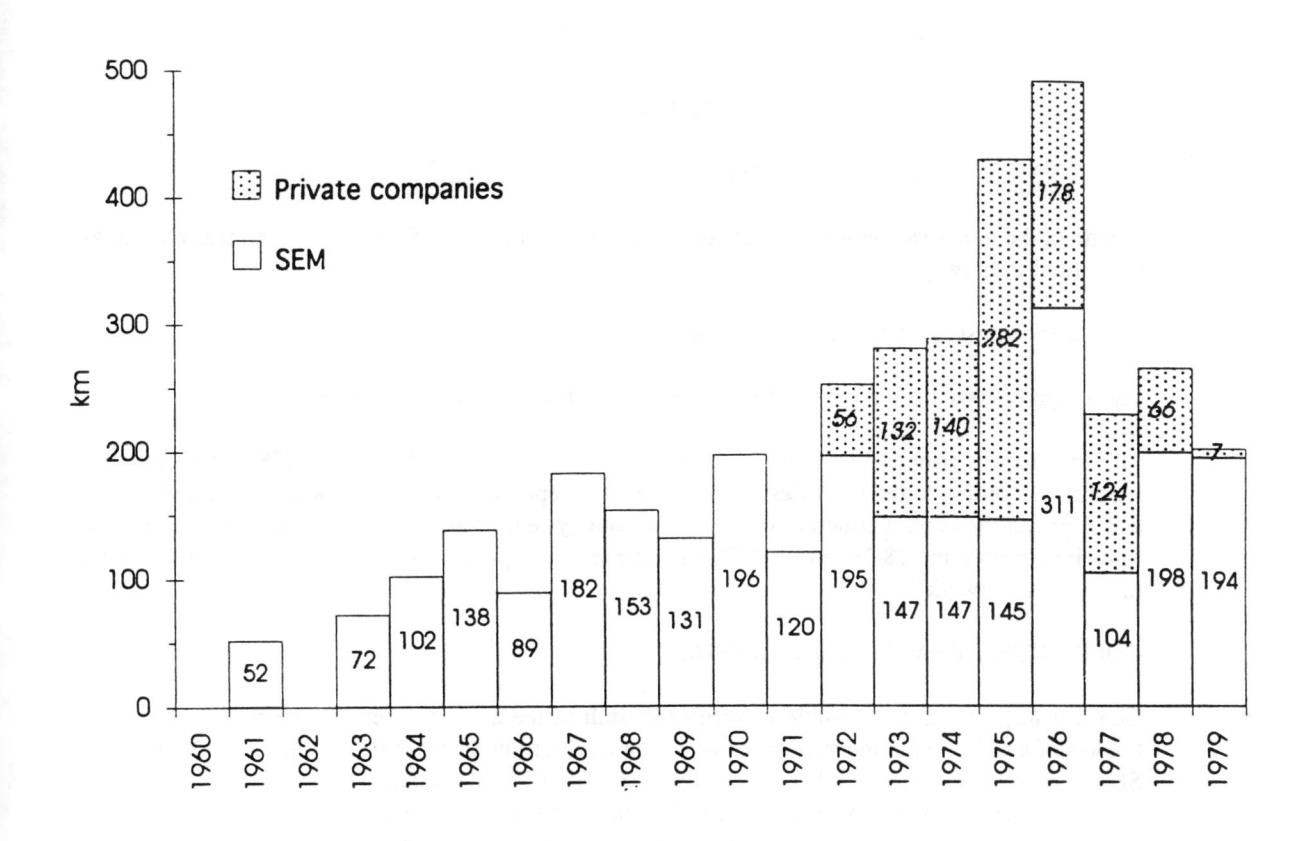

Figure 2. **Profit and loss of highway concessions**

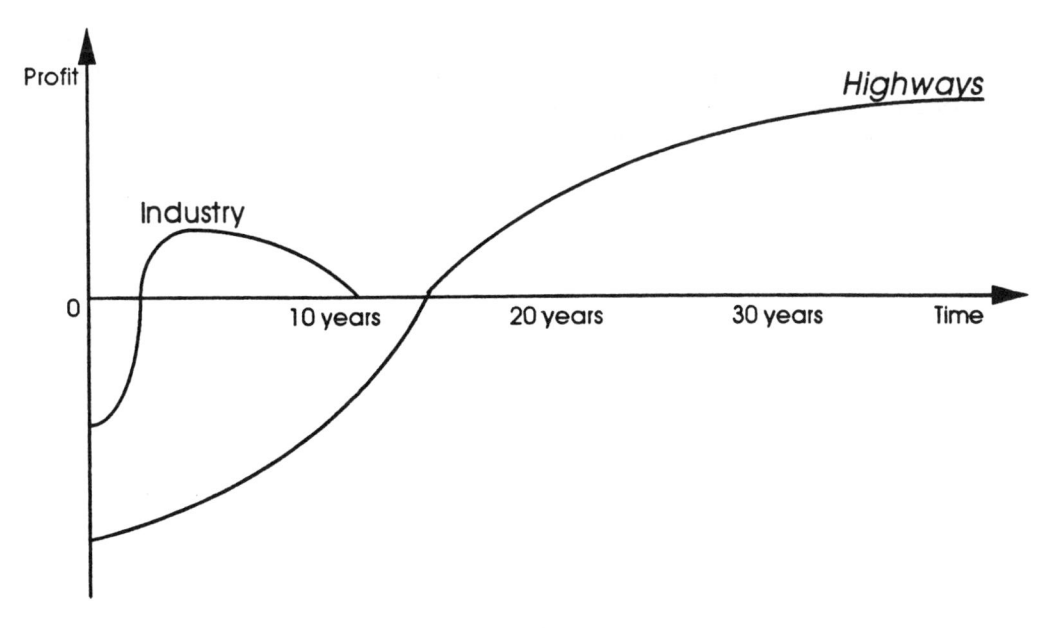

NOTES

1. Length of the motorway network under concession in operation in 1993, plus approximately 1 500 km of non-toll motorway.

2. See appended list for the meaning of acronyms.

3. These figures have been reconstituted from data supplied by Fayard, 1980, pp. 112-113.

4. This system was criticised by the *Cour des Comptes* (State audit office) in its 1986, 1990 and 1992 reports. According to the *Cour des Comptes*, these exceptional practices allowed an artificial balance and deprived the current structure of the concession system of any warning indicators. See esp. the May 1992 report, pp. 78-79, entitled "Road and motorway policy: assessment of the management of the national network".

5. COFIROUTE, AREA, APEL and ACOBA.

6. Consequently, it was not possible to verify the truth of the announcement by the private concession holders of a reduction in the average construction cost per km of motorway compared with that of the SEM. In 1969 the companies that were to form COFIROUTE stated that they could reduce the average cost to FF 3.3 million (compared with FF 4.3 million for the SEM, representing a saving of around 23 per cent). By 1978, the average cost of a motorway in open countryside had reached FF 10 million per km. See Fayard, 1980, pp. 69-73.

7. See note 5 above.

8. The fact that tolls are included in the retail price index may be one reason for this, even though their effect is only small.

9. This practice, which derives from a very broad interpretation of the law of 1955, corresponds to the notion of "overall concession". Specific concessions are not linked to each section under concession; each section covered by a new concession is added to the network operated by a company, giving rise to an extension of its overall concession.

BIBLIOGRAPHY

Cour des Comptes (1990), Public report of the *Cour des Comptes* (*Rapport public de la Cour des Comptes*), Vol I.

Cour des Comptes (1992), "Road and motorway policy: assessment of the management of the national network", (*"La politique routière et autoroutière : Évaluation de la gestion du réseau national", Rapport du Président de la République*), May.

FAYARD, Alain (1980), "Les autoroutes et leur financement", Notes et études documentaires, Nos. 4597-4598, December 10.

MERLIN, Pierre (1991), *Géographie, économie et planification des transports*, Paris, PUF.

Chapter Four

PRIVATE FINANCING OF PUBLIC INFRASTRUCTURE IN GERMANY

by

Sylvie Trosa
Formerly of the French Conseil
Scientifique de l'Évaluation

and

Martin Schreiner
OECD Public Management Service

INTRODUCTION

The German Government is currently investigating new forms of private and joint public/private finance for public infrastructure. The new approaches are being pursued in the fields of highway and national road construction and wastewater treatment plants.

This chapter is based on an analysis of documents produced by several ministries (see Bibliography) and on personal communication with ministry officials[1]. It deals with the following aspects:

- the reasons prompting the Government to advocate private financing for public infrastructure;

- the various organisational models considered;

- charging for the services provided;

- the view of the Budget Department at the Federal Ministry of Finance.

I. WHY PRIVATE FINANCING OF PUBLIC INFRASTRUCTURE?

The Government's strategy

"Privatisation and private financing of infrastructure will be two of the watchwords of economic strategy in the coming years" (The Federal Ministry for the Environment, Nature Conservation, and Nuclear Safety, 1993). In the context of the 1991 budget, the Federal Government set up a working party to investigate the possibilities of using private funding for public infrastructure, especially in the areas of transport and the environment. The working party delivered its conclusions in June 1991, the verdict being that increased private sector commitments were desirable.

The reasons put forward were the following:

- Because of a very serious lack of infrastructure in the *Länder* of the former GDR, where environmental problems in particular have not been taken into account, new financing solutions must be found. The state of the roads and of the infrastructure for environmental protection is almost catastrophic: numerous structures have been destroyed, the roads have not been maintained, many towns -- including such big ones as Dresden -- have no wastewater treatment plant.

- The current constraints on the Federal budget require utilising private finance, since the government no longer has the means to finance all infrastructure investments with public funds.

- Recourse to private operators provides for increased flexibility and saves substantial amounts of time.

- User charges increase total investment capacity.

- Augmenting both privatisation and contracting out support the Federal Government's general policy of reducing the role of government in favour of market solutions.

The report on the State of the Economy in 1993 remarks that "planning, construction, finance, and operation of infrastructure by the private sector not only eases the burden on public sectors' budgets, but also save time because private entrepreneurs are much more flexible than government in the way they proceed. The transition from direct administrative provision of infrastructure to contracting out would thus substantially alleviate the government's administrative burden" (The Federal Ministry of Economics, 1993, p. 54).

Several factors explain why time can be saved: arranging a global contract with an entrepreneur enables the latter to organise his work as he wishes, arranging contracts by mutual agreement (without going through the cumbersome public procurement procedures). In addition, private operators can resort to the various types of loan and financing as they wish, without having to obtain prior authorisation from the Ministry of Finance.

According to German government officials, time savings generated by using private finance are due to

- The professionalism of the companies involved.

- The companies' ability to have overall control over projects, without being constantly obliged to comply with public procurement procedures.

- The capacity to manage national projects without having to negotiate with all the levels of government. Efficiency gains from the latter, however, can only be reaped successfully if the planning process for the project in question has been fully completed in coordination with the *Länder*, municipalities, and citizens concerned. The planning result must be of such a quality that it can stand any judicial challenge likely to be brought up in the administrative courts.

Based on the findings of the working party's report, the Federal Cabinet decided on January 22, 1992 that private infrastructure financing should be analysed and introduced on an experimental basis, using the concession (pre-financing) model (the first pilot projects are the Nuremberg-Ingolstadt-Munich rail link and the Engelberg tunnel). The concession model also opens up the future avenue of raising user charges and fees[2].

To the extent that environmental concerns lie within the competence of local authorities, the Federal Government provides them with guidelines on which to base their decisions, concerning their mode of provision of new wastewater treatment plants. It has also set up a foundation of DM 2.5 million, which finances up to 75 per cent of the cost of feasibility studies (the municipalities covering the remaining 25 per cent), so that municipalities can decide which mode, private or public management, is likely to give the municipality the best cost/benefit ratio. The overall approach is an experimental one, the goal being to use pilot projects to test new solutions.

In general, the Federal Ministry of the Environment requires that (The Federal Ministry for the Environment, Nature Conservation and Nuclear Safety, 1993):

- the contracts be long-term, with provisions being made to deal with any defaulting on the part of contractors;

- effective quality controls be guaranteed;

- changes in legislation can be incorporated in contracts;

- stability of the level of charges can be ensured over the long term.

The Ministry also expects that the legal problems with regard to differential tax treatment of public and private service providers will be settled by the Federal Parliament.

Throughout official papers, there is much insistence on the private sector's ability to be more efficient than the public sector. Consequently, it is the government's intention to introduce the subsidiarity principle, implying that management under public control should be used only if public/private partnerships or private management are not feasible. Official papers are aware of the fact that there are still many legal and tax obstacles restricting the free choice of management methods. These obstacles also derive from German history and administrative culture.

Historically, in Germany contracting out has been used mainly for exceptional or large-scale projects (e.g. airports). It has not been standard practice for smaller scale infrastructure provision. All that has hitherto been contracted out is the actual construction work which, where roads are concerned for example, has always been performed by private companies. The management of the project and supervision of the work, on the other hand, and also all the planning studies, have always been in government hands. In this connection, the legal context is of particular importance in Germany. The constitution stipulates that the bulk of public utilities are the responsibility of the authorities, and traditionally the courts have taken the view that government responsibility was equivalent to management by the public authorities (the case, for example, of wastewater treatment which was deemed to come under the heading of public health). The acceptance of the concept that responsibility and management might not be in the same hands is advancing slowly. The main concern is that the contractor might not fulfil the requirements of continuity and equality of service. The principles of equal access to public services for all and of the need for continuity of these services are of paramount importance in Germany. The cultural change involved in drawing a greater distinction between the public authority responsible and the private executing body is all the more delicate since it has to be implemented first in the eastern *Länder* where the tasks are enormous, but public agencies' experience with private firms is least developed.

The decision of the Cabinet of July 1992 also states that concessions granted for private pre-financing of transportation projects will rely, initially, on funding from the Federal budget. The franchisees will only subsequently be able to resort to user charging. The debate on the related constitutional issues was on a fairly elevated level. The Federal Government made clear that while it is indeed the state that is constitutionally responsible for infrastructure provision, it is nowhere stipulated in the constitution that the state has also to manage and finance infrastructure projects. The government is responsible for the results, but not for the means.

The objective is that both management methods and public and private operators should systematically find themselves in an open competitive situation in principle, without any one solution having a greater chance of being selected than the other. The German Parliament decided on 22 October 1993 to amend the law governing the budgetary process *(Bundeshaushaltsordnung)* in such a way as to reinforce the principles of "value for money" and thrift, and to incorporate the mandatory search for private management solutions in the framework of government responsibilities. The new wording is as follows:

> *(1) The principle of "value for money" shall be respected when drawing up budgets. This principle shall mean looking first at the possibility of privatising or partially contracting out any government schemes.*
>
> *(2) Where major financial decisions are concerned, cost/benefit analyses shall be carried out. In certain cases, open invitations to tender shall be issued in order to determine whether private management alternatives are possible.*

A working party asked by the Chancellor to submit a report on private financing of public infrastructure concluded that "all federal government and *Länder* rules should be directed towards ensuring that public and private management solutions are approached in a completely equitable manner so as to guarantee that the formula giving the best benefit/cost ratio is selected" (The Federal Minister for the Environment, Nature Conservation, and Nuclear Safety, 1993, p. 2).

The task now is to embody these principles in the legislation of the *Länder* and municipalities by political persuasion, as coercion is not possible. This has already been done in the case of the *Länder* of Brandenburg and Thuringia. In order to encourage the spread of the new rules, the Federal Government is considering circulating standard specifications by way of indication. On constitutional grounds, however, the Federal Government cannot force the *Länder* and the municipalities to change legal rules governing public services that they are responsible for according to the Basic Law.

As in all countries, contracting can take two forms:

(1) the public authorities provide the company's resources either immediately or at a later date, the company not "paying" itself out of the prices set;

(2) there is an overall balance between private management and charging, as the enterprise is required to provide a service financed by the charges paid by the users.

It is the second point which is causing the main difficulty in Germany, since at present charging for the usage of highway infrastructure is unknown. To introduce it now would mean requiring payment for infrastructure which was previously free (paid for by taxes). As far as highways are concerned, the following issues are raised:

- Should only new, privately financed sections of highways have to be paid for by the users? What happens to the principle of user equality in such a case? This question is even more delicate because most of the new highways will be located in eastern Germany, where one finds the least ability to pay and where such a reform would cause the most political difficulties.

- If tolls are introduced on all highways, how will users react to this new charge?

As far as environmental problems are concerned, the call for private funds is mainly created by the situation in former East Germany, which is deemed catastrophic. In particular, wastewater treatment does not comply with European or West German standards. Only 30 per cent of all households are connected to a wastewater treatment plant. Most of the networks date from before 1945. 95 per cent of industrial wastewater is not adequately treated. To bring the wastewater treatment system up to the required standards requires an investment of between DM 110 and 150 billion over five years. It is impossible to finance this amount the traditional way. Consequently, the Ministry of the Environment is strongly in favour of employing private funding.

II. PARTNERSHIP MODELS

Four approaches are being experimented with: leasing, pre-financing, mixed models, and semi-public companies. As far as roads are concerned, pre-financing tends to be preferred.[3]

Leasing

- the authorities provide all the utilities and additional equipment needed before construction begins (drainage, access, etc.);

- a private company obtains a long-term leasehold *(Erbbaurecht)* or a similar type of property right on the land; it owns the motorway or infrastructure concerned and rents it to the government; when the lease expires, the government can either buy back (for example after 27 years), renew, or waive its rights and entrust them to the company;

- the rent paid by the government is based on the direct and indirect costs of financing the motorway; it should amount to 9 or 10 per cent of the investment costs;

- the operating costs will be met by the public sector.

In fact, leasing amounts to an arrangement to finance infrastructure investment indirectly from the Federal Government's budget, as the rent paid by the government is paying for the real cost of the infrastructure, but spread over time. Total construction costs do not have to be shown in the budget in the first year. It might seem that the cost of the appropriations is higher than in the case of direct financing from the government budget, government in this case having access to low-interest loans. However, the Ministry of Finance considers that:

a) There are legal ways to provide companies working for the government with low-interest loans.

b) "Even if a direct comparison of costs shows that the costs of private credit in the leasing context are higher, it is nevertheless a possible solution when it ensures that infrastructures are constructed and brought into service more rapidly" (The Federal Ministry of Finance, 1991, p. 32).

c) When leasing is used, the Federal Government budget does not have to bear all the investment costs in the first year. This implies that the cost can be spread out over time and consequently investment capacity is indirectly increased.

The Ministry of Finance insists on the fact that the choice of any legal solution must be preceded by a cost/benefit analysis, and that efficiency, rather than savings, must be pursued. These cost/benefit analyses are only just in their infancy.

At this stage, leasing is mainly considered for large projects. Since leasing is only possible if the financing plan is completed for the entire project, it is held against leasing that it will eliminate working in smaller tranches, which are easier to plan and implement. In addition, the rules governing bids for tender favour tranches. The administrative procedures for planning and tendering seem to be at odds with the financial requirements of leasing, consequently thwarting the budgetary flexibility to be gained by leasing. However, these criticisms would be applicable as well if pre-financing for larger projects is used.

The legal rules governing budgetary procedures (*Bundeshaushaltsordnung*) contain some leeway with regard to the leasing model. Problems concerning legal rules on taxation, however, generate difficulties for the feasibility of the leasing model for those infrastructure projects where a classical competitive market situation does not exist. The unresolved issues centre around the question of whether the common tax advantages of leasing based on the depreciation of the asset can be allocated with the lessor or not. To accommodate the special case of leasing of infrastructure projects, the income tax law and the law governing business relations would have to be changed. These points are currently being discussed at the Ministry of Finance.

Private pre-financing

Models based on private pre-financing of highways contain the following elementary structure:

- The Federal Government executes the planning work. Private consulting firms are hired to participate in the planning process.

- The Federal Government purchases the required tracts of land.

- The Federal Government and other relevant public authorities execute the planning procedure (*Planfeststellungsverfahren*). It is imperative that the planning procedure is successfully finalised and has stood up to all challenges brought up against it in the administrative courts, before the government starts the bidding process. The construction company that wins the competitive bidding builds the road (tunnel/bridge) and raises the necessary capital on its own.

- After the completion of construction, the state starts to pay for the project with annual payments over 15 years. Consequently, the private enterprise is exposed to a strong incentive to finalise the project as fast as possible. The annual payment will be fixed. It will not depend on the volume of the traffic. Hence the firm is protected against any economic risk. This will also be the case, if the contract includes operation and/or maintenance of the road (tunnel/bridge).

The guidelines issued by the Federal Ministry of Finance and by the *Länder* emphasize that contracts must not contain any cost indexation clauses. In addition, clauses providing for the authorities to step in in case a company defaults are not expected to be part of the contracts. However, the Ministry of Finance does not rule out the possibility that the government might be obliged to intervene in such a case. In this event, all charges and entitlements over the asset would revert to the state.

What is the difference between leasing and the pre-financing model? In financial terms, the difference is not great, since the government has to reimburse the real costs of the investment in both cases. The pre-financing model appears to be a substantially simpler formula because the government does not cede ownership of the infrastructure, and therefore does not have to buy it back on any due date. Contrary to the leasing approach, the pre-financing model does not generate difficult tax issues, whose legal aspects have not been properly solved yet. In general, the difference between the two approaches is legal rather than economic.

Mixed models

The highway is financed by the private sector, but the amount of rent paid by the government depends on the traffic generated. This model was adopted for the extension and renewal of the motorway A2 from Helmstedt to Berlin.

A private consortium combining banks and construction firms won a fixed duration contract to construct the motorway. After this period, the property rights will be transferred to the state for free. The government will pay a rental based on the traffic. The fees will differ depending on the type of the vehicle. From the point of view of the Ministry of Finance, this solution seems to have a number of drawbacks :

- the users do not pay any toll and thus do not feel accountable;

- it is only viable if the enterprise is able to shoulder any risks and thus costs resulting from insufficient traffic (otherwise, the government will have to step in);

- if the traffic should increase, the government will face a heavy burden to bear, which is very difficult to anticipate.

Semi-public (mixed) companies

As far as wastewater treatment is concerned, the organisational options at hand are more varied. Wastewater treatment is a public service that the municipalities have to provide on constitutional grounds. Consequently, the overwhelming majority of West German municipalities operates wastewater treatment plants either as a municipal agency (agency model/*Regiebetrieb* or *Eigenbetrieb*) or as municipality-owned company with limited liability (*Eigengesellschaft*). In former West Germany prior to unification, the absence of hard budget constraints made it superfluous to consider any changes of the mode of provision.

However, during the 1980s in the Federal State of Lower-Saxony, one experiment was undertaken to construct a small number of new plants that were both financed and operated privately (*Betreibermodell*). The model is especially suited for situations that require the construction of a new plant. After re-unification this model was transferred to the former GDR. So far, five new plants are already operating in the new *Länder* and several more are either under construction or in the planning stage.

Another option is to establish a co-operative company (*Kooperationsmodel*). The model consists of a corporation jointly funded and founded by the municipality and a private firm, realising a genuine public/private partnership in the form of a co-operative company. The municipality holds 51 per cent of the company's capital, the private firm 49 per cent, thus ensuring the municipality's final control. However, because of difficulties concerning internal organisation, the internal distribution of risks, and tax laws, this model has rarely been applied. Therefore, little empirical evidence as to its benefits is available.

The participation of private firms in the provision of wastewater treatment plants generates intricate questions concerning the interest rates charged on loans. In West Germany, municipality-owned companies with limited liability (*Eigengesellschaft*) enjoy the same low rates as the municipalities as borrowing entities themselves, as they are completely backed by the municipalities. The risk for a German municipality to default on its liabilities is practically zero, since they are backed by the *Länder*. The loans themselves are mostly provided by municipality-owned Savings and Loan Banks. Private firms, however, have to borrow at higher rates, reflecting their higher risk of default. Even deficiency guarantees provided by the municipality do not allow them to borrow at the same rate as the municipality. Within the private sector, credit quality varies as well. Large construction companies have access to the international financial markets, enabling them to borrow at lower costs, whereas small and medium-sized builder/operators are restricted to the domestic financial markets, exposing them to a handicap in the bidding process. In addition, private firms have to pay taxes, whereas public entities are tax-exempt. To level the playing-field, in September 1993 the Ministry of the Environment proposed that the taxation rules for both private and public entities should be equalized. Any operator, public or private, should pay a tax on the turnover at a rate of 7 per cent. As of fall 1994, the Federal Parliament has not implemented this recommendation.

III. CHARGING

Road pricing

Starting January 1, 1995, a time-based user charge (vignette) will be introduced for all trucks heavier than 12 tons on all German motorways. The annual (daily/weekly/monthly) fee for trucks with more than three axles will be set at DM 2500 (DM 12/DM 66/DM 250). For smaller trucks the annual fee will amount to DM 1 500. Foreign users will be charged the same daily or weekly rates, as appropriate. These fees represent a common solution of the BENELUX countries, Denmark, and Germany. Starting April 1, 1994, German truck companies will be compensated for the fee by a reduction of taxes for trucks that already fulfil the requirements of the E 2 emission norm (European Union norm). For political reasons, private cars are not going to be included in the vignette system.

The introduction of user charges for trucks serves as a means to harmonise the conditions of competition within the European Community, where German trucks are comparatively heavily taxed and have to pay tolls when using French and other southern European highways, whereas trucks from these countries are not taxed and use German highways free of charge.

An additional purpose of the user charge is to keep freight transport by rail competitive. Up to now, distortionary conditions have prevailed, as the road system has been indirectly subsidised by the state by not reflecting the full costs of its provision and maintenance in the current fuel and vehicle taxes. Despite previous intentions, the revenues from the user charge will not be earmarked for funding of transportation (which would have included railways), but will be considered as general revenues for the Federal budget.

The vignette system is being considered as an intermediate solution, until a workable electronic road pricing system is set up. A test of such a system with automatic fee control under all weather conditions will start in 1994 on a highway stretch of six kilometres between Bonn and Cologne. Different options based either on microwave or infrared technology will be tested. A key feature of the future system has to be its ability to scan cars passing at all speeds. It is intended to eventually create a common European Union standard.

The main goals of an electronic road pricing system are to:

- adequately price the scarce resource of "transportation infrastructure" by introducing pay-as-you-go user charges;

- steer network usage by peak hour/peak day related flexible fees;

- make optimal use of the existing network;

- strengthen the role of the railway system.

It is expected that a technically feasible system will have been developed by 1996. Total coverage of the highway network shall be completed by 1998 or later, costing around DM 3-6 billion. The existence of an electronic road-pricing system is essential for far-reaching plans to sell the entire highway system, or profitable parts of it, to a private stock company. More detailed information on this project, which might be on the agenda after the turn of century, if at all, is not available at present. A privatisation of the highway network in the long run, however, reflects the political will of the current ruling coalition.

Environmental charging

As far as wastewater treatment is concerned, within any of the organisational structures discussed above, the citizens continue paying the fees for the wastewater treatment to the municipality which in turn pays a contractual fee to the operating company and keeps the final legal responsibility for providing the service.

The private companies competitively tender on the basis of a certain fee per cubic metre wastewater containing a specific degree of pollution. The competing construction/operation companies' fees are intended to cover total cost of construction, operation, maintenance, and finance. The competitive bidding, combined with time savings during construction due to a privately managed and hence tightly supervised construction processes, plus the efficiency advantages inherent in a profit-driven company, embody the sources of the expected efficiency gains.

Concerning fresh water supplies, the Ministry of the Environment is envisaging a future solution under which the private firm would be responsible for investment, maintenance, and collection of charges. The public sector's role would be to ensure that the contractual obligations were fulfilled and the quality of service were provided.

Sophisticated contractual arrangements become essential to cover future changes and to manage risk. The most important elements of protection for the municipality in case of failure of the operating company are obtained by (1) not selling the land of the plant to the operator but keeping it as municipal property and handing it over on the basis of a long-term lease, and by (2) securing the right that in case of default the plant automatically gets transferred into the ownership of the municipality.

In the Ministry of the Environment, it is clearly acknowledged that the costs of credit for a private operator exceed the cost of credit a municipality faces. Even deficiency guarantees by the municipality, which the banks mostly require, do not provide the same rate; it lies still about 50 basis points above the interest rate for a municipal credit. An additional cost factor is created by the fact that private companies have to pay taxes, whereas exclusively publicly owned companies are tax-exempt entities. The private operators factor their long-term tax costs into their price, thus shifting the costs of taxation to the citizens of the municipalities. The private operators presently lobby to get a similar tax-exempt status granted. Their financial disadvantages are somewhat counterbalanced by having the same access to additional federal grants for wastewater plants as publicly managed plants. In the new States, model projects get federal funding up to 30 per cent of total cost.

The Ministry hopes that the banks will be willing to provide the private operators with credit at an interest rate as if a municipal deficiency guarantee had been granted, thus relieving the municipalities from the burden of being a co-bearer of the private firm's default risk as well. It hopes that the banks soon will move in that direction, since doing without this guarantee would create a more favourable inclination on the municipalities' side towards the private solution. According to the Ministry's assessment, a shortage of funds on the banks' side does not exist.

Given eastern public administration's lack of managerial skills and the private's sector ability to construct and start a new plant within nine to twelve months, higher costs of finance are outweighed by buying in time. This is especially important, as under the building and planning code both new residential and industrial developments must prove that their wastewater treatment is ensured by the time of their completion. Thus, a rapid provision of sewage treatment is imperative for new economic development to get the eastern States out of their still on-going adaptive crisis. Regions that lie ahead in their renewal of infrastructure are assumed to gain distinctive competitive advantages over lagging ones.

IV. THE VIEW OF THE BUDGET DEPARTMENT AT THE MINISTRY OF FINANCE[4]

The Budget Department supports on-going efforts to reduce the proportion of government spending as a percentage of GDP, but is critical of the currently tested models of pre-financing of public infrastructure, holding the opinion that pre-financing must not be confused with genuine privatisation of state assets or with contracting out tasks previously carried out by the public sector. In fact, the newly explored instruments of finance are considered to lead to a hidden expansion of future government expenditures.

There is some concern that the creation of various "shadow budgets" outside the Federal budget might put at risk the general strategy of Federal fiscal consolidation being pursued. The Budget Department also opposes the use of leasing models, for example, for new government or university buildings.

The following arguments are put forward against pre-financing and leasing:

- With pre-financing, government payment is just deferred into the future and spread over time. Goods are acquired by instalment payments. With the new highway projects, first annual instalments are due in 1998 and end in 2015. The Ministry of Finance regards this to be a commitment of public funds by paraleipsis. Future obligations are generated without any guarantee that the corresponding revenues will be forthcoming as well. The principles of sound budgeting are violated.

- Long-term commitments of this type constrain future changes of budgetary priorities. Budgetary flexibility becomes restricted and thus also the steering capacities of future governments.

- Both pre-financing and leasing imply that a third (private) party borrows for the state. The overall project costs are higher, because the private sector faces higher interest rates on the financial markets reflecting the higher risk. In addition, it factors in a margin of profit, cost of taxation and insurance and shifts them to the public budget. Ultimately, the tax payer pays for the higher bills.

- A crucial argument put forward is that the private firms involved do not bear any real risk. Even if they default, the state still is legally accountable for the provision of public infrastructure. Thus, eventually the state will have to bail-out defaulting companies or step in directly. A significant amount of real risk taking by the private firms can only be engineered, when feasible techniques of user charging are at hand.

- It might become more difficult for the government to both impose and implement new quality standards on the performance of privately operated public utilities.

Officials at the Budget Department also emphasize that from a macroeconomic point of view it is not relevant whether debt is held by the public or private sector. A general reduction of accumulated debt has to be achieved, and this goal cannot be realised with the new instruments of financing public infrastructure.

V. CONCLUSION

The fiscal strains created by reunification and their exacerbation by the recession of 1993 generated a far reaching willingness of policy makers and public administrators to consider new approaches of using private finance and public/private partnerships for the provision of public infrastructure.

At present, several new approaches concerning the finance of highway infrastructure are being discussed. Six pilot projects have been selected, which will be pre-financed by private construction/banking consortia. Far reaching schemes like the complete privatisation of the existing highway system are being discussed. Electronic road pricing systems to enable this endeavour are being tested.

In the five new *Länder*, private finance and operation are increasingly applied in the both ecologically and economically essential field of wastewater treatment facilities. Various organisational approaches are being explored. So far, it has not become evident that the private sector in principle provides actually cheaper and better wastewater treatment facilities, as the private firms continue to face higher cost of credit. In addition, complex issues concerning the laws governing taxation of private operators of wastewater plants are yet to be resolved on the Federal level. In the special case of East Germany, however, the shortage of seasoned and well trained public administrators creates an environment that requires the private sector to step in, especially since the rapid provision of wastewater treatment facilities proves essential for the future of local and regional economic development. The positive externalities created by the most rapid provision of services possible is considered to outweigh the private sector's higher cost of financing.

On the public sector's side, some uncertainty can be felt on how to deal with the specific, profit driven characteristics of the private sector and how to design and implement policies that really ensure that the private sector does not shift its entire entrepreneurial risks to the public sector. On all levels of public administration, knowledge about the requirements and methods of the financial markets should be expanded. New sets of skills may have to be acquired. The use of *ex ante* quantitative analyses, cost-benefit analyses and *ex post* evaluations should be augmented.

In addition, assessments of the future administrative and regulatory costs of large-scale privately managed monopolies of transportation infrastructures do not seem to be at hand. However, the general level of risk awareness is very high, as is reflected in the cautious approach selected by the ministries. The experiences derived from the pilot projects in both western and eastern Germany will be carefully evaluated by the Federal Audit Office and the Federal ministries. The results of these evaluations will be crucial for the further development of public policy.

NOTES

1. Interviews were conducted in July 1993, and January 1994 at the Federal Ministry of Finance, the Federal Ministry of Transportation, the Federal Ministry of Economics, and the Federal Ministry of the Environment, Nature Conservation, and Nuclear Safety.

2. On July 15, 1992, the Federal Cabinet stated: "Since the appropriations in the central government budget are limited, recourse to the concession model will afford increased opportunities to call up private finance, once charging becomes possible. We are waiting for European legislation to settle this point".

3. The Ministry of Finance constructed models in order to determine whether leasing or pre-financing was the least expensive. It is difficult, though, to draw any final conclusions because the models were designed in the context of the existing laws and regulations, which could be changed as was recommended by the "Second Report on Speeding up the Provision of an Efficient Infrastructure for Environmental Protection in the New *Länder* by Private Management", Bonn, November 29, 1993.

4. The position was derived from internal notes, including one dating back to 16 June 1982 (*Zusammenfassung der wesentlichen Gesichtspunkte, die gegen das Immobilienleasing im staatlichen Bereich sprechen*, "synthesis of the most important points speaking against leasing of buildings for purposes of the state"). The section represents the opinion of the Budget Department that is not necessarily shared by the whole of the Ministry of Finance.

BIBLIOGRAPHY

The Federal Minister for the Environment, Nature Conservation and Nuclear Safety (1993), "Second Report on Speeding Up the Provision on an Efficient Infrastructure for Environmental Protection in the new *Länder* by Private Management", Bonn, November 29 (*Zweiter Bericht zur Beschleunigung des Aufbaus einer effizienten Umweltschutzinfrastruktur in den neuen Ländern durch privatwirtschaftliche Organisationsformen, Bonn, 29.11.1993*).

The Federal Minister of Transportation (1993a), "Privatisation of Federal Highways", Bonn, May 4 (*Der Bundesminister für Verkehr, "Privatisierung der Bundesautobahnen", Bonn, 04.05.1993*).

The Federal Minister of Transportation (1993b), "Private Finance of Investments in Transportation Infrastructure within the Framework of the so-called Concession Model", Bonn, May 5 (*Der Bundesminister für Verkehr, "Privatfinanzierung von Verkehrsinvestitionen im Rahmen des sogenannten Konzessionsmodells", Bonn, 05.05.1993*).

The Bavarian State Ministry of the Interior (1991), "Guidelines on Planning, Financing, and Organisation of Municipal Services, Considering especially the Usage of Private Capital", Munich, December 11 (*Das Bayerische Staatsministerium des Inneren, "Hinweise zur Planung, Finanzierung und Organisation kommunaler Einrichtungen unter besonderer Berücksichtigung des Einsatzes von Privatkapital", München, 11.12.1991*).

The Federal Ministry of Economics (1993), "Report on the State of the Economy 1993", Bonn (*Das Bundesministerium für Wirtschaft, "Jahreswirtschaftsbericht 1993", Bonn*).

The Federal Ministry for the Environment, Nature Conservation, and Nuclear Safety (1991), "Guidelines for Wastewater Treatment, Bonn (*Das Bundesministerium für Umweltschutz, Naturschutz und Reaktorsicherheit, "Leitfaden zur Abwasserbeseitigung", Bonn*).

The Federal Ministry for the Environment, Nature Conservation and Nuclear Safety (1993), "Public-Private Partnership from the Government's Point of View", Bonn, April 19 (*Das Bundesministerium für Umweltschutz, Naturschutz und Reaktorsicherheit, "Public-Private Partnership aus der Sicht des Bundesregierung", Bonn, 19.04.1993*).

The Federal Ministry for the Environment, Nature Conservation and Nuclear Safety (no year given), "Privatisation of Municipal Wastewater Treatment - Pros and Cons", Bonn (*Das Bundesministerium für Umweltschutz, Naturschutz und Reaktorsicherheit, "Privatisierung der kommunalen Abwasserentsorgung - Ja oder Nein?", Bonn, o. J.*).

The Federal Ministry of Finance (1991), Report of the Task Force "Private Finance of Public Infrastructure", Bonn (*Das Bundesministerium der Finanzen, Bericht der Arbeitsgruppe "Private Finanzierung öffentlicher Infrastruktur", Bonn*).

Chapter Five

PRIVATE FUNDING OF PRISON OPERATIONS IN THE UNITED KINGDOM

by

John Moore
Independent Business and
Project Management Consultant
Dorking, Surrey, United Kingdom

INTRODUCTION

The objective of the chapter is to review the introduction of private finance and operation into the provision of prisons in the United Kingdom, setting down government policies, initiatives and plans, the progress towards implementation to date, and to adduce lessons learned in terms of benefits, weaknesses and deficiencies. While some lessons can be learned, it is too early to draw comparative conclusions as to the success of the programme.

The paper relates specifically to prisons in England and Wales. Prisons in Scotland are separately run by the Scottish Office and a different regime applies in Northern Ireland (Central Office of Information, 1994). In terms of progress towards private funding and operations, the lessons are to be learned from the service in England and Wales.

OVERVIEW OF THE PRISON SERVICE IN THE UK

The Home Secretary is responsible to Parliament for the custody and care of prisoners detained. For many years the Home Office has built, owned and operated the prisons and the prison services. There have been recent changes described below which transferred responsibility for building prisons and delivering the services to an Executive Agency under the Home Office. The provision of these facilities and services has now been further developed under the Private Financial Initiative with selective contracting-out to the private sector of escort services and provision and operation of custodial facilities.

At the end of 1992, there were about 52 000 persons held in prisons, as follows:

Country	Number of prisoners	Number of prisons
TOTAL, of which:	**52 000**	**155**
Scotland	5 000	20
N. Ireland	2 000	5
England and Wales	**45 000**	**130**

The prison population is almost entirely male (97 per cent), and about one-third of prisoners are held for offences against the person. There are separate prisons for women. 22 per cent are untried or unsentenced prisoners, mostly held in remand prisons.

The cost of operating the service runs at about £1 billion a year, of which staff costs account for 80 per cent. There are about 36 000 staff.

Many of the prisons date from the 19th century and need modernising. The government has spent increasing sums on new prisons and refurbishments over the past five years, in an attempt to reduce overcrowding and to improve conditions for both prisoners and staff. The investment has been as follows:

	Capital expenditure (in £ million)
1987/88	118
1988/89	205
1989/90	386
1990/91	480
1991/92	432

Prison Service responsibilities

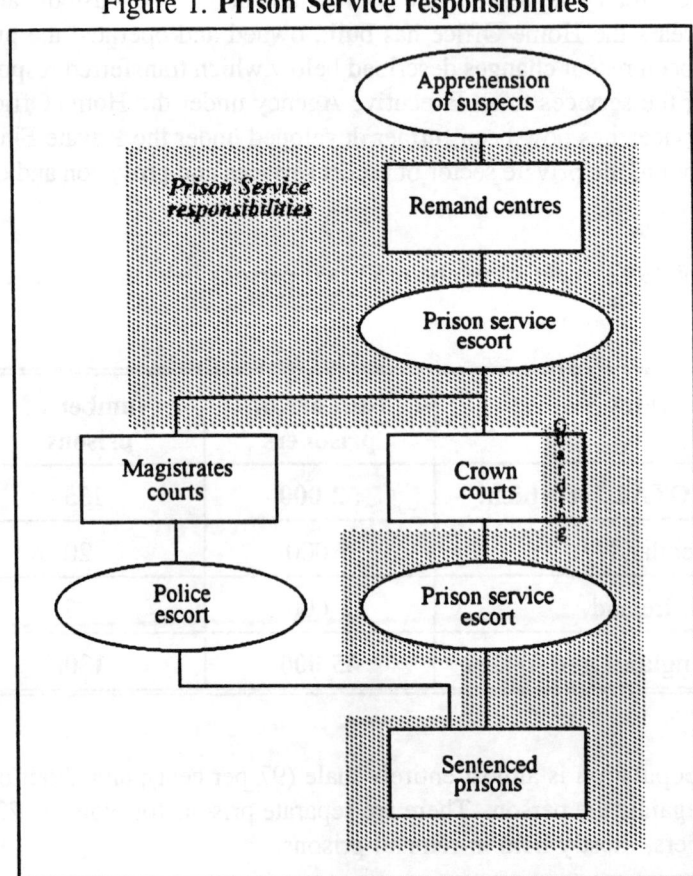

Figure 1. **Prison Service responsibilities**

All the work of looking after prisoners on escort to and from court and at court is being contracted out. The responsibility for the contracting out process, and for the contracted court escort and custody service, lies with the Prison Service, and in particular with the Contracts and Competition Group.

RECENT CHANGE IN THE PRISON SERVICE

The chronology of the development of policy and implementation is shown below.

Early 1980s	Home Secretary encourages private turnkey construction of prisons
1988	Home Secretary indicates little possibility of private involvement in prisoner custody
1988	*Next Steps* paper
1989	Home Affairs Committee proposes review of scope for private sector in custody of prisoners
1989	Home Office response to *Next Steps*
1990 April	Strangeways prison riot
1990 July	Court escorts custody and security paper published
1991 February	Woolf report on Strangeways riot published
1991	Remands Contract Unit established to manage contracting of prison management (later Custodial Contracts Unit) and the contracting of prisoner escort services.
1991	*Criminal Justice Act 1991* passed by Parliament, permitting privatised escort duties, private sector management of remand centres and new prisons, and also market testing
1991 July	Competitive tendering for management of Wolds remand prison
1991 September	White paper - Custody, care and justice published
1992 April	Wolds remand prison opened under private management

1992 February	Invitations to tender for escort services contracts for east Midlands and Humberside regions
1992 November	*Private Finance Initiative* announced, encouraging private finance into heretofore government funded services
1992 November	Escort services contracts signed for East Midlands and Humberside regions
1993	Statutory Instrument extends CJA 1991 to cover private provision management of existing and sentence prisons
1993	Further escort services contracts signed for Crown Courts at Stafford, Warwick, Worcester and Wolverhampton
1993 April	Prison Service executive agency constituted
1993 May	Blakenhurst local prison opens under private management
1993 May	HM Prisons Inspectorate inspects The Wolds
1994 February	Contractors pre qualification for design, construct manage and finance two new prisons at Bridgend and Merseyside
1994	Doncaster Cat B remand and short-term sentenced prison expected to open under private management
1994	Contracts expected for London area escort services

Up to April 1993, the provision and operation of the prisons was a department within the Home Office under the direction of the Home Secretary. In April 1993, the Prison Service was constituted as a separate "Executive Agency", still under the overall control of the Home Secretary but with a Chief Executive and a staff charged with responsibility for delivering the requisite services.

This formation of an executive agency was part of a government-wide initiative to improve the performance of delivery of services by hitherto government departments. The initiative was launched by the Cabinet Office paper "Next Steps" (Cabinet office, 1988) which identified and articulated the distinction between the role of civil servants in developing policies for ministers and defining standards of performance on the one hand, and the delivery of the services on the other hand. Executive functions carried out by the civil service were to be constituted as agencies operating at arms length within a policy and resources framework set by the sponsoring government department. Thus, there are now about 100 executive agencies, covering responsibilities such as vehicle licensing, issue of social benefits, management of estates, and patent matters. The executive agencies are retained within government ownership to enable adequate control in matters of public interest. Where government felt able, it privatised by sale to the public or to corporations those services (utilities, design services, for example) which were providing a service often in competition with the private sector and where the quality of the service was determined by commercial pressures rather than public interest.

The delivery of the prison service remains of public interest and hence the Prison Service was constituted as an Executive Agency under the Home Office. The Home Office response to Next Steps was set out in a paper in 1989 (HM Prison Service, 1989) which effectively retained control of the prison service but positioned it as an agency. In April 1993, that status was achieved. The Home Secretary retained responsibility for policy and standards of service, while the Prison Service is responsible for delivery to the defined standards, but firmly still within the Home Office and with a contract between the Home Office and the Director General of the agency. Funding continued to come from government but changes in government policy in regard to the introduction of private funds and private management into the service were already under way.

In the early 1980s the Home Secretary had become concerned at the cost and progress of construction of prisons, and brought in private contractors to build new prisons on a turn-key basis under conditions of competitive tendering and fixed price bidding. The contractors were not required to have any involvement in the subsequent operation of the prisons. This was not privatisation as such, but reflected an early impatience with the efficiency and speed of construction and was part of the wider approach to efficiency and effectiveness of government being developed by the Thatcher administration.

Although in 1988 the Home Secretary indicated that he saw little opportunity for the involvement of the private sector in prisoner custody, by 1989 the climate was already changing, and the Home Affairs Committee of the Cabinet was pointing to the need to review the scope for private custody. In 1991 the Remands Contract Unit was established to respond to the opportunities for private involvement under the Criminal Justice Act 1991. The Unit later became the Custodial Contracts Unit.

Following prison disturbances in 1990, Lord Justice Woolf prepared a report (Home Office, 1991) on the situation. This encouraged a response from the government in the form of a White Paper *Custody Care and Justice* (Home Office, 1991) setting out a programme of reforms for the prison service. The stated aim is to provide a better prison system with secure facilities for prisoners and protecting the safety of the public, prison staff and prisoners. This is to be achieved through more effective security and control, improved relationships within the prisons between staff and prisoners, and attention to work and rehabilitation programmes.

In 1991 the Criminal Justice Act 1991 passed into law. It was a major milestone in permitting private management into prison services. It provided *inter alia* specifically for prisoner escort duties to be carried out by prisoner custody officers who are authorised to perform such functions, and might include arrangements made by the Secretary of State entering into contracts with "other persons" for the provision by them of prisoner custody officers. It also provided for entering into contracts for the running of any prisons subsequently established and used for the confinement of remand prisoners. It was felt at that time that it was too sensitive an issue to allow private management of sentenced prisons. The Act also provided for subsequent modification by Statutory Instrument.

In 1993, by Statutory Instrument (which has to be decided on by Parliament) the Act was extended to cover all prisons.

The Criminal Justice Act 1991 also enabled "market testing". This was another strand of government policy whereby national and local government bodies were required to put out to competition the provision of services. In-house teams were eligible to bid, but their submissions/tenders were to be submitted to competitive bids from the private sector. In many cases the in-house teams are successful, and achieve substantial improvements in productivity.

The Act solely opened the way for contracting out the complete management of prisons and escorts, but did not provide for the contracting out of individual custodial services or parts of prison management functions. Consequently, market testing could not be extended to the latter. This somewhat impeded the functional market testing programme in the Prison Service. There are amendments to the 1991 Act contained in the Criminal Justice and Public Order Bill to be passed by Parliament in November 1994 that will overcome this difficulty.

In November 1992, the Chancellor of the Exchequer announced the *Private Finance Initiative* designed to bring the private sector into the provision of services and facilities (Central Office of Information, 1993; HM Treasury, 1992a-d, 1993a-e; Scottish Office, 1993; Chancellor of the Exchequer, 1993; Private Finance Working Group, 1993). The government had undertaken the major task of moving commercial operations out of government control, they had tried to improve the performance of construction with competitive, open tendering using private sector contractors, but they had not achieved the improvements in overall efficiency of investment which they sought.

As a generalisation, private sector involvement under the direction of government did not achieve the expected improvement in time, cost or operability. The contractor carried the risk for the cost, but he had no interest in subsequent operability. The public sector customer had too little appreciation of an appropriate balance between performance specification and cost, and would tend towards over-specification of quality. The *Private Finance Initiative* is an attempt to engage private sector expertise as much as finance in provision of facilities and services, and crucially to assign rewards and risks in fair proportions between customer and contractor.

The advantage of engaging a single contractor from the private sector in not only the construction of an asset but also in its operation was recognised. The combination of private finance for facilities and the return on that capital being dependent on the profitable and satisfactory operation of the facility should greatly reduce the scope for failure. In cases where there was no construction as such, the contractor's return could yet be tied to delivery. There are a great number of possible models depending on circumstances, but the government is determined to harness the best attributes and experience of the private sector while tying them fairly into achieving the required standard of service under conditions of shared risk.

In the *Criminal Justice Act* of 1991 the Home Secretary took powers to contract out to the private sector the management of prisons in England and Wales, and also the provision of escort and guarding functions.

OBJECTIVES

The objectives of the Home Office for the Prison Service (HM Prison Service, 1993) are to:

- keep prisoners in custody;
- maintain order, control discipline, and provide a safe environment;
- provide decent conditions for prisoners, meeting their needs including health care;
- help prisoners prepare for return to the community;
- deliver prison services using resources provided by Parliament with maximum efficiency.

Their stated vision is "to provide a service through both directly managed and contracted prisons of which the public can be proud and which will be regarded as a standard of excellence around the world" (HM Prison Service, 1993).

Efficiency and value for money are important. The service aims to reduce the total cost of the service by 5 per cent overall, with ten per cent of the prisons in private management during an initial phase.

EXPERIENCE OF PRIVATELY MANAGED PRISONS

The first privately managed prison is Wolds, Humberside, a remand prison which was opened on 6 April 1992. The prison is new, designed and built in one phase for the Prison Service specifically to hold those on remand (pending trial and possible sentence). The construction was by UK Detention Contractors (Mowlem and McAlpine). It is run by Group 4 Remand Services Limited under a five-year contract. It is designed to accommodate 320 prisoners on remand, including vulnerable prisoners and high-risk prisoners, and in May 1993 it had 306 inmates.

The Home Secretary informed Parliament on 3 February 1993 that private sector involvement is one way forward to a better service for prisoners and taxpayers. This was followed by a Member who said: "As to the experiment at The Wolds prison (rather than less accountability) bureaucratic accountability is difficult to test, whereas market testing contracts are open to challenge". Another Member said: "The Wolds has been an outstanding success" (Hansard, 1993a).

The Wolds was inspected by the independent HM Inspectorate of Prisons in May 1993 after 13 months of operation (Chief Inspector of Prisons, 1993c). The inspectors under Judge Tumin were positive about the prison. They praised staff attitudes and relationships with the prisoners and the adoption of respect in relations with individuals, and the regime which provided extended time out-of-cell, civilised mealtimes and quality food, daily visiting, and impressive education and leisure facilities. They had two principal criticisms.

First, there was a lack of clarity about some of the respective obligations of the two parties under the contract. The contract did not cover responsibilities for certain running costs and checks on costs were weak. HM Prison Service states, however, that it does not have to undertake financial checks of the contractor. Rather, it has to measure the contractor's output.

Second, they felt there to be a potential problem over the status of the Controller, the Home Office representative on the site charged with monitoring compliance and ensuring performance by the contractor and reporting on any allegations made against custodial staff. The Controller was significantly junior to and less experienced than the Director, a former prison service governor now employed by Group 4, and this had the potential for difficulty if (and this has not apparently arisen) there were to be a serious divergence of opinion about prisoner care. Monitoring of financial performance was weak. The chain of command in the event of a serious incident was deemed unsatisfactory.

The inspectors were also critical of the lax stance of inmates towards work and recreation. This is a feature of remand prisons where the inmates are transient and their stay tends to be of short duration, and they cannot by law be forced to work.

There have been no suicides and only one escape from within the prison (using disguise). There have been 64 incidents, including 29 attacks on staff and 21 on fellow inmates. The average for all prisons is six assaults per year, but the comparison is harsh because the Wolds figures are before adjudication and the national figure is after adjudication (Hansard, 1993b). The comparison for remand prisons suggests that the level of inmate-to-inmate assault is higher than nationally. There were 460 assaults in the six months to December 1992 nationally in remand prisons with an average population of 17 162 or 2.7 per cent (Prison Reform Trust, 1993a); at Wolds the level was 4 per cent. Vandalism is very low. HM Prison Send loses one prisoner a year through escape, and there was one suicide at Wormwood Scrubs (a mix of sentenced, lifer and remand prisoners) in the year preceding inspection (Chief Inspector of Prisons, 1991; 1993b). The report on Norwich was favourable, but did not comment on performance in this regard (Chief Inspector of Prisons, 1993a). There was no evidence in Wolds report that the regime or the quality of care was inferior to that offered in comparable prisons. However, Wolds's team is new, with many officers new to the service, and it is premature to conclude that Wolds is any less safely managed than comparable remand centres.

Blakenhurst local prison in Worcestershire opened in May 1993 under private management by UK Detention Services Limited. No inspectors report is available yet as it has been open for less than a year. However, in the six months to September there were apparently 16 assaults on staff and three on fellow inmates (Prison Reform Trust, 1994). This actually implies a higher assault rate compared with Wolds and with other directly managed establishments. Blakenhurst has introduced novel features to its regime with visiting every day of the week; and this has set a standard for the region which other prisons are now trying to follow.

In their defence, contractors point out that under the strict terms of their contract and because of the close supervision of the contract by the Controller in each prison, they are meticulous about recording incidents. In consequence, the number of reported incidents tends to be higher than in public prisons.

Doncaster Category B remand and short-term sentenced prison (a so-called local prison) will open in 1994, making the third privately managed prison after The Wolds and Blakenhurst. The contract was awarded to Premier Prison Services. It is noted that the Home Office has thereby awarded the first three contracts to three different contractors. This is good from the point of view of widening involvement by contractors and reducing the risk to the Home Office. It does not achieve the individual contractor's needs for a spread of contracts, although succeeding awards should mean that individual contractors begin to achieve a spread of contracts.

The future programme includes two new prisons, at Merseyside and Bridgend (South Wales). The procurement of these is currently in hand (February 1994), with interested contractors invited to pre-qualify for a short-list of five who will be invited to submit formal tenders (HM Prison Service, 1993). The competition is open; the invitations to pre-qualify were announced in the Official Journal of the European Communities (*Official Journal of the European Communities*, 1993). A date for the return of tenders will be set of no later than 30 November 1994.

Contractors were asked to pre-qualify in February 1994, and a short list of five companies is to be invited to tender for design, build, operate and finance the prisons. These will be the first where the construction is an integral part of the private contractor's responsibility. The successful tenderer will be required to design, build, operate and finance the new prison, and payment under the contract will begin on a per inmate basis by the Home Office from the time when the prisons begin to accept prisoners.

Merseyside and Bridgend will be category B security prisons with about 600 and 800 places, respectively. They should open in late 1997.

There will be one contract running for 25 years, covering design, construction and management. At the end of this period, the Home Office will have the right to take ownership of the buildings and will require that they are in satisfactory condition at that time.

It is fundamental to the approach that the contractor will be required to build and operate a secure and safe prison with a proper regime, and the two strands of the contract will combine these responsibilities under the one contractor. The building performance will therefore be an integral part of the performance of the management of the prisoners, and the return to the contractor will depend on both the performance of the buildings and the management and operation of the prison once in service.

The design, build, operate and finance contract will be taken by a consortium, usually containing a construction contractor for the building. The construction will usually be financed by a loan from a bank. The consortium and the bank will require a fixed price for the construction and require that the contractor building the prison has a substantial share of the equity in order that he is motivated to keep the capital cost to the agreed fixed price for construction. Alternatively, the construction contract might be put out to tender, where a consortium did not include a construction company. There appears no real reason to include a constructor.

Terms and performance measures

The terms of the contract are not yet finalised and their determination will be a feature of the tendering process. The Home Office is determined that payment should be related to meeting the objectives of the prison service and be output related. The Custodial Contracts Unit which is responsible for letting the contracts is therefore seeking bids which meet the prison service vision goals and values, meet the operational requirements, and comply with any fixed design and construction requirements.

The design of the prisons will be the responsibility of the contractor, and while the Prison Service design standards will be made available, the contractor is free to a major extent to incorporate his own ideas. However, the contractor will need to satisfy the Home Office that the final design meets the requirement to hold prisoners securely and to provide a safe environment within for both staff and prisoners, as well as protecting the public at large.

The contractor will have to provide assurance to the Director General of the Prison Service and the planning authorities responsible for the areas where the prisons are to be built that the safety of the public, staff and prisoners will be protected by a combination of physical and operational control and security measures. The facilities will have to comply with Prison Rules and other relevant statutory regulations, UK and European Union building regulations, Home Office fire safety specifications, and relevant requirements and regulations in regard to health, energy conservation, safety, and other conventions and obligations binding on the UK government. The planning application and negotiation with the planning authorities for the areas concerned will take time and undoubtedly there will be objections from the public. This delay is a risk for the contractor, who has spent money on preparation but cannot commence building until the application is granted. This could take twelve months or longer.

Payment for the prison will be made on some form of per-inmate basis, yet to be finalised. It is likely to be based on the Prison Service Code of Standards. The terms of the previous management contracts for Wolds and Blakenhurst have not been published. The contract performance terms are, however, likely to cover *inter alia*:

- retention of prisoners, and penalising for escapes;
- prison order, as measured by prisoner-to-prisoner and prisoner/staff assaults, and incidents;
- major prison disturbances and rioting;
- drug and alcohol reports;
- prisoner health, measuring sickness levels and suicides;
- visiting arrangements;
- nutrition standards and feeding;
- prison regime and time out-of-cells;
- education and training provisions;
- work provisions;
- leisure and recreation provisions;
- prisoner access to information, professional advisers, prison visitors' board;
- staffing ratios, officers to prisoners;
- efficiency of resources and costs.

It appears that no measures related to recidivism have yet been included in contracts, although the objective of restoring prisoners to normal life is one of the aspirations of the Prison Service.

The three components of prison management are illustrated below.

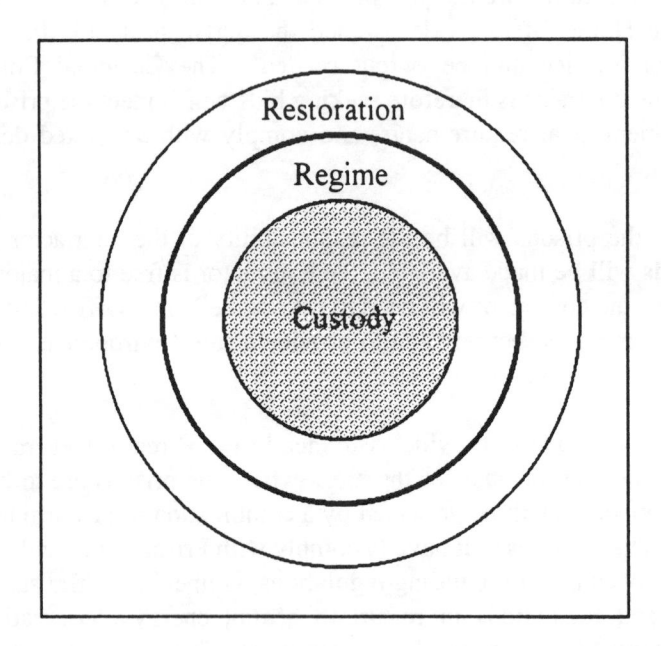

The core objective is the custody of the prisoner, but within a satisfactory regime. The Home Office has pointed out that the punishment is deprivation of liberty, and not the regime to which the prisoner is subjected in prison. The outer "layer" of the objective is the restoration of the prisoner as a decent member of society with education, training and the acquisition of skills. These three objectives are mutually interactive. A good regime is expected to reduce the problems of custody and to contribute to reducing recidivism. [63 per cent of young male offenders and 42 per cent of adult male offenders were re-convicted within two years of discharge from prison in 1986 (*Official Journal of the European Communities*, 1993).] However, the regime should not be over-generous to the extent of encouraging return. The successful contractor will be the one who strikes the right balance between these elements in his proposals (HM Prison Service, 1993).

Contractors' experiences

Contractors for the management of new prisons have had to create new businesses competent to run prisons. They have tended to bring in prison operation experience from the United States of America where private sector experience is already established. A number of issues have emerged.

There was no established prison operation experience in the UK, and new businesses have had to be created to meet the demand. Inevitably, there have been teething problems. The new contractors are managing new prisons but the inmates are often very familiar with the old regime and inclined to test out the new management. Contractors have noted that there are few sanctions which can be applied to prisoners; remission of sentence is automatic except in cases of severe bad behaviour. While some staff have been recruited from existing prisons, some are new to the service and they have had to learn the practicalities of managing relations with prisoners. The ideal of "new wine in new bottles", sending first time offenders to newly managed prisons, is not feasible in either remand or sentence prisons.

There are no prison governors with experience of running prisons to a contract within profit-determined budgets. Governors approved by the Home Office have been recruited, and they are having to learn the constraints and responsibilities of meeting the requirements of the contract and administering the prison within contractual terms. Contractors tend to favour an experienced governor because they believe this enhances their chances of success in winning the contract, although it might be better to appoint as governor someone more junior from the existing prison service who combines sufficiency of experience with personal ability to learn the new management style.

It is observed that the first three contracts were awarded to three different companies. Despite the fact that this was a random outcome of the bidding procedures, it satisfies the Home Office objective of reducing their risk with a spread of contractors, and assists in widening the experience to several contractors quickly. However, contractors are anxious to establish more depth to their prison business to reduce their own risks. There is a need to establish a solid business in providing contracted services to prisons, and eventually with the emergence of some informed business-wide body representing the contractors which can share experience and develop common industry approaches. There appears to be a sufficiency of organisations now involved to enable this to happen.

It has been reported that some organisations, both direct contractors and support services such as banks, are cautious about and reluctant to involve themselves in prison services because they fear adverse public and shareholder reactions. A national body could help in establishing the image of the industry as caring and effective, and well able to meet the best standards expected in prisoner custody and care. To the extent that the only image which can be successfully promoted is that based on reality, it is vital to the new business that experience of their services is of the best.

Insurance is one cost borne by the private contractor which is not a direct cost on the existing prisons. Insurance is reported as difficult to obtain and expensive, although as the business matures this problem should ease.

Contractors avoid importing restrictive historic trades union practices into their new prisons, and tend to favour staff associations over union recognition. The Prison Officers Association is not recognised by the three new managements. A strike or industrial action could severely damage this emergent business. However, the Criminal Justice and Public Order Bill makes it clear that organised industrial action would be unlawful. Prison officers, as constables, are not covered by traditional employment legislation, and may not take industrial action, although this interpretation is subject to a judgement of the courts.

Concern has been expressed over the number of prisoners to be held in the new prisons. No guarantees of numbers have been given by the Prison Service. Average length of sentence for indictable offences has risen from 8.1 months in 1981 to 14.7 months in 1991 (*Official Journal of the European Communities*, 1993) but the average prison population has been static for three years, at just under 46 000 in England and Wales. It has, however, risen significantly during 1993 by 5 000 or so. Contractors would like some guarantee as to inmate numbers and they feel particularly vulnerable to changes in prisoner numbers as they believe they are operating on the margin of the demand. The point has also been made that numbers should be limited to the capacity of the prison to avoid overcrowding and consequent management risks.

In the longer term, the private sector is concerned that the whole approach to crime and punishment might change, in a way which reduced prisoner numbers or favoured public sector prisons. A change of government to one favouring the public sector is an obvious risk, but a change of approach to punishment and rehabilitation could have effects on the prison population upwards or downwards.

At present, privately run prisons operate to a strict contract in which the services and regimes are defined by the Prison Service, and prisoner allocations are made by the Prison Service. Under these circumstances, the method of reimbursement based on per capita payments might be considered to favour the Prison Service. It might be fairer on the contractor (and possibly on the prisoner also) for the Home Office to consider paying a two-part tariff comprising a fixed element related to the fixed costs of the establishment and a per capita payment to cover variable costs per prisoner.

Contracts are not made public. However, one might assume that contractors are likely to request terms of payment which go at least part of the way to providing protection for them as well as the Home Office. The tariffs are likely to include some degree of recognition that the supply of prisoners is entirely at the Home Office's discretion and that the contractor has a substantial fixed cost. Some formula with a plus and minus provision around an average occupancy is likely to be included.

The biggest problem faced by the contractors used to be their lack of total resource. However, the current Criminal Justice and Public Order Bill provides for mutual aid between prisons. Staff from contracted prisons will be able to go to the aid of directly managed prisons at times of crisis and vice versa. In any case, the private sector has its own back-up arrangements which have relied on other staff of the contractor's associated companies and now tend to rely on help from the other contractors or from the court escort and custody service.

Escort services

An important part of the Prisons Service's responsibilities is the escorting of remand prisoners from the remand prisons to the magistrates courts for trial where the police then take charge. In the case of prisoners appearing before the Crown courts, they guard them in court and escort them to the relevant local prison if they are awarded a custodial sentence. After that a process of allocation takes place.

In 1988, a firm of management consultants was asked by the Home Office to investigate the scope and merits of private sector involvement in remand centres and escort and court duties. Their report was published in March 1989 and informed much of the government's discussion paper *Court Escorts, Custody and Security* published in July 1990 (Home Office, 1993). During 1989, the Home Office were already in discussions with the private sector as to the comparative costs and efficiency of private escort services. Firms involved included Group 4 and UK Detention Services.

In November 1991, the contract to run Wolds was awarded to Group 4. As a remand prison, it was involved in custody of prisoners awaiting their court appearances. It had an interim escort responsibility under that contract from April 1992 when The Wolds was expected to open.

Invitations to tender for the provision of escort services for the East Midlands and Humberside regions were issued to twelve companies in February 1992. The contract was awarded to Group 4 Court Services Limited starting on 5 April 1993.

UK Detention Services has been awarded escort services contracts for Stafford, Warwick, Worcester and Wolverhampton Crown courts. This is an extension of their responsibilities under their contract to manage Blakenhurst prison. The escort service in London was tendered in 1993 and the contract signed in December 1993 with Securicor. The service will be phased in beginning of 1994 and will be fully contracted out in July 1995.

It is too early to make sound judgements or comparisons as to the performance of the contractors compared with the public service. However, there have been teething problems over performance of the fundamental requirement that prisoners should be secured. In the first year, there were 40-odd escapes. By contrast, there were 147 escapes from prison service escorts during 1992 in England and Wales. Six per cent of the escapes were from the one contractor (Home Office, 1990; Prison Reform Trust, 1993b). There is some disagreement as to whether the contractor or the Home Office were at fault for some of these escapes, but this is indicative of the problems which inevitably accompany such a major change. Escapes from custody is a key performance indicator for the Prison Service whose objective is to reduce the total number year-by-year. It is important to realise that -- pending the approval of the current Criminal Justice and Public Order Bill by Parliament in November 1994 -- all types of escort services can be contracted out. Currently, 20 per cent of all escort services are being contracted out. It is the policy goal of HM Prison Service to contract out 100 per cent of escort services by 1995.

Market testing

Market testing of prison management is being tried in a number of functional areas. For prison management, the Prison Service has not published their basis for selection but will probably select candidates on the basis of no more than one per prison region. In order to maximise early returns and improvements, candidates will be selected on the basis of high costs and poor regimes. This has already had a beneficial effect on existing prison managements because prison governors do not want to be market tested and they are therefore striving to improve in order to avoid selection. This strategy is highly beneficial and requires little effort.

Market testing of prison management was put into effect first in the management of Strangeways prison. There was a very serious riot at Strangeways prison in April 1990, causing the deaths of three people and the virtual destruction of the prison, which was extremely old. Lord Justice Woolf headed an enquiry into the riot that recommended certain reforms and inspired the government White Paper *Custody, Care and Justice* (Home Office, 1991a-b; Prison Reform Trust, 1992). It did not pronounce on agency status as a means of managing the prison, but affirmed the need for a formal contract between the Director General of the prison service and the Home Secretary and the need to delegate certain authorities within that contract down to individual prison governors. The White Paper endorsed this and articulated improvements to standards of care and the responsibilities of the prison service for care of offenders, and provided useful input to the formulation of contracts with the private sector.

The management of the reconstructed Strangeways prison was "market tested". The existing management team was required to bid for running the prison in open competition with private sector companies. In the event the contract was awarded to the in-house management team, but the process of putting together a competitive bid is leading to reductions in costs and improvements in service and efficiency.

In 1992 it was decided to put out to tender the education services at prisons previously provided by the Local Education Authorities. Teachers were employed by the local colleges of further or higher education to teach in prisons, and answerable to the local prison governor. Tenders were invited from private companies in competition with the educational establishments.

Unfortunately for the Home Office, a major obstacle arose in the form of the TUPE regulations (Transfer of Undertakings Protection of Employment) which are founded in the European Union's Acquired Rights Directive. In essence, this regulation applies to the situation where the services of an employee are transferred to a new employer and requires that the new employer provides the same terms and conditions of employment to the employee. TUPE was held to apply to any local education establishment which wished to bid to continue providing education services to prisons where they already provided the service. This had the effect of favouring change and favouring new bidders, because TUPE required the existing service providers to retain the same staff on existing terms, reducing their scope for economy and efficiency.

Half the new contracts were awarded to companies or educational bodies new to prisoner education. It is too soon to say what the effect of contractorisation will be, but the benefits should lie in a more focused, efficient and responsive service provided that the prison governor defines precisely the service he requires. On the debit side, widening the provision has tended to break the traditional links with the local education authorities and has thereby potentially reduced possibilities for continuity of education for the prisoner between prison and his release into the local community (Prison Reform Trust, 1993c). This problem could be resolved by careful definition of the requirement on the contractor to integrate with the local education system.

TUPE is widely considered to be an impediment to change. Contractors have mentioned it as a major obstacle in bidding. It does not apply to new prisons with new staff, as there is no previous obligations to employees. However, in the case of bidding for the management of an existing prison or in the provision of services under contracting out and market testing, existing staff have to be offered their previous employment rights, including redundancy entitlements which are often quite high for public servants. This has been upheld by the European Court. In some cases the government has eased the problem by accompanying transfer with a cash payment to the new contractor which accommodates redundancy payments post transfer. However, contractors believe that they can offer as good terms as the public sector and can address the TUPE problem adequately.

Other services have been, or are currently being, market tested, and the Custodial Contracts Unit claims it is open to suggestions from contractors on any aspect of prison operation. The prison dog service was mooted but did not proceed. Wider powers are being sought in the Criminal Justice Bill currently at the committee stage in Parliament (Criminal Justice and Public Order Bill, 1994).

The Prison Officers' Association is an independent trade union claiming membership by 95 per cent of prison officers. They say that privatisation has "so far failed to deliver the goods and is frankly providing an embarrassment for the government" (Prison Officers' Association, 1994). They refer to the resources of the service to quell disturbances, and point out that its members have never failed to respond to an emergency when additional resources have been needed to be bussed in to deal with rioting prisoners and burning prisons. Some accommodation will have to be struck between the public prison officers and the private operators.

Public reactions

Public reaction has been muted. There is no significant reaction either in favour or against the introduction of private operations into the service. The government has itself been concerned to ensure that standards of care and custody are at least as good from a private operator as is available from the state-run establishments. Thus the Home Secretary voiced concern in 1988 lest the profit motive should intrude to the detriment of standards of care. This theme has not been picked up markedly by the public, although there have been letters in the press and some television and radio comment.

The Prison Reform Trust is a registered charity dependent on voluntary subscriptions and donations for its work. Its objectives are to create a just, humane and effective penal system. It has studied privatisation in prisons and has stated its opposition to involving the private sector in running prisons. It believes this to be "fundamentally wrong in principle", and goes on to say that experience of the private sector prisons in the USA gives rise to considerable concern about the treatment of prisoners in private prisons (Prison Reform Trust, 1993d). It produced a review of The Wolds after twelve months of operations pointing out some of the early teething problems and it has been critical of the escort services in their first year (Prison Reform Trust, 1993a).

The strongest public reaction has been evinced at the public enquiries which are statutorily necessary before the local planning authority grants a planning permission for new prisons. However, here the public's concern has not been the well-being of the prisoners, but rather that a private operator might be less concerned about the impact on the local environment and the local community.

In his report on The Wolds remand prison, Judge Tumin's inspectors reported that the staff had encountered hostility from the local community, sometimes taking the form of hostility at the personal level (Chief Inspector of Prisons, 1993c). The Chairman of the Board of Visitors reported "constant sniping" from the media, and that staff wearing Group 4 uniforms had been spat at by children in a nearby village. The escapes from escorts and the one escape from The Wolds had caught the attention of the media and made Group 4 staff rather more visible and vulnerable. That said, there has been little informed opposition to the changes by the public at large.

Risks/lessons learned/observations

Policy objectives are to improve custodial service programme; to improve regime (e.g. time out of cells, visit duration and number, hours of productive work, education and training, etc.) to cut costs, and improve efficiency.

The first lesson is that change of this fundamental nature takes time. Both the Prison Service and the private sector has to adjust. The Prison Service has to find ways of contracting and operating within a contractual environment. The private sector has to build its competence from scratch. Both parties have to learn from experience.

The programme has to be large enough to ensure that a number of contractors end up each with several contracts. This reduces risk for the contractor -- he has several prisons -- and for the Home Office it reduces the risk by having several contractors. Fourteen prisons in private hands may be just sufficient.

There is no experience of prison management in the private sector and both management and staff have to be recruited and trained. It takes two months to train a prison custody officer and he cannot serve until he has been certificated by the Home Office.

A proper prison care industry has to be built up, with a professional industry body and competent membership, providing standards and sharing experience. It needs to address the image of the business and be seen as caring and responsible.

The definition of a clear customer-contractor relationship in the contract is integral to and crucial to the privatisation process. It is beneficial in defining the respective responsibilities of the parties, the services to be provided, the standards of delivery and the basis for remuneration.

The structure of responsibilities has to be clear. The Governor is responsible on behalf of the contractor for delivering the service to contract within the budget, but there needs to be a competent and sufficiently senior compliance officer from the prison service on site to monitor standards of performance and advise on meeting the required standards of regime, the latter being a statutory requirement (Prison Reform Trust, 1991).

Unlike some privately provided services (for example road use charges) there appears to be little possibility to transfer responsibility for payment for prison operation from the public purse to the end user. Under these circumstances, the operations of the prisons will remain a direct charge on government. The advantages to government are therefore restricted to savings associated with improved efficiency of operations and reduced costs.

So far as the provision of the buildings is concerned, the public purse is spared the initial investment, but instead has to pay the contractor an annual charge for the facility which will cover interest and capital recovery. Because the cost of money is higher for the contractor than the government, the net present value of the forward lease payments will be higher for the privately provided prison.

There is risk in separating the construction contract from the management contract for new prisons. It removes the incentive on the contractor to get it right.

Payment terms are per capita/prisoner. While the prison operates to contract terms defined entirely by the Prison Service, there is a case for the customer (the Prison Service) to pay a two-part tariff covering fixed costs as well as per capita variable costs to better reflect the risks to both parties.

There could be scope for an incentive payment to encourage better performance. This might include perhaps a payment based on qualitative independent opinion as to performance, perhaps based on the prison inspection (although these would have to take place more frequently to be useful). An additional discretionary element for excellent performance could also be tried, giving motivation by carrot as well as stick.

Contractors are vulnerable to under-supply of prisoners. A payment system which comprised a fixed as well as a per capita payment would reduce the profit risk and reflect the control which the Home Office has over terms.

Market testing has a beneficial effect on the management and administration of existing prisons.

The employee protection afforded by TUPE is a disincentive to privatisation of existing establishments and services.

Where a consortium is bidding, the structure and ownership of the consortium is important. To avoid the risks of over-run on construction costs by the member responsible for the building, the construction should be on fixed price and that member should hold a substantial proportion of the equity in the design, build, operate and finance company. Alternatively, the consortium might not include a constructor, but seek open tenders to protect their positions.

The public image of companies involving themselves in prisoner custody and care is a matter of concern to the contractors, and they will work hard to maintain standards and project them to the public and their shareholders.

The private sector encounters some hazards not a feature of the public sector. These include insurance, cost management, and handling prisoners "brought up" under publicly run regimes.

While there have been some widely publicised problems in the first year of operation of newly-contracted prisons and escort services, these are seen as teething problems which contractors are rapidly remedying and learning to overcome. Their remuneration and long-term returns depend on it.

The private sector needs to develop to the point where they have sufficient resources in prison and manpower numbers to achieve the necessary credibility in the eyes of the prisoners to enforce security, discipline and the regime. Until the sector matures, they may well have more difficulties than the public prisons. The Home Office can recognise this problem by moving rapidly ahead with market testing and privatisation.

BIBLIOGRAPHY

Cabinet Office (1988), *Improving Management in Government: The Next Steps*, Cabinet Office paper, HMSO.

Central Office of Information (1994), *Britain 1994 - An Official Handbook*, Her Majesty's Stationery Office (HMSO).

Central Office of Information (1993), *Breaking New Ground, the Private Finance Initiative*, November, produced for HM Treasury by Central Office of Information, TRSY J081120NJ.

Chancellor of the Exchequer (1993), "Private finance initiative to transform capital projects in the 1990s", Speech to the CBI, 26 May.

Chief Inspector of Prisons (1991), *HM Prison Wormwood Scrubs*, Home Office, April.

Chief Inspector of Prisons (1993a), *HM Prison Norwich*, Home Office, January.

Chief Inspector of Prisons (1993b), *HM Prison Send*, Home Office, February.

Chief Inspector of Prisons (1993c), *The Wolds Remand Prison*, July, Home Office.

Criminal Justice Act 1991, HMSO.

Criminal Justice and Public Order Bill 1994, Bill 9 51/2, HMSO.

ERICKSON, Charles (1992), *Development and Principles of direct supervision in American Prisons*, Group 4, Ltd., November.

Hansard (1993a), House of Commons Debate (Session 1992-1993), Vol. 218, cols. 422-443, 3 February 1993.

Hansard (1993b), House of Commons Debate (Session 1992-1993), Vol. 218, cols. 1094, 1005-6, 11 February 1993.

HM Prison Service (1989), *Review of Organisation and Location above Management Level*, HM Prison Service response to Next Steps.

HM Prison Service (1993), "New prison programme: briefing for potential tenderers", 15 December, private paper.

HM Treasury (1992a), "1992 Autumn Statement: public expenditure plans", 12 November.

HM Treasury (1992b), "Private finance", press release, 12 November.

HM Treasury (1992c), "Redefining the mixed economy", press release, 23 November.

HM Treasury (1992d), "Private finance: guidance for departments", 9 December.

HM Treasury (1993a), "Joint ventures, guidance for departments", 16 March.

HM Treasury (1993b), "Leasing, guidance for departments", May.

HM Treasury (1993c), *Competition and the PFI*, consultation note, September.

HM Treasury (1993d), "Private finance projects list", 9 September.

HM Treasury (1993e), "Private finance", referring to specific privatisation projects in the Chancellor's Autumn budget statement, press release 122/93, 30 November.

Home Office (1991a), *The Woolf Report*, HMSO, 5 February.

Home Office (1991b), *Custody, Care and Justice*, Government White paper, September, Cm 1647, HMSO.

Home Office (1993), *Information on the Criminal Justice System in England and Wales - Digest 2*, Department of Research and Statistics, April.

Home Office (1990), *Government Court Escorts Custody and Security*, July.

HURL, Bryan (1992), *Privatisation and the Public Sector*, Heinemann Educational.

MATTHEWS, Roger (1989), *Privatising Criminal Justice*, Sage Publications.

Official Journal of the European Communities (1993), "UK-London: two announcements of pre qualification procedures for the operation of prisons", 18.11.93, No S 225/90 and 91.

Prison Officers' Association (1994), *Prisons in Peril*, briefing, February.

Prison Reform Trust (1991), "Management and structure of the prison service", December.

Prison Reform Trust (1992), *Implementing Woolf*.

Prison Reform Trust (1993a), *Wolds remand prison - contracting out: a first year report*, April.

Prison Reform Trust (1993b), *Court Escort Services*, July.

Prison Reform Trust (1993c), *The Future of the Prison Education Service*, July.

Prison Reform Trust (1993d), *Manifesto for prison reform*.

Prison Reform Trust (1994), *Privatisation Factfile 4*.

Private Finance Working Group (1993), first meeting, 15 December.

Scottish Office (1993), "Treatment of build own operate and transfer schemes in the provision of local authority schemes in Scotland", Local Government Finance Group, circular ref 18/1993, 19 August.

Chapter Six

**PRIVATE FUNDING FOR ROADS
IN THE UNITED KINGDOM**

by

John Moore
Independent Business and
Project Management Consultant
Dorking, Surrey, United Kingdom

INTRODUCTION

The objective of the chapter is to review the introduction of private finance and operation into the provision of road transport infrastructure in the United Kingdom, setting down government policies, initiatives and plans, the progress towards implementation to date, and to adduce lessons learned in terms of benefits, weaknesses and deficiencies. While some lessons can be learned, it is too early to draw comparative conclusions as to the success of the programme.

BACKGROUND

The UK road network comprises over 3 000 km of motorway in a total road network of over 360 000 km (Central Office of Information, 1994):

TOTAL length of UK road network, of which:	362 400 km
Motorways	**3 160 km**
Other trunk roads	12 330 km
Other roads	346 910 km

The system is used by some 25 million vehicles of which 20 million are private cars. The estimated usage in 1992 was some 400 000 million vehicle kilometres. Motorways carry 15 per cent of all traffic, and other trunk roads 17 per cent: combined, these two account for over half of all goods traffic in Great Britain. In 1992, accidents killed 4 230 persons and injured quarter of a million. The government is committed to reducing congestion on roads and to reducing accidents, by a combination of road improvement schemes, traffic management and new roads. The government's Citizen's Charter commits the department to improving services to motorists.

The UK has a relatively low proportion of motorways and trunk roads for the number of vehicles using them compared with other advanced European countries. However, there is a basic skeleton of trunk routes linking the main centres. In England, the level of provision of other roads is high in relation to land area, and there are therefore numerous alternative routes which, although slow, can be used over shorter journeys. Thus, the case for new motorways is strong because the present network is congested in some areas, but the commercial possibilities for tolled private roads are limited by the availability of alternative publicly-provided roads. The best possibilities for private tolled roads are estuarial crossings where the alternatives are lengthy and time-consuming for the driver. Thus privately financed or tolled crossings have been provided across the Thames, the Severn and to the Isle of Skye, and new crossings are planned for The Forth and the Tamar. There are some plans for tolled motorways. These privately funded schemes are described below.

The Secretary of State for Transport through his Department of Transport is responsible for all forms of transport, and directly for the construction and the costs of maintenance of motorways and other trunk roads. County Councils, Metropolitan and District Councils and London Boroughs are responsible to him for operating and maintaining trunk roads on his behalf and for the costs of non-trunk road maintenance. The Scottish Office and the Welsh Office are responsible for trunk roads in their regions (Central Office of Information, 1994). They are designated as the Highway Authority responsible for the provision, operation and safety of highways.

The expenditure on new trunk roads in 1993-94 will be about £1.4 billion. Maintenance of trunk roads is running at £550 million a year, an average of £40 000 per mile per year (Central Office of Information, 1994).

EVOLUTION OF POLICY ON PRIVATELY FINANCED ROADS

In 1919, when the Department of Transport was constituted, an annual tax on motor vehicles was introduced to pay for the construction and maintenance of the public road network and a Road Fund was created for this purpose. Over a period of time and by 1937, the Road Fund was no longer used exclusively for road provision and became absorbed into the general pool of taxation income. Use of roads continued to be free of direct charges and their provision was a charge on the national general taxation.

Vehicle fuel duties were introduced in addition to retaining the Vehicle Excise Duty. In 1993, fuel duties were 30.6 pence per litre for petrol, 25.8 pence per litre on unleaded petrol, and 25.1 pence for diesel. These were about half the retail prices of the fuels. Vehicle Excise Duty was £125 for a private car and up to £5 000 for certain heavy goods vehicles. The government has attempted since 1968 to raise enough revenue from these duties to cover the track costs, track costs being defined as the construction costs and the running costs of the road network but excluding finance charges. In 1993, the Chancellor announced that fuel tax would be increased in real terms by at least 3 per cent a year as part of the policy of cutting emissions of pollutants.

Tolls were only charged on a few locally-administered river crossings such as the Mersey tunnel, Tyne crossing, and, more recently, the Humber and Tamar bridges. The principle of tolling was therefore established, recognising the advantage to the user of savings in time and fuel which these crossings conferred. The level of tolls was set by local public inquiry run by an inspector who then reported to the Department on the appropriate level of tolls.

Construction of motorways and new trunk road schemes were financed by the public sector, and contracts let under competitive tender to the private sector to undertake construction. Traditionally, the Department used independent consultants to carry out the planning, design the road, and supervise construction. More recently, the department has looked for package design and construct contracts.

The development of government policy towards privately financed roads then unfolded relatively quickly, with a mix of policy and practice, each encouraging the other, and with mutual stimulation between the Department of Transport, the Treasury and private companies. The overall chronology is illustrated below:

Date	Milestone event
1985 July	Government announces scope for privately financed new estuarial crossings
1988 June	Second Thames crossing concession awarded
1988	*Next Steps* initiative defined Agencies for delivering services more effectively
1989	*New Roads by New Means* announces policy on finance and BNRR as first private road
1989	*Roads for Posterity* announces expanded road programme
1990 April	Second Severn bridge concession awarded
1991	New Roads and Streetworks Act enables tolls on **new** roads
1992 May	Concession for BNRR agreed
1992 November	Private Finance Initiative announced by Treasury
1992 November	Chancellor announces private build operate finance for new roads plus private operation of existing roads
1993 May	*Paying for Better Motorways* consultation paper on road costs, charging and electronic tolling
1994 February	Transport Secretary solicits electronic tolling proposals
1994 Spring	Announcement of shortlisted tenderers for Forth crossing

In July 1985 the Government announced that it would explore the scope for privately financed new estuarial crossings, chief amongst these being the need for a new Thames crossing to enable the M25 London orbital motorway to function fully. The M25 was to be opened in 1986 and it was clear that the existing Thames crossing using the Dartford Tunnel under the Thames East of London would be inadequate for the traffic flows. A new bridge was built using private finance. Following this a second crossing of the Severn was needed and a concession agreement was signed with the private sector in 1990.

These examples demonstrate that the Department of Transport were early in engaging private sector resources, but there was a wider desire in government to introduce private finance into many aspects of the government's responsibilities for delivering infrastructure and services to the public. In November 1992, the Chancellor of the Exchequer announced the *Private Finance Initiative* designed to bring the private sector into the provision of services and facilities (Central Office of Information, 1993; HM Treasury, 1992a-d, 1993a-e; Chancellor of the Exchequer, 1993; Scottish Office, 1993). The government were intent on improving the performance of construction with competitive, open tendering using private sector contractors and bringing in private finance. The private finance was believed to introduce an additional element of discipline into the management of the contract.

In their paper *The Next Steps* of 1988, the government articulated their concern about the efficiency and quality of functional services delivered from within the Civil Service (Cabinet Office, 1988). In essence, they argued that while government departments were good at formulating policy and monitoring implementation, they were not so effective as the private sector in delivering services to the public. The principle of getting the delivery of services out of the direct control of government was set down. Sections of the Civil Service which delivered services which could be better managed as free-standing agencies were either to be separately constituted as Executive Agencies run at arm's length by departments of state, or privatised by sale to the private sector. The licensing of road vehicles was one such function which was reformed as The Driver and Vehicle Licensing Agency to operate under a chief executive to a contract defined with the Department of Transport. The Transport (and Road Research) Laboratory is also now an agency and there are now over 100 agencies across government. A Highways Agency is currently proposed to assume responsibility as the Highway Authority for roads. This is welcomed by the private sector. The Agency would have an arm's length contract with Department of Transport defining motorway performance standards and overseeing implementation of road management and construction, eventually contracting with the private sector to deliver the services.

As a generalisation, so long as private sector involvement was under the close direction and control of government it was not expected to achieve real improvement in the time and cost of construction or operability. Engaging a private contractor, even under competitive tendering conditions, reduced the risk for the cost and time, but he had no interest in subsequent operability. The public sector customer had too little appreciation of an appropriate balance between performance specification and cost, and would tend towards over-specification of quality. The *Private Finance Initiative* (PFI) is an attempt to engage private sector expertise as much as finance in the provision of facilities and services and to couple this with responsibility for subsequent operation. Crucially, the PFI attempts to assign rewards and risks in fair proportions between customer and contractor.

The advantage of engaging a single contractor from the private sector in not only the construction of an asset but also in its operation was recognised. The combination of private finance for facilities and the return on that capital being dependent on the profitable and satisfactory operation of the facility should greatly reduce the scope for failure. There are a great number of possible models depending on circumstances, but the government is determined to harness the best attributes and experience of the private sector while tying them fairly into achieving the required standard of service under conditions of shared risk.

In 1989 the government published a consultation paper *New Roads by New Means* (Department of Transport, 1989). This set out the policy of involving the private sector in construction, finance and operation. The government's objective was to bring the abilities of the private sector to bear on new road provision and operation. The government sought genuine privately financed and owned schemes constructed and operated without government intervention or finance, or even government guarantees against risks. Shadow tolls were effectively proscribed as unhelpful in achieving the necessary motivation of contractors or the road user. Road schemes would be let in competitive tendering, and tolls would only be regulated by the government where the operator had a monopoly position on use of a route (i.e. most river crossings). The contractor would carry the environmental responsibilities. He would be permitted to benefit from planning gains.

An expanded road programme was announced in the White Paper *Roads for Prosperity* (Department of Transport, 1991); as a white paper, the programme was subject to revision to accommodate resources and budgets, but it articulated an expansion of construction of motorways, trunk road and major bypasses. Motorway expenditure was to provide for widening existing motorways and the provision of feeder-distributor roads alongside them.

In 1991 the *New Roads and Streetworks Act 1991* enabled tolls to be charged but only on new roads. As such it did not cover widened motorways or the existing network. It also enabled a highway authority (Department of Transport or a local authority) to use the planning process for new roads and bridges operated by private companies. The public has to be informed of the proposed toll and of the line of the route, and either or both are subjected to public inquiry if there is a valid objection. If either are found wanting, the road cannot proceed. The Act also requires a Concession Statement to be published outlining the key points of the concession agreement on a new road (the detail of the agreement remains private).

In May 1993 the Green Paper (essentially a consultative paper) *Paying for Better Motorways* was published by the Department (Department of Transport, 1993). This paper opened the debate on charging for motorway use with a review of the costs of road provision and how revenue could be achieved through tolling and charging. In addition to the Government's aim of recovering costs, the Government were considering the contribution which direct charging might have on traffic volumes and were mindful of their commitment to the Rio Earth Summit to reduce carbon dioxide emission (traffic contributes about one quarter of the carbon dioxide generated each year).

A number of mechanisms for recovering payments from users were paraded in *Paying for Better Motorways*. In terms of their effect on the user, they ranged from shadow tolling which would have little direct impact on users, through permits to use and tax on fuels, to direct measurement of use and related charging. It was also seen that direct charging could offer the opportunity to increase private sector finance and management in road construction and operation.

The principle of shadow tolling is that roads are operated and maintained by the private sector, and the use of roads is measured, but the Government pays the revenue. The motorist is not therefore aware of his consumption. It would have attraction for the private sector, but shadow tolling is ineffective in achieving the Government's aims, stated to be:

- achieving more finance for road capacity;
- forestalling the economic, environmental and accident costs of congestion;
- facilitating private finance and management;
- stimulate awareness of the real costs of road provision;
- improve the competitive position of rail and public transport generally (Department of Transport, 1993).

The weaknesses of fuel taxes are numerous. They are not selective between users and apply equally to all classes of vehicles on all roads, and do not relate adequately to the costs of relieving congestion and the use of alternative routes, nor to the real costs of the different axle loadings on road wear. The vehicle excise duty can be used to distinguish classes but are unselective between users in a class. No combination of fuel tax and vehicle duty can accurately reflect the real costs of individual journeys. Permits are seen as blunt instruments.

The paper therefore concludes that tolling is the solution with direct measurement of use and charges born by the user. The technology is not yet tested, and the earliest schemes might rely on manned toll booths. These have deficiencies in discriminating between vehicles and can cause delays but would open the way to acceptance of tolls. A form of electronic tolling has been introduced on the new Dartford crossing; about one quarter of users are equipped with credit tags which are debited automatically every time the vehicle makes the crossing. Full electronic tolling would include the ability to vary charges during the day and by location to reflect demand levels, to charge by costs incurred, and to inform the user of the real costs of providing/using specific sections of route. The preferred technology is probably that based on "smart cards", which could be debited at slip-road controls or their passage recorded against a credit account for regular users.

Legislation to allow tolling on existing roads would still be necessary.

In his 1992 Autumn Budget Statement to Parliament, the Chancellor of the Exchequer suggested that as a transitional step the government might invite private contractors to design, build and operate roads for which they would receive payments from government based on use. This might be accompanied by a network-wide charging regime, to encourage private management of the network.

Private contractors could be invited to tender for franchises to operate existing roads against specified levels of service and performance standards. These might include improvements to the franchised roads to meet increased demand. The tariff charged to the government by the contractor would be part of the tendering process of selection. This would bring private finance into the improvement of roads. It would also accelerate the introduction of electronic tolling systems.

A small step in private sector influence in developing motorway services was made in August 1992 when it was announced that responsibility for development of motorway service areas (stations supplying fuel, restaurant and conveniences along the motorways) would pass to the private sector. This has had the effect of speeding up the provision of these facilities and providing for their financing.

Views of observers

The Chartered Institute of Transport responded with a paper *Mobilising Private Investment* in October 1993 (Chartered Institute of Transport, 1993). They concluded that there was need to stimulate private investment because government funding was limited and the road system inadequate. They pointed out that although government can borrow money more cheaply and is better able to absorb statutory risks, the private sector should be better at identifying market demand, reducing costs and managing risk so far as it lies within their powers. The private sector will require commercial levels of return commensurate with the risks. Road projects exhibit high uncertainty in the planning stages, given particularly the protracted nature of the planning inquiry processes in the UK. They also claim that payback is slow because of slow build-up of traffic on new roads, but this is not always true (e.g. the M25). Furthermore, the asset is not realisable in the event of failure.

They also point out the difficulty of identifying profitable new projects within a dense network of freely provided motorways, but the introduction of some form of permit or direct user charging on existing roads could mitigate that problem. (In an announcement of December 1993, the Secretary of State firmly ruled out permits as un-rewarding in benefits.)

The CIT referred to the distinction between direct benefits of new roads to the user, and the indirect benefits to the nation of economic and environmental benefits. Only the government can properly account for the latter, and to the extent that these are nationally desirable, government should consider financial contribution to schemes where these benefits are significant in deciding the investment. The range of options proffered for government involvement included:

- lump sum grant from government;
- annual revenue grant;
- co-equity investment by government;
- deeply subordinated loan by government.

The British Road Federation (BRF) is a private organisation representing commercial and private road users, and it campaigns for safe and efficient roads. Its response to the Green Paper was to welcome the acknowledgement of the need for better roads (British Road Federation, 1993). It supported proposals to charge for usage, provided that revenues were used to improve the road network, and the level of public provision for road improvement and maintenance was at least maintained in real terms. It sought reduction of the time to complete new roads and endorsed the need for the formation of a road management executive agency, the Highways Agency.

The BRF doubted that the technology to enable electronic tolling would be available inside a decade, and the costs of building the system could absorb resources better used on developing roads. They believe there to be little scope in the UK for purely private road schemes, and advocate joint public/private partnerships in road construction, the payment of shadow tolls and franchising of individual existing roads.

The Automobile Association (AA) and the Royal Automobile Club represent private motorists. They "reluctantly accept key aspects of the government's proposals but only if the Treasury plays fair and guarantees that the roads budget is not cut again". The AA said:

> *The Treasury has hammered Britain's motorists twice in 1993 [Note: two Budget increases in fuel tax and an increase in Vehicle Excise duty] and they will find it hard to believe that motorway charging is not just another form of taxation for little return. Motorists must have firm guarantees that the deeply damaging cuts in the roads programme announced by the Chancellor on Tuesday will not be repeated in future and that all revenue from motorway charging remains genuinely additional to current roads spending. Once introduced, motorway charging must be matched by corresponding cuts in other motoring taxes.*

(Automobile Association, 1993)

The reference to cuts follows the Chancellors announcement that the programme of road schemes was to be reduced following an overall review of government expenditure.

The Trades Union Congress (TUC) and the Freight Transport Association agreed (National Economic Development Office, 1991). They believed that responsibility for provision should remain with government, and roads should be financed from taxation.

The environmental group Council for the Preservation of Rural England responded by rejecting the proposals for motorway charging (Council for the Preservation of Rural England, 1993). They support the principle of using price as a mechanism for demand management but only as part of a strategic transport policy framework compatible with environmentally sustainable principles. They say that there may be a role for charging on a geographical self-contained basis which does not permit avoidance of charge by the user. The polluter should pay for all pollution, whereas the proposals to charge tolls only on motorways confines the decision to whether the motorist is prepared to pay to use the motorway system rather than the much more environmentally important issue of whether he is prepared to use an alternative to the car or lorry. They favour taxing fuel as part of a coherent package of transport and energy measures including greater investment in alternative modes of transport.

The tenor of objections is therefore to accept tolling in principle but requiring that the transfer of charging from indirect taxation to direct charges on users does not reduce overall expenditure on roads and is accompanied by commensurate cuts in indirect taxation of the motorist.

Permissions, planning and land use

Before construction can start, permission has to be granted for the use of the land needed for the purpose of constructing and operating a motorway. There are two ways this is achieved: Act of Parliament, or existing planning legislation. This latter route involves public consultation over the proposals, followed by publication of the draft scheme/proposal together with draft orders for side road works and the compulsory purchase of land. There is opportunity for objections to be raised and a public inquiry is then held under an Inspector appointed by the Secretary of State.

Authorisation by Act of Parliament also provides for public objection but through petition to a Committee of Members of Parliament who will consider representations and report them to the House during consideration of the enabling Bill. The New Roads and Street Works Act of 1991 was passed to enable the highway authority to use procedures of the 1980 Highways Act to obtain authorisation for new privately funded toll roads and bridges without resorting to the complexity of a Parliamentary Bill. These procedures provide for publication of the line of route and the toll for public scrutiny and possible objections. A public inquiry will be held to consider objections.

The public inquiry results in a recommendation to the Secretary of State who makes the decision. If the inspector recommends significant changes to the proposals, a second round of inquiry procedures may be necessary.

Delays to road schemes have been very substantial. The Department has recently proposed ways of reducing the delays.

Some commentators have suggested that the levels of compensation paid to adversely affected property owners along the route is too low (National Economic Development Office, 1992). Householders receive compensation downwards from about 12 per cent of the market value of their property according to the level of disturbance and the extent by which the property value is diminished. Commentators argue that there would be fewer objectors if the compensation were higher. There are two flaws in this: the majority of objections come from persons not eligible for compensation but who are concerned about the environment, and higher compensation reduces the financial return.

In August 1993, the Secretary of State for Transport announced new rules for public enquiries aimed at speeding up the process. He hoped that the changes would reduce by between three and five years the time taken for a road proposal to move from planning to opening, which can currently take more than thirteen years. Allowing three years for construction, he is suggesting halving the time for enquiry. The improvements will come from reducing bureaucratic processes and defining carefully and restricting the scope of the inquiry. However, motorway protesters have been adept in the past at finding ways of extending the scope of inquiries, for example the M25 intersection inquiry at Leatherhead, and it may not prove possible to achieve all the expected saving of elapsed time.

The Department will be implementing these proposals from 1994. Proposals to be tried out include:

- giving formal standing to a pre-inquiry meeting at which procedural points would be resolved;
- The Inspector being allowed to set a timetable for the inquiry;
- statements of evidence to be prepared and exchanged between parties prior to the inquiry;
- summaries only to be read at the inquiry;
- inspectors having the right to refuse evidence which they believe irrelevant or repetitious.

Implementation was confirmed in February 1994 (*The Times*, 23 February 1994).

CURRENT STATUS OF PROJECTS

The current status of the programme for road projects considered for private finance is shown in Figure 1 below.

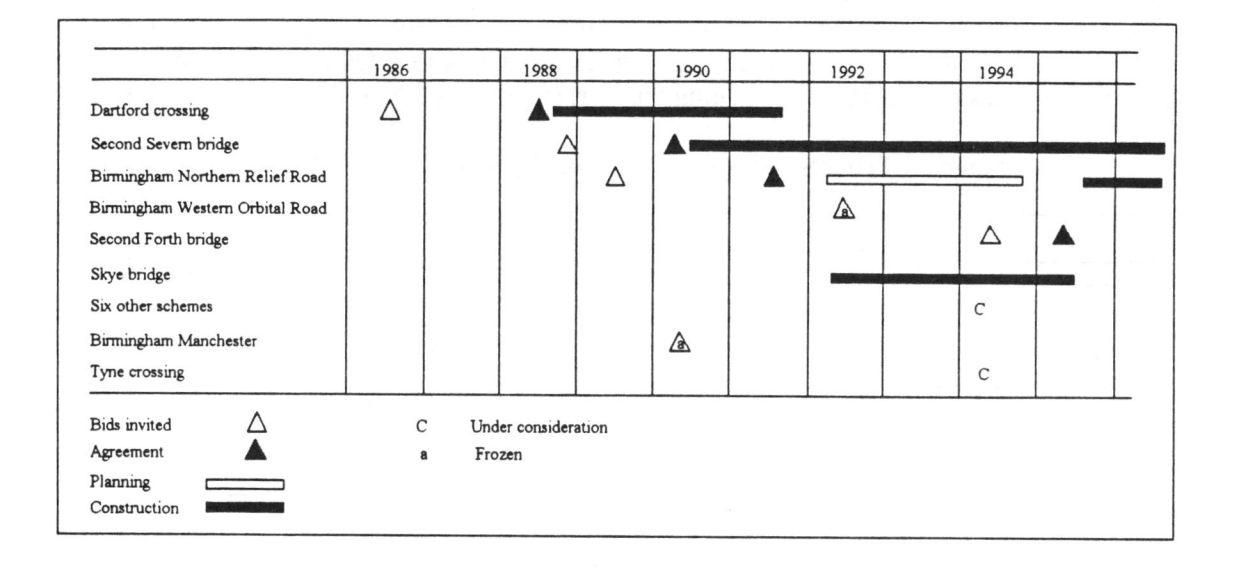

Figure 1. **Programme of private-financed proposals**

	1986	1988	1990	1992	1994
Dartford crossing	△	▲━━━━━━━━━━			
Second Severn bridge		△	▲━━━━━━━━━━━━━━━━━		
Birmingham Northern Relief Road			△	▲ ▭▭▭▭▭	━━
Birmingham Western Orbital Road				⚠	△ ▲
Second Forth bridge					△ ▲
Skye bridge				━━━━━━━━━━━━━━	
Six other schemes					C
Birmingham Manchester			⚠		
Tyne crossing					C

Bids invited	△		C	Under consideration
Agreement	▲		a	Frozen
Planning	▭▭▭			
Construction	━━━			

The principal schemes are described below, but the distinctive differences between estuarial crossings and roads should be noted.

Birmingham Northern Relief Road

This route was first published in 1980 as a relief route around the north of Birmingham and outside the M6. Traffic congestion was already high and a relief route was needed. Much of the existing motorway was on viaduct or elevated and widening the M6 would therefore be prohibitively expensive. A preferred route for a new motorway of 40 km in length was published in 1986 with a public inquiry in 1988. The results of that inquiry were never published, but the Department published its Green Paper in 1989 and accompanied this by a statement that the BNRR would be the first road to be built under the new initiative.

Prospective bidders were invited to pre-qualify and a short list of three were then invited to tender for design, build, operate and finance it. The concession was finally agreed with Midland Expressway in early 1992 (Adams, 1992; Midland Expressway Limited, no date).

Midland Expressway Limited is a private incorporated limited liability company. It is a joint venture between Trafalgar House and the Italian Iritecna, whose subsidiary company Autostrade has experience of motorway operation. Finance is not yet agreed and funding agreements will await the approval of the scheme after the public inquiry. It will take the form of private debt capital of some £300 million, but with a substantial equity base likely to be a condition of the lenders in order to ensure that the contractors build economically and operate the system efficiently.

The programme is shown below, but is already delayed by the planning process. It is unlikely that the public inquiry will begin until Spring 1994, with construction commencing no earlier than late 1996 or even during 1997. The contractor is providing extensive support for their application before the inspector, including comprehensive environmental impact assessment and much public consultation (Midland Expressway Ltd., 1993). In excess of 6 000 objections have been received. Although this is not an unusual number for a high-profile new road inquiry, it indicates that the inquiry is likely to be extended in time. The contractor carries the risk of this delay to the extent that he has already invested considerable money in getting thus far, at a guess perhaps of the order of £20 million.

Figure 2. **Progress of the planning and procurement of BNRR**

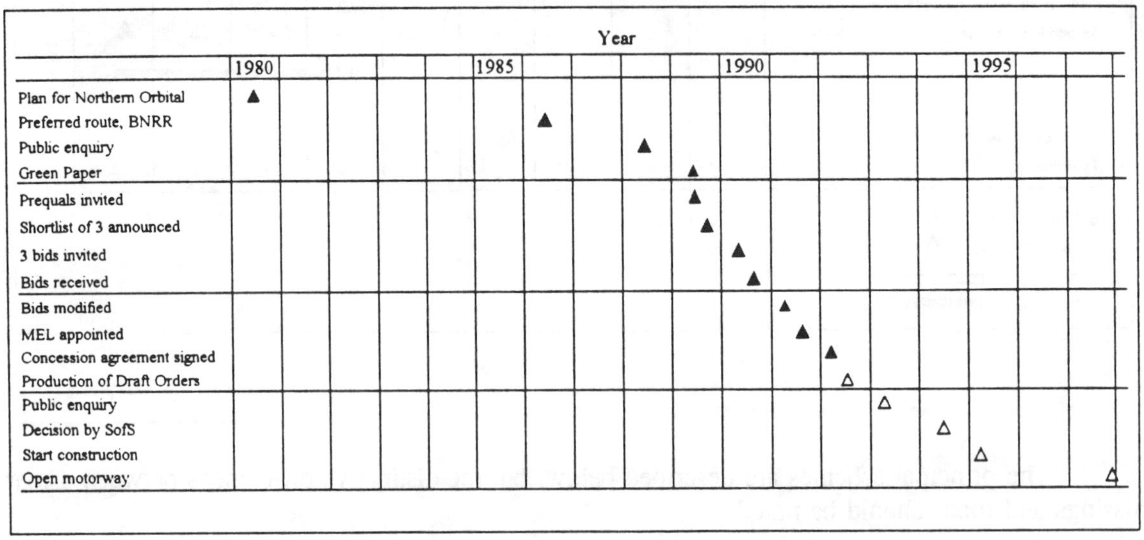

The concession agreement granted MEL a 53-year-long concession comprising three years construction and 50 years operation.

MEL's published objectives are to provide a facility which will give the level of service for which users would be most prepared to pay. Emphasis was placed on designing a road which would offer safe, attractive and reliable flow conditions, convenient access points and ease of use. It would be environmentally acceptable. MEL recognised that the scheme design would come under exceptional public scrutiny as the first privately financed and operated motorway.

The motorway will be free of congestion with traffic levels controlled by tariffs. Prices of £1.50 a car and £3.00 for trucks were proposed as markers for tariffs in 1990.

One of the risks to be carried by the private operator is that of environmental contamination following an accident involving a noxious chemical. The possibility of serious ground contamination could arise, and the operator will wish to insure against the consequences of such an eventuality. This will be a significant cost, and not one which affects roads in the public sector.

Western Orbital Route

This is proposed as a design build operate and finance road, relieving the M5 and M6 west of Birmingham.

Pre-qualifications were sought in February 1992, but support was small with only four submissions. The problem emerged that it was not viable as a wholly privately funded scheme, and the government withdrew the project for re-consideration as a joint public-private scheme. The project is currently likely to be held until the introduction of general motorway tolling.

Proposals for a Birmingham Manchester route in parallel with the M6 were also shelved in February 1992 for lack of viable propositions compatible with environmental or technical requirements.

Thames bridge crossing at Dartford

This new bridge crossing was necessitated in order to alleviate the congestion on the M25 at the crossing of the Thames. There was a twin two-lane tunnel at Dartford but this was inadequate for the volumes of traffic.

Various schemes were formally submitted to the Department but failed to satisfy the criteria set by the government. A proposal was then put forward by Trafalgar House plc for a bridge crossing downstream but adjacent to the tunnels. The bridge company Dartford River Crossing Limited was incorporated with a share capital of £1 000, and the construction financed by loans totalling £184 million raised from a syndicate of banks and an insurance company (Dartford River Crossing Ltd., 1991).

The terms of the concession were that the company would build own and operate the bridge for a maximum of twenty years or until the loan had been retired, whichever was the sooner. The bridge would then be transferred into public ownership. Tariffs were set, with the agreement restricting price increases to the Retail Prices Index.

The company charges tolls and is responsible for operation and maintenance of the bridge. It is required to be maintained in good order for the eventual transfer into public ownership. Traffic volumes have exceeded expectations and there is every indication that the terms of the agreement will be satisfied well inside twenty years (14 years is the current estimate). An electronic tag system based on pre-payment credit cards is available for drivers which is used by about one quarter of the vehicles. The card is debited on each crossing trip, and the driver alerted when the pre-paid credit runs low.

This example has enabled a crossing to be provided free of charge on the public purse, financed by the private sector and paid for by the user. However, it should be noted that the government provided the approach roads to the value of £36 million.

The timescales of this development were short. The planning process for a crossing is much shorter than that of a new road, as there are very few private individual objectors. There were some delays occasioned principally by technical issues concerning the safety of the bridge for motorists under high wind speeds. It was also necessary to transfer ownership of the tunnels to the new company so the bridge and tunnels could be operated and maintained as an entity, which required a Bill to pass through Parliament. This was achieved in June 1988, and construction began in July. The bridge was opened in October 1991.

Figure 3. **Dartford river crossing programme**

	Year									
	1980				1985				1990	
Guidelines on private sector schemes	▲									
Various second crossing proposals				▲┈┈┈▲						
Trafalgar House proposal approved						▲				
M25 opened						▲				
Parliamentary Bill							▲			
Royal assent								▲		
Construction started								▭▭▭		
Bridge opened									▲	

Second Severn bridge

There is an important crossing for the M4 into South Wales over the Severn Estuary. When opened, the first Severn Bridge carrying the M4 was inadequate technically even to meet the design capacity, and demand grew to the point where a second crossing was required. The first bridge was built with public money and operated with tolling by the public sector.

Bids were invited by the Department in December 1988 from private companies to provide a second bridge, take over the first bridge and operate both under a concession agreement. A concession agreement was signed in April 1990 with a joint venture company Severn River Crossing Limited whose Members are John Laing plc (construction company), GTM-Entrepose (operators through Cofiroute of motorways in France), Bank of America and Barclays de Zoete Wedd. The concession was granted for a maximum period of 30 years. The user will pay a toll; tolls are to be linked to the Retail Prices Index (Laing GTM, 1990).

The bridge is due to open in Spring 1996. It will be 5 km in length.

The motorway approach roads are not included in the crossing contract, and they will be built and paid for by the Welsh Office and the Department of Transport.

Figure 4. **Second Severn crossing programme**

	Year		
	1985	1990	1995
Guidelines on private sector schemes	▲		
Various second crossing proposals	▲		
Laing/GTM proposal approved		▲	
Concession agreement		▲	
Planning and consents		▬▬▬	
Construction			▬▬▬▬▬
Bridge opened			△

Detailed planning was carried out through to 1992, with construction commencing in May 1992. The approach roads were subject to planning inquiry, the bridge crossing required Parliamentary authorisation.

Second Forth bridge

In March 1992, the Scottish Office published a consultation document *Setting Forth* to elicit public and corporate interest in new links by road and rail across the Forth Estuary at Edinburgh (The Scottish Office, 1992). A new road bridge was proposed, to alleviate congestion, together with measures to improve toll collection and consideration of differential pricing also aimed to reduce delays and congestion.

This was followed in mid-1993 by an invitation for contractors to submit proposals to the Scottish Office to design, build, finance, maintain and operate a second Forth road bridge and associated road links, and to take over maintain and operate the existing bridge (Secretary of State for Transport, 1993). Pre-qualifications were sought by 2 November 1993, with tenders required from a short-list drawn up early in 1994 for submission by Autumn 1994. The concession is expected to be signed in early 1995, with statutory procedures completed to enable construction to commence before April 1996.

The contractor will be expected to assume all project risks, including traffic volumes, geological problems and wind shielding. The Scottish Office acknowledge that legislative and procedural risks may have to be managed by the Office. The concession will be for a limited period.

The conditions set for the selection of the short-list include technical and project management competence, but also seek a sound experience in major project financing, and experience of operating and maintaining "civil engineering projects of this nature". The approach to environmental aspects and properly addressing the requirements of public consultation will be examined.

CROSSING SCHEMES DIFFER FROM ROADS

The three crossing schemes described above differ from the private road scheme of BNRR and others in ways which are significant.

Estuarial and river crossings can be very bankable, as evidenced by the very high gearing of the financial packages. The term "pinpoint equity" was coined for the Dartford crossing. The crossing provides substantial savings in journey time and fuel costs to users as the alternative is a lengthy detour. Tolls can be levied which the motorist is prepared to pay, setting them against his savings of time and fuel. They tend not to involve lengthy public inquiries and can be enabled by Parliamentary Bill. The environmental aspects are no more difficult than for a road proposal.

It is important to the success of the operator that he assumes control of any existing crossing in order to enable tolling and also the effective management of traffic flow during periods of maintenance.

By contrast, the new private road proposal has to operate within a dense network of adjacent roads free of charges, which tends to limit the level of charges to that which the motorist is prepared to pay to avoid congestion and save time. They involve extensive and extended public consultation and public inquiry because of the number of private individuals who feel threatened by the new road.

Risks and rewards

The government are anxious to ensure that the new road will operate to the specified standard and be in a fit state to take over at the end of the concession period. They are also determined to limit and fix their financial participation in the project.

The contractor wishes to achieve a return on his investment commensurate with other opportunities for investment and the risk. He therefore wants to be satisfied as to demand, revenues, costs, and time to implement.

Paying for Better Motorways set out the risk issues (Department of Transport, 1993). They are:

Design. The contractor offering design build operate and finance will design to optimise the total costs and usability of the road. The design has to be subjected to public inquiry at quite an advanced state of design, which may introduce changes to the design. The public inquiry and the European Commission will be concerned about the environmental impact, and this may necessitate changes.

Construction cost. All risks during construction can reasonably be born by the contractor, having carried out due diligent enquiries and investigations. Ground conditions can be discovered which occasion extra unforeseen costs, and there may be a case for government to underwrite these.

Time to opening. This is a big risk for the contractor, as finance charges by the end of the planning process can be £4 000 to £5 000 a day and by the end of construction will be £50 000 to £100 000 a day. Once investment starts, the road needs to open as soon as possible because revenue depends on it. Delays can arise in: planning which can be protracted, site labour problems, unforeseen ground conditions, weather, and political or public opposition. The skill of the private sector construction manager lies in finding ways of overcoming these impediments, but government can assist by ensuring that statutory processes or the enforcement of the law is effective and prompt.

Demand and revenue. This is the other big risk; will the traffic flows be adequate, and will the tariffs be sufficient for a return. Fears have been expressed that traffic may only build up slowly on some new routes, and that alternative routes may continue to attract users. The contractor can offer some attractions of service and congestion-free motoring, but the scope to attract traffic appears limited. As experience develops however means may be found to attract and retain users with suitable marketing, and perhaps through some form of direct public participation in the company.

Maintenance. The operator will be responsible for maintenance, and this gives the constructor the incentive to design for durability and maintainability. Where and to the extent that the Highway Authority might require to determine timing of maintenance (e.g. to suit other road maintenance closures) this cost should be born by the Authority. The government will seek to ensure that the highway is maintained to standards in order that it is fit to acquire at the end of the concession. This remains a hazard for government which will be defined in the contract but will require vigilance in monitoring application.

Safety and Environment. This has not been referred to in the public literature listed, but the risk of action by injured users and the real possibility of serious contamination in the event of spillage of noxious chemicals is real. The contractor will probably not be able to afford to shoulder these risks himself, and he will insure against the eventuality if this is economic. Public liability insurance is obtainable, but the consequential costs of pollution could prove uninsurable. Government may have to underwrite some or all of this.

The Department has expressed its encouragement for private companies to put forward new schemes where they might perceive opportunity. There have been one or two such speculative un-solicited schemes put forward, but not successfully. Several commentators have referred to the risk to private companies in advancing un-solicited proposals, in that there is no real protection for the promoter from subsequent competitive bids and the possibility that the work put in by the original promoter proves nugatory.

The private sector will need to make a return on capital commensurate with the risk and commensurate with returns elsewhere. Infrastructure projects tend to be high risk, low return and long duration investments. Motorways are such. Utility companies understand this type of investment, but in the UK at present they enjoy good returns and there is no evidence that they have been seriously attracted into road projects. There might be scope for European utilities to enter this market. Managers of commercial and industrial companies acting on behalf of shareholders are cautious. Construction companies have shown interest, but look very carefully for evidence of future traffic flows before making un-solicited proposals or entering bids. Again, the distinction between the captive demand from a crossing and the demand for a new road is clear in their differing enthusiasms for the two types of business.

Proposed tolling on roads

The availability of roads free of charges is the principal difficulty standing in the way of private new roads, or the private operation of existing roads. Shadow tolling is no solution as the motorist does not pay directly for use.

The Secretary of state for Transport is therefore keen to introduce a national system of tolls for motorways. In February 1994, he stated that the government were considering a variable pricing scheme for the entire public motorway network with higher charges at peak times to reduce congestion and even out traffic flows. He also mentioned the benefits it would have elsewhere in the economy in encouraging flexible working hours and greater use of public transport (*The Times*, 24 February 1994).

He announced that no decision would be taken on charges for at least two years. In setting charges he would have regard to protecting alternative local roads by setting tariffs below the point at which they might cause traffic to divert onto alternative routes.

Electronics and software companies have been invited to submit suggestions for developing a national measurement, recording and charging system. Currently available systems in the UK and overseas are not sufficiently advanced to permit non-stop electronic charging at high speeds on multi-lane systems, and they all suffer from difficulty in simplifying prepayment or in recovering payment from the user post-journey. All present systems have to provide for the alternative of cash payment at the point of use. Prepayment cards capable of debiting remotely as the vehicle passes collection points are favoured because of the difficulties of recovering in arrears. Quarterly billing for motorway use is a novel concept to the user, who might none-the-less get used to paying his motorway bill like his telephone and gas bills. It is hoped to have some workable system proposals by September 1994. Workable systems means addressing not only the sensor, recording and information processing, but also the mechanisms for prepayment, or billing and post-payment of users, including visitors from overseas.

A number of new road proposals await the imposition of national tolling or at least the ability to toll adjacent routes if the new road is to be commercially viable.

Tarmac submitted some thoughtful ideas to the Department on *Paying for Better Motorways* (Tarmac Construction, 1993). They favour tolling, and the introduction of private companies to finance, build and operate motorways. They proposed full privatisation of the motorway network under a regional structure of independent operating companies. This would give the necessary scale to each business, and provide the requisite flexibility in operation and maintenance.

By introducing tolling, the government will effectively transfer charges from the public purse to the user. There may be resistance to this when it is appreciated that the network has already been paid for by the taxpayer. To ameliorate this, there may have to be some relief of existing road user taxes. The level of charges suggested by the government, 1.5 pence per mile for cars, is adequate to cover the running costs of motorways, but the provision of a new road needs about 5 pence per mile. A regional business could compromise on the difference, using a slightly higher tariff from existing motorways to support the capital investment in new roads.

ACHIEVEMENTS TO DATE

The achievements for estuarial crossings has been significant. New crossings have been provided with only minor public finance, relieving some points of major congestion in the motorway system. The achievement in new roads is almost zero; only the BNRR is anywhere near realisation.

Committed investment of private funds probably totals between £500 and £600 million with associated public works of one tenth of this. But it is entirely estuarial crossings. Spread over the period, the expenditure, say £50 to £100 million a year is small compared with current annual public spending on new trunk road construction of £1.4 billion.

It is not yet demonstrable that a competent private sector business has been established to operate and maintain roads and bridges in a safe state, and fit to hand over to public ownership at the end of the concession. A road system comprises not only the pavement but also bridges, communication systems, service areas, and maintenance service areas, and each of these has special requirements if it is to be maintained in good order. Experience to date is too short, and the number of companies engaged and the number of management staff is still too small to constitute a dependable base.

Several companies have pointed out the need to develop a sound base of business. The European Round Table of Industrialists comprises leaders of the major industrial companies in the European Union. They argue for "portfolio investment" in infrastructure rather than "project investment" to provide a spread of risks (European Round Table of Industrialists, 1992). In order to achieve a sufficiency of investments in roads, it may be necessary to develop private investment on a pan-European basis; the UK is simply not a big enough base.

CONCLUSIONS

It is too soon to judge the success of the initiatives, with only one privately financed road which is still in the planning stage. The only successes have been the relatively easier river crossings.

Full engagement of the private sector in roads provision awaits the introduction of tolling, almost certainly electronic, on all motorways, and this is still some years ahead. Both existing and new motorways need to be tolled, to prevent distortions in use and unfair competition between existing and new roads.

The introduction of charges for motorways is regressive taxation and there may have to be some accompanying reduction of existing motor taxes. Tariffs will have to be set which provide not only for running costs but also to cover new construction.

Development of the technology for tolling is moving forward, but full implementation probably has to proceed in close conjunction with the development and implementation of similar technology across Europe.

The finance is available for private road construction, but banks are cautious about risk, particularly revenue risks, until it is clear that any new road does not have to compete with existing "free" provision of alternative routes for the user.

The private sector will only invest if it can be reasonably sure of making a return commensurate with the risk and comparable with other investment opportunities. Utilities could take more interest as they understand the inherent characteristics of infrastructure investment, but there appears little interest at present, perhaps because they are achieving good returns from their existing businesses.

Mixed schemes of public-private finance may be necessary for some new roads to achieve the necessary returns for the private sector.

The asset created in a private road scheme is unrealisable in the event of failure, although in such an event the restructuring of the finances might render the asset viable as a commercial operation. This is not of course a sound basis for the initial investment decisions. The banks are therefore particularly cautious about financing roads.

The private sector is reluctant to shoulder all the responsibility and risk for the extended process of public inquiry. He incurs costs and finance charges for an indeterminate time. Government proposals to reduce the time of inquiries should greatly assist.

There are imperfections in the market. The private sector cannot easily obtain any advantage from the national benefits of a new road, such as relief of congestion elsewhere or reduced emissions to the environment.

The private operator incurs charges which are not born by the public road, notably insurances and higher costs of borrowing.

Government has a key role to play in reducing risk to the investor, through improving and facilitating statutory and administrative processes and enforcing the law where it is being flouted to delay new roads.

Bidding is expensive, and serious bidders will only commit themselves if schemes are viable and the risks reasonable. Pre qualification offers a route to selecting a short-list of bidders who are then more likely to put forward acceptable tenders. Remuneration of bidding costs, while welcomed, does not markedly change the enthusiasm of the bidders if the scheme is a good one, and poor schemes unlikely to proceed will not attract serious bidders anyway.

Risks can mainly be shouldered by the private sector, but the risks of delay consequent on planning and on statutory processes and the enforcement of regulations and law are for government. The risk of environmental contamination is also likely to need government underwriting.

A regional structure of private motorway management has attractions in creating a viable scale of operations for investing companies, and permitting flexibility in operation and maintenance management and resources.

Speculative proposals have attractions but at present they are almost impossible to protect from competition once they are publicised. A regionally organised business would enable them to be protected and this should encourage proposals.

The business of managing roads is embryonic in the UK, and expertise has still to be imported. Indigenous capability will grow quickly if and when the network is operated on a commercial basis with privately managed tolling.

BIBLIOGRAPHY

ADAMS, M.G.W. (1992), *Birmingham Northern Relief Road: The UK's First Tolled Motorway*, paper to Planning and Transport Research and Computation International Association (PTRC), September.

ASCHER, A. (1987), *The Politics of Privatisation: Contracting Out Public Services*, Macmillan Education.

Barclays de Zoete Wedd (1993), *Privatisation World-wide: the Barclays Group Approach.*

British Road Federation, (1993), Response to *Paying for Better Motorways*, 16 August.

Cabinet Office (1988), *Improving Management in Government: The Next Steps*, HMSO.

Central Office of Information (1993), *Breaking New Ground, the Private Finance Initiative*, November, produced for HM Treasury, TRSY J081120NJ.

Central Office of Information (1994), *Britain 1994 - An official handbook*, HMSO.

Chancellor of the Exchequer (1993), "Private finance initiative to transform capital projects in the 1990s", Speech to the CBI, 26 May.

Chartered Institute of Transport (1993), *Transport Infrastructure: Mobilising Private Investment.*

Council for the Preservation of Rural England (1993), Response to *Paying for Better Motorways*, September.

Department of Transport (1989), *New Roads by New Means*, Green Paper.

Department of Transport (1991), *Roads for Prosperity*, White Paper.

New Roads and Streetworks Act, 1991.

Dartford River Crossing Limited, (1991), *Europe's Fastest Growing River Crossing.*

Department of Transport (1993), *Paying for Better Motorways*, HMSO Cm 2200, May.

European Round Table of Industrialists (1992), *Growing Together - One Infrastructure for Europe*, May.

HM Treasury (1992a), "1992 Autumn Statement: Public Expenditure Plans", 12 November.

HM Treasury (1992b), "Private finance", press release, 12 November.

HM Treasury (1992c), "Redefining the mixed economy", press release, 23 November.

HM Treasury (1992d), "Private Finance: Guidance for Departments", 9 December.

HM Treasury (1993a), "Joint Ventures, Guidance for Departments", 16 March.

HM Treasury (1993b), "Leasing, Guidance for Departments", May.

HM Treasury (1993c), "Competition and the PFI", consultation note, September.

HM Treasury (1993d), "Private finance projects list", 9 September.

HM Treasury (1993e), "Private finance", referring to specific privatisation projects in the Chancellor's Autumn budget statement, press release 122/93, 30 November.

Institution of Civil Engineers (1992), *Infrastructure - The Challenge of 1992*, Thomas Telford.

Institution of Civil Engineers (1994), *Ways to Pay*, New Civil Engineer - Motorway charging 1994.

Laing GTM (1990), *Second Severn Crossing*.

Midland Expressway Limited, Various technical and commercial brochures for BNRR.

Midland Expressway Limited (1993), *Birmingham Northern Relief Road, Environmental Statement*.

National Economic Development Office (1991), *Private participation in infrastructure*, Construction Industry Sector Group.

National Economic Development Office (1992), *A New Approach to Road Planning*, Construction Industry Sector Group.

Planning and Transport Research and Computation International Association (PTRC) (1987), "Public Transport Planning and Operations: Proceedings of seminar", Summer Annual Meeting, 7-11 September.

Planning and Transport Research and Computation International Association (PTRC) (1992), *Financing Transport Infrastructure*; proceedings of seminar, 20th Summer Annual Meeting, 14-18 September.

Scottish Office (1992), *Setting Forth* - a consultation document on Forth of Firth transport links, March.

Scottish Office (1993a), "Treatment of build own operate and transfer schemes in the provision of local authority schemes in Scotland", Local Government Finance Group, circular ref 18/1993, 19 August.

Scottish Office (1993b), *Second Forth Road Bridge*, September.

Secretary of State for Transport (1993), Statement to the House of Commons on motorway charging, response to Parliamentary Question 294, 2 December.

Tarmac Construction (1993), paper responding to *Paying for Better Motorways*, September.

The Times, 23 February 1994.

The Times, 24 February 1994.

Chapter Seven

**PRIVATE SECTOR OWNERSHIP AND OPERATION OF PRISONS:
AN OVERVIEW OF UNITED STATES EXPERIENCE**

by

Harry S. Havens
Former Assistant Comptroller General
United States General Accounting Office

INTRODUCTION

This chapter provides a brief summary of the US experience of using private sector firms in constructing and operating institutions for the incarceration of individuals convicted of violations of criminal law. This involvement has taken many forms and has evolved greatly over the years. Some of these experiences have been judged successful; others less so.

The justification for using private firms to carry out governmental functions is commonly stated in some combination of the following:

-- the private sector, by avoiding some of the bureaucratic and other constraints faced by government, can achieve greater efficiency and lower costs;

-- with fewer impediments to innovation and stimulated by the profit motive, the private sector has greater inclination and opportunity to experiment with novel techniques, thereby increasing efficiency gains and possibly achieving greater effectiveness.

-- on construction projects, the private sector can avoid some of the political and bureaucratic impediments that often delay public construction projects, allowing the private sector to complete such projects more rapidly.

Objections to increasing the role of the private sector often challenge the efficiency and effectiveness arguments, on grounds that the evidence is far from conclusive on either point. Skeptics also stress the importance of meaningful competition in achieving gains in efficiency and effectiveness, along with the difficulty of assuring it in many circumstances.

The special case of private operation of prisons raises additional issues. These center on the risks associated with giving a profit-motivated firm control over an involuntarily confined individual. The risks to the prisoners -- exploitation and inadequate concern for health and safety -- are accompanied by risks to the government that has made such a delegation of power. A government may find it difficult to withdraw from an unsatisfactory arrangement, and under US law it may be held liable for substantial monetary damages in the event of a violation of a prisoner's rights.

This chapter attempts to assess these arguments. It starts by presenting a brief historical background and then describes a "standard model" for the construction and management of public prison facilities in the United States. It then describes the role of the private sector in that standard model before proceeding to a discussion of several alternatives embodying considerably greater private sector involvement. The paper concludes with a discussion of some of the important concerns that have been expressed about the private sector models and the difficulties that may be anticipated in countering the adverse incentives created by the profit motive.

HISTORICAL BACKGROUND

It is likely that the average US citizen today would assume that the confinement of convicted felons is an entirely governmental function. When we think of prisons, we think of the famous ones, such as Alcatraz or San Quentin, all of which have been operated by the federal or state governments. In actuality, however, penal institutions operated by the government are a relatively recent development. Until the mid-Nineteenth Century, for example, England avoided the need for the long-term incarceration of large numbers of convicts by "transporting" (banishing) many of them, first to the American colonies and then to Australia. Upon arrival, the prisoners were effectively sold as indentured labor, an apparently profitable transaction for the merchants who handled the transporting process (Feeley, 1990).

In the early years of independence in the United States a comparable practice emerged, that of "leasing" prisoners to those who wished to employ the convict labor, most commonly in agriculture or mining, but occasionally in factories. One study described the practice as follows:

> *The state was paid [by the contractor] a stipulated amount for the inmates' labor, the inmate received no compensation, and the conditions of work were often highly exploitative, since the contractors supervised the operations and had an obvious interest in maximizing their production.*

(Mullen et al., 1985)

In some parts of the South and West, this practice persisted until well into the Twentieth Century. Some attribute its demise to outrage over the many abuses involving cruelty and exploitation that were revealed by investigative reporters and legislative inquiries (US General Accounting Office, 1991). Others ascribe it to opposition from "free" labor who objected to the unfair competition (Mullen et al., 1985).

Thus, the private incarceration of convicted criminals is not a new invention. Rather, it has a long and decidedly checkered history that should give some pause to those who endorse extensive use of this approach to solving the very serious problems of the US penal system.

ORGANIZATION OF THE US PENAL SYSTEM

The federal structure of the United States introduces a degree of organizational complexity that may not be found elsewhere. It may minimize confusion in later discussions to describe that complexity at this point.

Institutions for the confinement of convicts or of those accused of crimes are found at several levels of government. The federal government, through the Bureau of Prisons, operates prisons for the confinement of persons convicted of federal crimes. In addition, the Immigration and Naturalization Service operates detention facilities for confinement of illegal aliens and the US Marshals Service operates facilities for the detention of unsentenced federal offenders.

State governments, commonly through a Department of Corrections, operate prisons and other facilities for those convicted of violating state criminal laws. County and city governments operate jails and other detention facilities, usually for the confinement of those awaiting trial or sentencing (including those being held at the request of state and federal law enforcement officials, as well as local police) and for those convicted of relatively minor offenses. In county governments, these facilities are commonly managed by the Sheriff, who is often an elected official of the county government.

Most criminal laws, such as those against murder or armed robbery, are enacted and enforced at the state level of government. Thus, not surprisingly, most convicted criminals are housed in facilities that are constructed and operated under state laws. It was recently estimated, for example, that of the total costs of the corrections system in the United States, 70 per cent was incurred by the states, 5 per cent by the federal government, and the remainder by county and city governments. One recent study reported the prison population of the United States as including 57 689 in federal prisons and 650 703 in state prisons (US General Accounting Office, 1991).

The United States also has a wide variety of types of facilities for the detention of criminals. These include prisons, which are usually classified as maximum security, medium security, or minimum security on the basis of the risk to public safety posed by the inmate population. The minimum security category blends into other types of facilities, such as prison farms. As noted earlier, jails (often involving a relatively high degree of security because of the diversity of the inmate population) serve to house those awaiting trial and those serving relatively short sentences.

There are also several types of specialized facilities for housing particular categories of prisoners. Juvenile offenders are usually assigned to institutions limited to young prisoners. The criminally insane are usually confined in specialized mental hospitals. Addicted criminals may be assigned to drug treatment facilities.

Prisoners approaching the end of their sentence may be transferred to pre-release centers or "halfway houses" where the terms of confinement are considerably less strict. For example, the individual may be permitted to leave the facility during the day to engage in gainful employment.

After release from prison, a former inmate (as a condition of parole) may be required to submit to various levels of supervision to assure good behavior. Finally, some states are experimenting with intensive supervision (ranging from daily reporting of activities to electronically monitored house arrest) as an alternative to incarceration.

A STANDARD MODEL OF INCARCERATION FACILITIES

Because of the diversity of types of detention facilities and the decentralization of the prison system, it is not possible to describe a "standard model" of such facilities in great detail. However, there are certain characteristics which are common to many of them. Some of these characteristics will be described in this section of the paper as a basis for the later discussion of ways in which the private sector is, or may become, involved in the detention process, both as part of the standard model and in deviations from that model.

Virtually all prisons and jails are owned and operated by one or another level of government. That is, the government acquires the land and arranges for the construction of the facility. Once the facility is ready for operation, the staff are comprised primarily of civil servants, some of whom (commonly designated "corrections officers" in state and federal prisons and "deputy sheriffs" in county jails) have been granted police powers with regard to the inmate population.

The construction of state, county, and city detention facilities is usually financed by bonds issued by the government. In most cases the issuance of such bonds must be approved by the voters in a referendum. The delays involved in obtaining this approval and the frequency with which the voters have rejected these proposals, along with other debt and tax limitations at the state and local level, have been a significant factor in the growth of private sector involvement in prison construction, as will be described later in the paper.

At the federal level, prison construction funds are provided in the regular budget process, with no requirement for special voter approval. At all levels of government, once a detention facility has been placed in service, the regular operating costs are financed through the annual (or in some states, biennial) budget process.

Some detention facilities generate considerable income from the sale of goods and services produced by inmates, although the extent of these "prison industries" has been severely constrained by laws limiting the use of prison labor in competition with free labor. Most prison industries are restricted to producing goods for use by the government, not for sale in the commercial marketplace (Mullen *et al.*, 1985). Inmates may receive a wage for working in the prison industry, but it is quite modest, well below wages paid in the general economy. The disposition of prison industry profits varies. In some cases, it is paid to the state government and handled the same as profits from other state-owned business operations. In other cases, it may be retained by the prison or by the state Department of Corrections, supplementing the appropriation for operating expenses.

Private sector involvement in the standard model

Even in the case of a detention facility that is owned and managed by the government, there is considerable scope for private sector involvement. The actual construction of the facility, for example, is almost invariably done by private firms under contract to the government. The design is usually produced by an architectural firm, which may also be employed to help supervise the construction process. The actual construction is often segmented into several contracts covering different elements of the structure (foundations, walls, electrical equipment, etc.). These contracts are commonly on a fixed-price basis and state law typically requires that the contract be awarded to the firm offering to do the work for the lowest price.

In recent years it has become more common for the government to enter into a single contract covering the entire design and construction process. The firm obtaining this contract (called the "general contractor") is then responsible for parcelling the segments of work among "subcontractors" and for managing and integrating the work of these subcontractors to produce a finished structure.

Private sector involvement in state-owned and operated facilities does not necessarily come to an end with the completion of the construction phase. With increasing frequency in recent years, state corrections departments have contracted for the provision of essential services for the inmate population.

In food service, for example, the traditional arrangement has been for food to be prepared in the prison kitchens, using inmate labor supervised by state employees. Today, it is not unusual to see this service performed by a private firm under contract, with the firm being paid a fixed daily amount for providing meals of a specified nutritional content for each prisoner.

Health services and routine maintenance of the physical plant, along with the education and training of inmates, are other functions which are now frequently performed under contract by private firms. One reason these firms are able to provide the service at lower cost is their ability to capitalize on economies of scale (such as through the bulk purchase of supplies) (Fitzgerald, 1991). In addition, they avoid the rigidities of public sector salary and other personnel management practices.

Private sector involvement is even greater among specialized institutions. Drug treatment centers, for example, are now commonly owned and operated by private organizations, as are many juvenile detention facilities and, especially, half-way houses. The contract usually calls for the state to pay the firm a fixed daily amount for each inmate who is housed in the facility.

Problems in the public sector model

It is generally acknowledged that there are severe problems in the corrections system in the United States. While the problems are not new, their severity is usually attributed to the extremely rapid growth of the prison population, leading to extreme overcrowding of existing institutions. Federal courts have ruled that an unreasonable degree of overcrowding violates the constitutional rights of the inmates and have ordered many state corrections departments to relieve this overcrowding. One recent study reported that 41 states and the District of Columbia were under court order to relieve overcrowding at one or more their prisons (US General Accounting Office, 1991). This leaves the state with two choices; it must build more prisons or it must release enough prisoners to make room for those newly convicted.[1]

Both options have been pursued to varying degrees in most states. Each, however, faces serious obstacles. Granting early parole is very unpopular because of growing public concern about crime and the high rates of recidivism among released convicts. But building prisons is not popular, either. As noted earlier, proposals to issue bonds to finance the construction of prisons are regularly defeated at the polls. One observer notes that, in the 1980s, 60 per cent of jail bond proposals were defeated in local elections (Fitzgerald, 1991). It is evident that much of the US public has not yet accepted that the logical implication of its demand to "lock up the criminals" (a demand reflected in voter approval of mandatory minimum sentences and life imprisonment for repeat offenders) is the construction of more prisons in which to confine them.

PRIVATELY FINANCED CONSTRUCTION OF DETENTION FACILITIES

One response to the dilemma posed by voter opposition to the issuance of state or local bonds to finance jail or prison facilities is to circumvent the voter opposition by financing construction with private funds. In this arrangement, a private firm may borrow the funds to finance construction, acquire the land, build the facility, and then lease it to the government. The lease may be a "straight lease," in which ownership remains with the private firm, or it may be a "lease purchase," in which ownership shifts to the government after a specified period of time, usually twenty to thirty years. Both forms have been observed.

State laws typically prohibit contracts for periods exceeding one year, so the lease is usually for one year, with options to renew the lease annually thereafter. While this creates some financial risk for the private owners, that risk seems small, as will be discussed later.

In terms of achieving the desired increase in prison capacity, privately financed construction has the decided advantage of avoiding the need for voter approval of a bond issuance. In reality, of course, this does not avoid the eventual cost to the government of financing the facility. It only redirects that cost from the amortization of bonds to the payment of rent. State constitutions, however, treat the two types of transactions differently.

While the primary motivation for private financing of prison facilities appears to be the avoidance of unpopular bond referendums, the proponents of this approach claim other advantages, as well. A private firm, for example, may be able to avoid the bureaucratically tedious and politically charged question of where to locate a prison by building it on land the firm already owns or can acquire in a voluntary sale.

The firm also avoids many of the regulatory procedures governing the award of public contracts, permitting it to initiate and complete construction more rapidly. A corrections official from New Mexico said that it took a private firm nine months to construct a new facility, while it would have taken the state government three years because of the required studies and the delays associated with the legislative appropriations process (US General Accounting Office, 1991). In addition to accelerating the availability of the facility, the avoidance of delays in the construction process usually leads to reduced costs by avoiding inflationary increases in prices and wages, and by minimizing the required working capital.

The private firm also is less subject to the bureaucratic traditions governing design and construction methods. It is argued that this freedom permits it to adopt innovations in both areas, with potential savings in both capital and operating costs and greater effectiveness of the new facility. One author claimed that private prison builders lower their costs by 15 per cent and more below government costs by using innovative design and building techniques (Fitzgerald, 1991).

A private firm usually pays commercial interest rates on the money it borrows to finance the project, without the benefit of tax exemption of interest paid by state and local government on their bonds. The private firm, on the other hand, gains the advantage of large tax preferences available to owners of real property under federal and state income tax laws. Some believe that the latter outweigh the former, giving the private firm an advantage in financing costs (Mullen *et al.*, 1985).

One state's experience with privately-financed construction has been described as follows:

> *Missouri switched to a lease-purchase arrangement for its most recent project, a 500-bed maximum-security facility. For this effort, it hired an architectural firm to write the request for proposals (RFP), which was extremely detailed. Nearly $2 million was spent in the design of the facility. The resulting RFP was put out to bid, and eight firms submitted proposals. Many entered into joint ventures with communities in Missouri, which were anxious to obtain the new facility. The firm that wrote the RFP also evaluated the proposals.*

The winning city was Potosi. The builder assumes all the costs until the building is brought on line, so he has a strong incentive to complete it on time. The price of the project is fixed: $4.6 million each year for the next thirty years. Since Missouri, like most states, can only contract for periods of one year, the builder is also accepting a large risk in assuming that it will be leased for the full thirty-year period. However, as a result, he is being extremely responsive to the state's needs. The state knows it is getting exactly what it pays for.

(Sevick and Cikins, 1987)

This favorable attitude toward privately financed construction of prison and jail facilities appears to be found frequently among corrections officials at the state level of government. It seems to reflect real satisfaction. A caution must be added, however, that it may also reflect simple relief at finding a practical way to bypass voter reluctance to finance public construction of those facilities.

GOVERNMENT OWNERSHIP WITH PRIVATE MANAGEMENT

A few governments have taken the approach of contracting for prison services one step further; they have contracted for the overall management of the detention facility. This has been justified by the argument that the private firm can operate a facility more efficiently and effectively than is possible for the state corrections department.

Being exempt from the rules and regulations of the civil service system permits the firm to hire, fire, and reassign staff and to establish wage levels different from those of the civil service employees in the standard model. The firm can also avoid the "layering" of managerial supervision that commonly characterizes government bureaucracies. It is argued that this greater flexibility in staffing arrangements can lead to greater efficiency in operating the facility. It is also argued that the firm, being free from the traditions of the corrections profession, has more flexibility to innovate in the handling, treatment, and rehabilitation of inmates, leading to improvements in effectiveness, as well as efficiency.

Others have expressed considerable skepticism about these claims of greater efficiency and effectiveness on the part of private sector managers. The data on these points are sketchy, of questionable reliability, and are best viewed as inconclusive. As the same issues arise in the next category of privatization initiatives in the corrections field, they will be discussed in that context.

PRIVATE OWNERSHIP WITH PRIVATE MANAGEMENT

Some governments have taken the privatization process in prisons to what might be considered the final stage, combining private ownership with private management. The state commonly pays a daily rate for each of the inmates housed in the facility.

This arrangement seeks to take advantage of the savings presumed to be available with regard to both the construction phase and the continued management of the facility. It builds on the extensive experience of private ownership and management of specialized institutions such as drug treatment facilities, juvenile detention facilities, and halfway houses. In recent years, however, it has been extended to other types of facilities.

As of 1990, the capacity of private prisons planned or in service was reported to be 15 687. The states of California, Kentucky, Texas, New Mexico, and Louisiana were operating private prisons to house relatively small proportions of their general inmate populations, while Florida was in the process of contracting for a private prison. Most of these facilities house minimum to medium security inmates within two years of parole. However, the New Mexico facility houses women at all security levels and the planned Florida facility will house 1 000 medium to maximum security male prisoners (US General Accounting Office, 1991).

At the federal level, the Bureau of Prisons contracts with three local governments in Texas that are, in turn, using private prisons to house about 1 000 minimum and medium security adult male deportable alien offenders who generally have two years or less remaining in their sentences. The Immigration and Naturalization Service contracts for seven facilities with 873 beds for detention of aliens in process of deportation, with detention periods averaging less than 30 days. The Marshals Service has contracted with nine local governments who have, in turn, contracted with private firms for detention of unsentenced federal offenders (US General Accounting Office, 1991).

A more recent source reported that the total population of private prisons had risen to more than 20 000 by the middle of 1993 (Ng, 1993).

Uncertain cost comparisons

It is argued that private ownership and operation of prisons maximizes the efficiency and effectiveness gains of privatization. The facility, being constructed, financed, and owned by the private firm, avoids the need for voter approval of government bonds as well as the rules governing public construction contracts. Thus it is claimed that the facility can be constructed more quickly and at lower cost. The private owners have a strong incentive to complete the facility as rapidly as possible in order to begin housing prisoners and collecting the daily fees from the government for doing so. As noted earlier, private management of the completed facility is said to bring opportunities for greater efficiency and effectiveness through freedom from bureaucratic restraints.

A number of studies have been undertaken in an effort to establish whether or not the claimed savings, especially in the ongoing management of the facility, are real. None has succeeded in resolving the issue. One study estimated annual savings of four to eight per cent, but this involved the comparison of a single private prison with a hypothetical public prison, relying on untested assumptions about the costs of the public prison (Logan and McGriff, 1989).

Another study found that private facilities were one to ten per cent more costly, but with slightly higher quality of services. This study involved a comparison between actual prisons on both the public and private side, but the sample was small and the assumption of comparability of the paired facilities was questionable (Urban Institute, 1989).

The US General Accounting Office concluded from its review of the available data that private operating costs appeared to be lower, but that there was no assurance of similar operating standards. Overall, it judged that the data on costs and services were inconclusive.

Cost comparisons of this sort are notoriously difficult. The difficulties start with the problem of identifying truly comparable facilities. A newer facility is usually less expensive to operate than an older one because of more efficient layout and, particularly, because of reduced maintenance. A facility located in or near an urban area is likely to have higher labor costs than one located in a rural area. Labor costs also differ considerably from one region of the country to another. A more highly secure facility is more expensive to operate than a facility requiring a lower level of security.

On each of these dimensions, the average private prison is likely to have an inherent cost advantage compared to the average public prison. Private prisons are generally newer, located in relatively low wage locations, and house inmates requiring lower levels of security. As one observer notes,

Public minimum security prisons have operating costs about 20 per cent below those of both medium- and maximum-security prisons; comparing the cost performance of private prisons [mostly of the minimum-security type] with all public prisons would thus be seriously misleading.

(Donahue, 1989)

Moreover, even if the prisons were classified at the same level of security, the prisoners may be different. There is anecdotal evidence that some state corrections officials consciously assign the better-behaved prisoners to the private facility, keeping the more troublesome ones in the public prisons (Donahue, 1989). The motivation for this is unclear, but if it is a common practice, it obviously would contaminate further any attempt to compare either the costs or the effectiveness of public and private prisons. At this point, therefore, the relative cost and effectiveness question remains unresolved.

In addition to the debate about issues of efficiency and effectiveness, however, other concerns and objections have been raised to increased privatization, some on grounds of principle, some based on more pragmatic considerations.

Incarceration as an inherently governmental function

Some have argued that the involuntary confinement of a person and the treatment of that person while confined is solely a responsibility of the state and conclude that it is improper to delegate that function to a private party, whose interests may conflict with the objectives of confinement (Walzer, 1991). Those holding this view may argue exclusively from their concept of the role of government in society or may also cite the history of widespread abuse of those incarcerated in the private systems of an earlier era and the difficulty of avoiding repetition of that experience.

Advocates of privatization commonly counter this argument by pointing out that the decision to incarcerate and the terms of the incarceration would remain exclusively in the power of the government. Only the implementation of that decision would be delegated. One observer commented as follows:

> *The state does not own the right to punish. It merely administers [that right] on behalf of the people and under rule of law. There is no reason why subsidiary trustees cannot be designated, as long as they, too, are ultimately accountable to the people and subject to the same provisions of law that direct the state.*

He goes on to say,

> *The law may specify that those authorized to use force in particular situations should be licensed or deputized and adequately trained for the purpose, but they need not be state employees.*

(Logan, 1991)

Many governmental powers have been delegated to private parties. For example, limited police powers have been granted to private security guards. These are employees of private firms who provide security services (under contract) for the protection of private, or in some cases public, buildings or other property.

Proponents argue further that abusive treatment of prisoners can be prevented by the proper structuring of the contract, by appropriate governmental oversight, and by inmate access to the court system for redress of grievances. They further argue that the self-interest of the firm, desirous of retaining the contract, would be sufficient incentive for it to install management systems strong enough to prevent such problems from arising. Thus, they maintain that the profit motive can be harnessed to the interests of the state, providing standards of custody at whatever level the state wishes. The next sections of this paper discuss that assertion in greater detail.

Implications of the profit motive

Opponents of privatization often express concern about the adverse incentives facing a private, profit-motivated corrections system.

The desire to maximize profits may lead the firm to economize in inappropriate ways. To reduce labor costs, for example, the firm may hire less qualified staff. For example, one private firm's plans for correctional staff at a new facility reportedly called for less than 50 hours of training, compared to the 320-hour program mandated for public employees (Bowditch and Everett, 1991).

The private firm may be tempted to skimp on food or health services, or on services such as education and training that are intended to help rehabilitate the inmate (Donahue, 1989). The desire to spread the firm's fixed costs over as large a population of prisoners as possible may encourage overcrowding. If the firm employs prison labor for the production of salable goods and services, it may exploit that involuntary labor by overworking the inmates or underpaying them in order to maximize profit margins.

Opponents also point out the perverse incentives resulting from the private operator's desire to have his prison filled with inmates who pose as few problems as possible. One issue concerns the role played by corrections officers in the decision to release inmates.

Early release (parole) is commonly granted to prisoners who have behaved properly during the term of incarceration. These decisions are based in large part on the reports of corrections officers, the only people who have direct observation of the prisoner's behavior. The employees of a private firm may face a significant perverse incentive in making its reports to the state parole board. Problem prisoners are more difficult (and more expensive) to manage than are cooperative ones. Thus the firm has an incentive to encourage early release (or transfer to another institution) of the difficult prisoners and retention of the cooperative (and more profitable) ones.

The supporters of privatization counter that many of these problems already pervade the public prison system, stimulated by inadequate governmental funding of the corrections system, and could hardly be worse in a privatized system. In a private system they could be prevented by proper structuring of the contract (including appropriate incentives for performance) and by public oversight.

Historical experience makes it clear that, in the absence of strong safeguards, the profit incentive in a private prison system creates an environment conducive to exploitation and abuse. We will next turn to the potential for creating the needed safeguards.

Structuring the contract

The proponents of privatization look to the nature of the contract between the government and the private firm as the means of avoiding the problems posed by their opponents in the debate. This raises two questions. Can an appropriate form of contract be negotiated? If negotiated, can it be enforced?

It seems clear that a simple contract, under which the firm is paid a specified daily rate for the prisoners housed in its facilities, would create strong perverse incentives. To protect against the most easily recognized problems, certain conditions would need to be written into the contract covering such matters as qualifications of staff, nutritional content of food, access to health and other services, and living space for inmates. For example, one contract with a county government for the operation of a private prison work farm includes a requirement for the firm to meet or exceed the Standards for Prisons and Jails issued by the American Corrections Association, a professional organization of corrections officials (Mullen *et al.*, 1985).

It is certainly possible to draft a contract containing such conditions; enforcing that contract may be a different matter, as will be seen later.

Replacing the adverse incentives with positive incentives for effective performance will be considerably more difficult. The objectives of the corrections system are numerous and diverse. At minimum they include the following:

-- maintaining security for the public from the risk of escape by dangerous felons and for the inmate population from the risk of violence by other inmates and abusive guards;

-- assuring adequate care for prisoners during their term of incarceration, including food, living accommodations, health services, recreation, etc.;

-- promoting the rehabilitation of prisoners so that, upon their eventual release, as many as possible will become productive members of society rather than committing additional crimes; and

-- accomplishing these goals at minimum cost.

It is certainly possible to devise contractual incentives for effective performance of any one of these goals. Writing a contract that adequately reflects all of them in a balanced combination would be a much more difficult, complex task. Even if this could be done, it is not clear that it would have the intended effect.

In general, managers function most effectively when they can focus on a small set of clearly understood goals. The more complex the goals, the more difficult it becomes to keep all of them in mind and to manage the inevitable conflicts among them. Thus, the more numerous and diverse are the incentives included in a hypothetical contract for the incarceration of prisoners, the less likely those incentives are to have a major effect on the private firm's activity.

Enforcing the contract

The effective enforcement of a contract requires several conditions.

-- the terms of the contract must be clearly stated and the criteria for compliance must be understood by both parties to the contract;

-- techniques must exist to determine objectively whether or not the criteria are met;

-- each party to the contract must have an effective avenue for redress in the event of default by the other party.

In many contractual relationships, enforcement is a relatively simple matter, at least in principle. In the sale of an automobile, for example, the terms are clear. The buyer agrees to pay the seller a particular sum of money in exchange for delivery of the specified vehicle. If the buyer fails to pay, or the seller fails to deliver the agreed item, a default occurs. The party suffering the default may be able to sue in court for damages. In any event, that party can usually revoke the unfulfilled contract and deal with someone else. The buyer, for example, can choose to purchase a different automobile from another seller.

The enforcement of a contract for the incarceration of prisoners is unlikely to be as simple as this example. First, the terms of the contract are likely to be complex, particularly if the contract includes numerous performance incentives, creating abundant opportunities for ambiguity. Compliance with the criteria must be measured objectively if the contract is to be enforced fairly. Yet many of the needed measurements can be obtained most efficiently only through reliance on observations and reports from individuals whose motives may be suspect. For example, physicians who are employees of the contractor may have an incentive to under-report illnesses and injuries if health status of the inmate population is a material factor in the contract.

Because of the potentially perverse incentives, governments would be unwise to judge performance exclusively on the basis of reports submitted by the contractor. Rigorous external oversight will be required if the government is to have assurance of compliance and the ability to detect significant deviations from the terms of the contract. But effective oversight is costly. Since one of the primary reasons governments are considering contracts for the incarceration of prisoners is to reduce the cost of the corrections system, there is room for skepticism that those governments will make the needed commitment to the required oversight mechanisms. One observer comments

One might wonder whether a public that has refused to put up the resources to bring public prisons up to minimal standards will resist the temptation to turn a blind eye to the conditions of confinement in bargain-rate prisons.

(Donahue, 1989)

The means of redressing contractual failure also raise some questions. In theory, if the private firm fails to perform in accordance with the contract, the government can simply revoke the contract and put the prisoners somewhere else. In practice, that may be quite difficult, a prospect that arouses considerable concern on the part of those who are skeptical of the private prison alternative. In their view, competition is an essential element of any successful privatization program.

Yet competition will be especially difficult to assure among private prisons because of the high capital investment required to create a private prison. The high entry and exit costs create a considerable barrier to competition (Donahue, 1989; Bowditch and Everett, 1991).

No contractor will build a facility unless he is assured of the assignment of prisoners (or other financial considerations) that will make the facility profitable for him. In view of the budget constraints faced by most state governments, it seems unlikely that the state would pay for the construction of excess space with the only justification being to assure the existence of competition for current contractors. Thus there may be no alternative private contractor.

The tactic of moving prisoners from a persistently unsatisfactory private facility to a public prison may prove equally infeasible. Contractual incarceration arrangements are emerging in an environment of severe overcrowding in public prisons. Barring an unlikely expansion in the public prison system or a significant decline in the prison population, there may be no room in the public prisons.

In the short run, therefore, the government may have no other facility in which to house the prisoners currently held by the non-performing contractor. Money damages may be an equally unrealistic course of action in the face of a contractor threat of immediate closure of the facility.

One writer, discussing the general issue of privatization, commented as follows:

Efforts to compensate by other means for the missing discipline of competition will seldom be fully successful. Those public services for which it is technically or politically impossible to keep contractors in a state of healthy insecurity offer, at best, limited potential for privatization.

(Donahue, 1989)

If that assessment is correct, one would be wise to exercise considerable caution in the privatization of prison facilities, in view of the barriers to entry and the reluctance of governments to construct alternative facilities of their own.

Government liability

Under US law, a prisoner who is abused or otherwise mistreated may file suit against the responsible government agency and recover substantial monetary damages if the suit succeeds in court.

In recent years, these damage awards have become a major item in the cost of many state corrections systems.

It is not yet clear how the law would be applied in the case of a prisoner incarcerated in a private facility under contract to the government. Early decisions suggest, however, that the contractor and the government would be jointly liable for any damages. One assessment of the liability issue concluded as follows:

> *Just as juveniles are wards of the court, inmates can be considered wards of the state, and a private contractor essentially as an extension of the state. Thus, if a contractor errs, the state has retained its authority and may share the liability.*

(Mullen, et al., 1985)

Thus, governments may be exposing themselves to substantial unanticipated costs in view of the perverse incentives for the private contractor, uncertain effectiveness of public oversight, and the difficulties of enforcing contractual standards.

CONCLUSION

There is a growing trend in the United States toward the provision of government services by private firms under contract. That trend has now begun to penetrate the corrections system, including not only the specialized facilities where private firms have long operated, but also facilities for the incarceration of the general prison population. It seems clear that there is an appropriate role for the private sector but the extent of that role remains uncertain.

In the construction of prison facilities, it is evident that there are advantages of extensive private sector involvement. Private management of the construction process leads to savings in time and probably in cost. Private financing of prison construction avoids the need for voter approval for the issuance of government bonds although any apparent cost savings from this are largely illusory.

In the operation of prison facilities, the evidence on private sector involvement is considerably less convincing, particularly with regard to facilities housing the general adult prison population. With respect to costs, the data are anecdotal, at best, and contaminated by the absence of valid comparisons. The same is true with regard to effectiveness, with the added caution that some of the most important effects, such as successful rehabilitation and reduced recidivism, will not be measurable until the passage of a considerable period of time.

In summary, if additional prison capacity is required, as it is under present conditions in the United States, private management of the construction process, including private ownership of the prison (leased to the state) appears to combine considerable advantages in terms of time and, perhaps, cost with relatively little risk for the government.

Contracting for the private delivery of some services where the private sector has a demonstrable cost advantage, and where the price and quality of those services can be assured through the availability of competitive vendors, also appears to involve relatively little risk for the government.

Contracting for the overall management and operation of a secure detention facility should be approached with caution, despite the apparently growing popularity of that approach in the United States. It can carry substantial risk to the government and to the implementation of public policies for the management of the corrections system, and there is room for considerable skepticism about the effectiveness of available safeguards.

NOTE

1. A number of experts have criticized the US criminal justice system for what they view as its excessive rates of incarceration. They suggest that the problem of prison over-crowding is an unnecessary and self-inflicted problem. That issue, however, is beyond the scope of this chapter.

BIBLIOGRAPHY

BOWDITCH, Christine, and Ronald S. EVERETT, "Private Prisons are Not More Efficient than Public Prisons," in Stacey L. TIPP, ed., *America's Prisons: Opposing Viewpoints*, Greenhaven Press, San Diego.

DONAHUE, John D. (1989), *The Privatization Decision*, Basic Books, New York.

FEELEY, Malcolm M. (1990), "The Privatization of Punishment in Historical Perspective" in *Privatization and Its Alternatives*, William T. Gormley, ed., University of Wisconsin Press, Madison.

FITZGERALD, Randall (1991), "Private Prisons are More Efficient than Public Prisons" in Stacey L. TIPP, ed., *America's Prisons: Opposing Viewpoints*, Greenhaven Press, San Diego.

LOGAN, Charles and Bill McGriff (1989), "Comparison Costs of Public and Private Prisons: A Case Study," *NIJ [National Institute of Justice] Reports*, September/October, reported in US General Accounting Office (1991), *Private Prisons: Cost Savings and BOP Authority Need to be Resolved*, GAO/GGD-91-12, February.

LOGAN, Charles H. (1991), "Private Prisons are Just," in Stacey L. TIPP, ed., *America's Prisons: Opposing Viewpoints*, Greenhaven Press, San Diego.

MULLEN, Joan, *et al.* (1985), *The Privatization of Corrections*, National Institute of Justice, US Department of Justice, Government Printing Office, Washington.

NG, Raymond, "Private Prison Census Shows Continued Growth," *Privatization Watch*, Reason Foundation, Los Angeles, August 1993.

SEVICK, James R. and Warren I. CIKINS, eds. (1987), *Constructing Correctional Facilities: Is There a Role for the Private Sector?* The Brookings Institution, Washington.

Urban Institute (1989), *Comparison of Privately and Publicly Operated Corrections Facilities in Kentucky and Massachusetts*, Urban Institute, Washington, August, reported in US General Accounting Office (1991), *Private Prisons: Cost Savings and BOP [Bureau of Prisons] Authority Need to be Resolved*, GAO/GGD-91-21, February.

US General Accounting Office (1991), *Private Prisons: Cost Savings and BOP [Bureau of Prisons] Authority Need to be Resolved*, GAO/GGD-91-21, February.

WALZER, Michael, "Private Prisons are Unjust," in Stacey L. TIPP, ed., *America's Prisons: Opposing Viewpoints*, Greenhaven Press, San Diego.

Chapter Eight

**PRIVATE AND PRIVATE SECTOR ROLES
IN THE CONSTRUCTION OF HIGHWAYS:
AN OVERVIEW OF UNITED STATES EXPERIENCE**

by

Harry S. Havens
Former Assistant Comptroller General
United States General Accounting Office

INTRODUCTION

The purpose of this chapter is to provide a brief overview of the respective roles of the public and private sectors in the provision of highway infrastructure in the United States.

US transportation systems are characterized by a diversity of ownership arrangements, both among systems and across time. Each of the transportation modes -- highways, railroads, aviation, pipelines and waterborne commerce -- reflects a different set of public/private sector relationships. These diverse patterns were determined in large measure by historical circumstances, not as the intended outcome of a deliberate policy.

The US system of roads and highways is the focus of this chapter for two reasons, the first being its central role in the nation's overall transportation network. In addition, however, initiatives are being explored, involving a potentially considerable expansion in the private sector role, that may have relevance in other circumstances.

The chapter begins with a brief discussion of the historical development of the US highway system. This is followed by a description of current arrangements for financing and constructing highways, including a discussion of the typical role of the private sector construction industry. This provides a basis for comparison in the next section, which describes initiatives for the construction of privately owned highways. Observations are summarized in the concluding section of the chapter.

HISTORICAL BACKGROUND

From colonial times until the end of the 19th Century, the US road transportation network was crude, at best, and in many areas almost non-existent. In the colonial period, most commerce depended on coastal and international shipping and most of the immigrant population was located within a few miles of the coast or of easily navigable rivers. The roads to the interior were, for the most part, unimproved trails originally used by the indigenous tribes. Some city streets in the larger settlements had been surfaced in line with European practices of the time. In addition, there were several thousand miles of privately financed roads, ferries and bridges, linking some of the larger population centers, which were operated as toll facilities (turnpikes). For the most part, however, water transportation remained the most convenient and efficient mode of travel throughout this period.

The US Constitution, ratified in 1789, a few years after independence from Great Britain, gives the federal government the authority to "establish ...post Roads," (US Constitution, Article 1, Section 8) but this responsibility was largely ignored before the Twentieth Century. One writer describes this period as follows:

The federal government entered road building briefly by allocating part of the proceeds from the sale of public domain lands to internal improvements and utilizing some of the funds to construct the Cumberland (National) Road to Wheeling on the Ohio River to protect the Old Northwest Territories, later extending the Road to Illinois. This federal effort was discontinued in 1838, in part because railroads were expected to supplant highways and in part because road building was thought by many federal officials to be a matter of states rights.

(Hazard, 1977)

While the federal government considered road building a matter for the states, they, in turn, considered it a local responsibility. The cities and counties, with little in the way of revenue sources or capacity to borrow for capital investment, were unable to undertake much road construction, even if they had been inclined to do so.

Thus the US system of public roads and highways languished, even during the period of westward expansion. Private turnpikes were never very profitable and most succumbed to canal and rail competition by the middle of the Nineteenth Century.

Internal commerce continued to rely initially on coastal shipping. The late Eighteenth and early Nineteenth Centuries saw the construction of numerous canals, such as the Erie Canal in New York State, connecting the Hudson River at Albany to the Great Lakes at Buffalo. The emergence of New York City as the preeminent commercial and shipping center of North America is often attributed to the completion of the Erie Canal, permitting economical transportation access to the west. The predominance of water transportation was also facilitated by the network of rivers flowing into the Mississippi, providing access to much of the future United States between the Appalachian and Rocky Mountains.

The first viable transportation alternative to waterborne commerce came with the invention of the steam engine and the subsequent development of the railroad. It soon became evident that the railroad was, for much of the country and for many goods, a more efficient means of transportation than was available through the combination of coastal shipping, river boats, and canal barges.

Railroads soon became the preeminent mode of transportation, a process that was accelerated by the interruption of shipping on the Mississippi River during the US Civil War of the early 1860s. Rapid expansion of the rail network was strongly encouraged by generous public subsidies, such as large grants of land (alternating one square mile blocks along the right of way) to railroads building lines in the undeveloped western states. The development of roads and highways continued to languish on the presumption that (as happened in England) the railroads would soon provide quick and easy access to all significant centers of population.

The notion of universal access to the railroad system was never fully achieved in the United States. In addition, even where the railroads were available, farmers were still required to transport their commodities to the towns served by the railroads. By the late Nineteenth Century, the problems of moving bulk commodities by wagon over unimproved roads led to the emergence of a Good Roads Movement, focusing primarily on what came to be called "farm to market roads."

The initial responsibility for road building remained with the counties but, in time, the states became involved. Most of these roads were improved only by the expedient of grading and adding gravel; hard surface highways remained rare. Nevertheless, the basic elements of a highway system were beginning to emerge. County roads served purely local needs, such as permitting rural areas access to the population center of the county. State roads allowed access among population centers across the state.

With the invention of the automobile in the late Nineteenth Century, pressure intensified for the development of adequate roads and highways. While the machine was invented in Europe, it was in the United States that efficient mass production techniques lowered costs to the point that most families could own an automobile by the 1920s. This greatly increased the mobility of the US population, but it also added to the pressure for more and better roads and highways. Automobiles could function on gravel roads, but were much more efficient (as well as being a good deal safer) on hard surface highways.

The increased mobility of the population also stimulated a recognition, for the first time, of the need for a national system of highways in the United States. The state road system, naturally, concentrated on linking people and facilitating commerce within the state. They often had little interest in devoting scarce road-building resources to meeting the needs of those wishing to travel between states. As a response to this gap, beginning during the First World War and accelerating in the 1920s, the federal government began contributing to the construction of highways. This assistance, for the construction of what came to be called "federal" or "US" highways, was channelled through the states. It was used for building highways meeting construction standards laid down by the federal government along routes approved by the federal government.

The final component in the US highway system came with the decision in 1956 to create the 43 000-mile network of high-speed, limited access Interstate highways. The construction of this network, which is only now approaching completion, has been financed almost entirely by the federal government but with the funds again channelled through the states, who must use the funds on specified routes and must comply with federal construction standards.

CURRENT PATTERNS

Financing and ownership

The current patterns of responsibility reflect the historical development of the US road and highway system. The federal government has played a central role in financing the construction of a national highway system, but has directly managed very little of that construction. The primary exceptions involve roads entirely within property owned by the federal government, such as military reservations and national parks.

The federal government has financed the construction of the Interstate system of high performance highways by providing grants to the states covering 90 percent of the cost of construction. Other components of the national highway system typically receive federal aid for a substantially lower share of the costs.

The federal aid is financed by revenue from certain dedicated sources. The largest of these is the tax on motor fuels, but other revenue sources are included, such as the excise tax on rubber used to manufacture tires. Funds are distributed to the states through a complex formula involving population, road miles, and other factors.

The states actually "own" the highways constructed with federal aid and manage the process of constructing them. Until recently, the states were financially responsible for all costs of maintenance and repair. However, this created a perverse incentive for the states to defer maintenance, allow highways to fall into disrepair, and then use federal funds for major reconstruction. To reduce this incentive, states are now allowed to use a portion of the federal highway assistance for routine maintenance and repair.

State roads and highways are typically funded by the state using the proceeds of fuel taxes, license fees, and other forms of usage charges. These revenues may be used either directly, on a pay-as-you-build basis, or to amortize bonds issued to finance the construction.

In a few locations involving high density travel, primarily in the eastern part of the United States, states have constructed some new high performance highways financed by tolls. The same mechanism has been used to finance the construction of some bridges and tunnels. This has typically been accomplished by establishing a specialized government-owned corporation (often called an "authority") which issues bonds to finance the construction. Proceeds of the tolls are then used to repay the bonds and to pay for maintenance and upkeep. When the bonds have been repaid (usually over a period of thirty or forty years), the tolls may be discontinued. If the tolls are continued, the proceeds may be used for major renovation, for expansion of capacity, such as the addition of lanes, or may be diverted to help finance other projects.

County roads and city streets are typically financed largely with local funds and local governments manage the process of construction, maintenance, and repair. A modest amount of federal assistance is available for these projects (such as for extending the Interstate system into major cities) but that assistance is generally channelled through the states. It is common for local governments to finance major local road projects through the issuance of bonds which are repaid from general revenue sources, of which the most important is usually the property tax.

A frequent exception to this local pattern is found in the construction of roads and streets to serve new industrial, commercial, or residential facilities. In these cases, the developer typically constructs the roads serving his project and, as a condition of approval for the development, may also be required to finance improvements in adjacent roads and streets which the government believes are likely to become congested as a result of the development. In the case of a residential development, these privately constructed streets are then commonly turned over to the government after the development is completed. For commercial and industrial facilities, responsibility for maintenance and repair of interior roads and streets usually remains with the owner of the property.

Construction process

On any major public construction project in the United States, the usual arrangement is for the government to contract with one or more private firms to perform the actual work. This is also the case with highway construction. Only on minor repair work (repairing potholes, for example) or routine street cleaning or cutting grass on the right of way would it be typical for public employees to do the work.

The process by which the decision is made to construct a highway varies considerably from one state to another but the following discussion outlines a reasonably typical approach. Based on an analysis of traffic patterns and of anticipated growth in traffic, employees of the state Highway Department (sometimes called the state Department of Transportation) will suggest the need for a new highway or a major expansion or renovation of an existing highway. Typically, the proposal will describe the route in general terms and include a preliminary estimate of the cost. This proposal is subject to various approvals within the state government, often including action by the state legislature. Approval from the US Department of Transportation may also be required if federal financial aid is involved. The approval of other federal agencies may be required in some circumstances, such as if the project raises environmental concerns or if it is proposed that the highway pass through property owned by the federal government.

Once the necessary approvals have been gained, the state highway engineers (who are usually civil servants with training and experience in civil engineering) define the project in greater detail. After analyzing land contours and anticipated traffic flows, the precise route is decided, including such features as interchanges and intersections, which will define the needed right of way. At this point land acquisition can begin. Some of this can be accomplished through voluntary sale or even donation of the land. (A large landowner may donate land in exchange for the construction of an interchange that may substantially increase the value of his remaining holdings.) If a voluntary transaction cannot be arranged, the state may seize the needed land, leaving it to the courts to determine the fair value to be paid for the land that was taken.

The highway engineers also prescribe the detailed specifications of the construction project. This includes such matters as the gradients to be maintained, drainage arrangements, and standards to be satisfied for construction elements such as the foundation and the pavement. Typically, this design work would be performed by government employees but some elements, such as the design of a bridge, may be contracted to a private firm of architects. Once the detailed design has been completed, the project is ready for the contracting process.

The procedures for awarding public construction contracts to private firms differ from one state to another but typically follows one of two general approaches. One is for the state to award separate contracts for each segment of the work. One contract may be awarded for preparation of the right of way, which would typically include grading the land to specified contours and constructing culverts and channels for required drainage. A separate contract may be awarded for constructing the crushed rock foundation required to stabilize the roadway. A third contract may be awarded for laying and finishing the surface pavement. Separate contracts are often awarded for the construction of bridges or tunnels. Additional contracts may be required for other aspects of the project, such as grading the shoulders of the highway, plantings to reduce soil erosion, and installation of signs.

The alternative approach is one in which a single overall contract is awarded to one firm that serves as the construction manager or general contractor. Under this arrangement, the general contractor typically performs a substantial portion of the work using his own employees and parcels out other segments to "subcontractors." It is generally believed that this approach leads to more rapid completion of the project and, perhaps, to lower costs because of the incentives at work on the general contractor.

State law typically requires public construction contracts (under either of the two approaches) to be on a fixed price basis, and to be awarded to the low bidder on the basis of sealed bids. This is intended to prevent one potential contractor from knowing the price being offered by another, supposedly giving each contractor an incentive to offer the best price he can.

Unfortunately, collusion among contractors is not unknown. There have been cases, primarily involving relatively small, locally managed projects, in which a group of contractors agreed in advance as to which of them would receive a particular contract. The other contractors would then offer prices high enough to assure that the selected winner would have the low bid. The selected winner can then inflate his bid (while still keeping it below the others) and collect higher profits. On occasion this collusion has been accomplished with the knowledge and assistance of corrupt officials, who may receive a share of the inflated profits. Such collusion can be very difficult to detect, and may be revealed only when one of the conspirators, dissatisfied with his share of the profits, makes the collusion public.

Throughout the construction process, state highway engineers typically exercise close supervision of the project. The inspection process is often virtually continuous, with engineers testing such elements as the soil compaction and the adequacy of the crushed stone roadbed. As the pavement is laid, engineers will usually take samples of the concrete or other surfacing materials and submit them for laboratory analysis to assure conformity with the contract specifications. If a contractor fails to comply with those specifications, he may be required to repeat the work.

The financial risks to the government of public highway construction appear to be relatively modest, provided the contracts are awarded on a fixed price basis in a truly competitive environment. In principle, the fixed price contract shifts all risk to the contractor.

As has been seen in other situations, such as military weapons system procurement, if a contractor assumes too much risk, the costs of adverse developments may come back to the government despite the presumed fixed price of a contract. That seems unlikely in this situation. The technical risks seem small in view of the detailed design work, involving conservative application of proven technologies, that is typically performed by the state highway department, the probable infrequency of design changes during construction, and the detailed oversight that is usually maintained during the construction process.

Furthermore, the public highway construction process, unlike the weapons procurement process, does not involve a severe imbalance of expertise. The engineers and managers in the state highway departments are, for the most part, trained engineers and career civil servants who expect to remain in this profession for the balance of their careers. The entire process, of course, generates considerable political pressure with regard to the selection of highway projects, the alignment of routes, and the location of interchanges. In many cases, however, these decisions are made in an explicitly political fashion by elected officials, not by the technical staff of the highway department. This is not inappropriate, in view of the role that highway construction often plays in the economic development priorities of the state and in its allocation of limited budgetary resources.

The standard practice of awarding contracts on the basis of competitive sealed bids seems generally to provide a reasonable safeguard against inflated costs. However, it is not a foolproof system. As noted earlier, there have been instances of collusion among the bidders, sometimes coupled with corruption of public officials. There have also been cases in which the competitive bidding process was ignored or manipulated in order to award a contract to politically influential firms.

Another risk of this process is that a firm may submit an unrealistically low bid because of error or incompetence. The firm may then find itself under great pressure to reduce costs, perhaps by performing shoddy work or using substandard materials. The safeguards against this are twofold. First, most contracting agencies are authorized to disregard unrealistic bids or those from "unqualified" firms. Those agencies are likely to scrutinize carefully any bids that are substantially below expected costs.

The second safeguard is the continuous inspection process during the construction period, which is usually adequate to reveal poor quality work or substandard materials.

For a state-owned toll road, there is always the risk that inadequate traffic could leave the public authority unable to repay the bonds used to finance construction. Such bonds usually do not carry an explicit state guarantee. Nevertheless, the state would be under considerable pressure to make good on the authority's debts to avoid endangering the state's ability to borrow for other projects. To date, however, this does not appear to have been a serious problem, perhaps because road builders in general have tended to underestimate future traffic volumes.

In summary, in the typical highway construction endeavor, the project is designed in detail by government engineers and the actual construction work is performed by private firms under contract to the government, but with close supervision by employees of the contracting agency.

NEW INITIATIVES

The scarcity of financial resources at the federal, state, and local levels of government has led to the exploration of alternative ways of providing needed highway capacity. State and local governments, in particular, have found it increasingly difficult both to maintain existing streets and highways and to construct the additional highway lanes needed to accommodate growing volumes of traffic. This problem has been exacerbated by tax limitation initiatives, such as those in California, that have sought to constrain the size of government by limiting government revenues. These measures, coupled with limits on the borrowing power of state and local governments, have severely restricted the ability of those governments to undertake infrastructure expansion such as the construction of additional highway capacity.

At the same time, governments in the United States (unlike some in Europe) have generally been unwilling or unable to take the steps that might serve to slow that rate of traffic growth, such as by restricting automobile access to congested areas or heavily subsidizing alternative, non-highway modes of transportation. There have been some exceptions, such as the construction of mass transit systems in a few major cities and the development of traffic lanes (or even entire highways) for which access is limited to vehicles carrying multiple occupants. As a rule, however, the usual response to growing volumes of traffic remains the construction of additional highway capacity.

As actual or projected congestion increases in the face of the limited ability of governments to construct the required capacity, consideration has turned to the possibility of privately financed highways. At present, this possibility is approaching reality in one case in Virginia, several proposals are in the advanced stages of development in California, and the idea is being seriously considered in at least one other state, Arizona.

Virginia toll road

In recent decades, the Washington, D.C. metropolitan area has expanded dramatically to the west, in the direction of Dulles International Airport. Beyond that airport lies a considerable amount of farmland, much of it held in relatively large blocks, that appears likely to lie in the path of future development. At present, however, there is limited highway capacity from that area to centers of employment to the east.

A state-owned toll road currently extends about 13 miles from the Washington Beltway west to Dulles Airport, parallel to a highway for which access is restricted to those travelling to and from the airport. A proposed private toll road, for which construction began in September 1993 and is expected to be completed in 1996, would extend from the end of the state-owned toll road to intersect with another existing state highway in the vicinity of the town of Leesburg. Access to the new toll road would be permitted at any of 10 entrances along its 14 mile length.

It seems clear that the scheme would facilitate the development of the area between Dulles Airport and Leesburg. Indeed, this is probably essential for its economic viability. While there appear to have been a few holdouts, most of the landowners have readily agreed to sell or donate land for the right of way, in the expectation that development will substantially increase the value of their remaining holdings.

Because of the private nature of the activity, public information about its business operations is limited. Ownership is in the form of a partnership, Toll Road Investors Partnership II, L.P. (TRIP II).[1] A US subsidiary of the Italian firm Autostrade International is one of the general partners and will be responsible for the operation of the highway after its completion. Brown and Root, a construction firm with world-wide operations, is a limited partner and the general contractor responsible for the actual construction work on the project.

All necessary financing has been arranged privately, with no state guarantees of the debt. A consortium of investors, primarily insurance companies, has committed $258 million in long term financing, with an average maturity of about 30 years. The remainder of the required financing for the project is from a group of banks and from equity contributed by the partners. The total cost of the project is estimated at $326 million.

While not involved in the financing, the state does play a considerable regulatory role in the project. The firm is chartered by the state of Virginia and is subject to regulation as a public utility. Under the terms of the charter, the firm has agreed to limit its tolls to amounts required to provide a rate of return of 14 percent on its invested capital for the first six years. Proposals to increase tolls are subject to approval by the State Corporation Commission, which is empowered to enforce this limit and will presumably determine the appropriate rate of return after the six-year limit expires.

The charter also provides that the highway be constructed to the standards used by the Virginia Department of Transportation for its own highways, and that the highway be turned over to state ownership after a period of 42 years. To assure compliance with the construction standards, state highway engineers will perform continuous inspection and testing of the construction work.

The direct financial risks of the project appear to have been assumed entirely by the partners in the private firm. There seems little likelihood that those risks could be shifted to the government. Neither the state nor the affected county government appears to have taken any actions that commit them to the completion or subsequent economic success of the project. If the partnership were unable to complete the project with available funds, some would undoubtedly urge the state (or the county) to finance its completion. However, the traffic loads necessary to generate intense public pressure for completion of the highway are unlikely to materialize until after the project is finished. Unless the project were very close to completion, therefore, the scarcity of highway construction funds at the state level and the limited borrowing capacity of the affected county would probably preclude any significant government assistance.

If traffic volumes prove insufficient to repay construction costs, the risk of financial failure would be borne first by the partners. Limited partners are typically liable only to the extent of amounts previously invested. General partners are commonly liable for any debts of the partnership, as well. If these resources prove inadequate, ownership of the project might shift to the partnership's creditors. The new owners in that eventuality would remain subject to state regulation and would have no obvious basis for seeking financial relief from the state.

One risk to the public interest of such a private highway lies in the owner's potential for extracting monopoly profits from its users. To some degree, this is restricted by the terms of the charter but enforcement may require close scrutiny by the regulatory authority. There are many ways of disguising profits, such as through inflated management fees and other expenses, which may be detectable only by a thorough examination of financial records. Competition, the preferred means of precluding monopoly rents, does not seem to be a plausible option in this case.

A final element of public risk relates not to the project itself, but to its indirect consequences. If, as anticipated, the highway leads to substantial population growth in the surrounding area, it will generate rapid growth in demand for public infrastructure such as schools, secondary roads, and water and sewer facilities, and for services such as police and fire protection. In Virginia, as in most states, these facilities and services are financed primarily at the county level of government, where tax revenues are heavily dependent on the tax on real property.

If the development consists largely of low density housing, with the occupants commuting to other parts of the metropolitan area for employment, the tax base of the county could be severely strained. Experience elsewhere has demonstrated that "dormitory suburbs" often generate infrastructure and operating costs that, at least in the short run, are disproportionate to the increase in taxable property values. It remains to be seen if the counties affected by the new highway will be able to attract commercial and industrial development sufficient to offset the budgetary consequences of the likely residential development.

Private highway proposals in California

For many years, one of the defining characteristics of the state of California has been its high level of investment in public infrastructure and services. The California state highway system has probably made the citizens of that state the most mobile population on earth. The reliance on automobiles to achieve that mobility, however, has created an ever-increasing demand for additional highway capacity to relieve congestion. In recent years, the ability of state and local governments to finance highway construction has been severely constrained by voter-enacted limits on the growth of government revenues.

This conflict between the demand for increased highway capacity and the limits on governments' ability to finance that construction has led to the exploration of privately financed alternatives. To date, proposals have been developed for eight private toll roads in California. Four of these proposals have been endorsed by state authorities and are in various stages of development; one is reportedly under construction (Gomez-Ibanez and Meyer, 1993)[2].

The process of developing private toll roads started in California with the enactment in 1989 of a state law authorizing the California Department of Transportation (Caltrans) to enter into agreements with private companies for such facilities. Caltrans invited proposals and received eight. After review, four were selected for further consideration.

The first proposal was to build an eleven-mile extension of an existing freeway, State Route 57 (SR-57), through Orange County south of Los Angeles. The objective was to relieve congestion on other arteries, so the highway would be accessible only to passenger vehicles. To minimize land acquisition problems, the road would be built on a platform elevated over a normally dry river bed (the Santa Ana River). (This route had been considered for the construction of a public freeway, but was rejected because of the high cost of construction.) One innovative feature of the SR-57 proposal was that tolls would vary by time of day.

A second proposal involves an eleven mile extension of existing State Road 125 (SR-125) in eastern San Diego County. It is intended to serve growing residential communities in eastern San Diego County, as well as handling the growing truck traffic generated by manufacturing facilities in Mexico immediately to the south.

The third project was another in Orange County. This would involve building a ten-mile toll road on the median strip of an existing freeway, State Road 91 (SR-91), for the purpose of relieving congestion on that highway. A novel feature of this proposal is that tolls would vary by the number of occupants of a vehicle. Those containing three or more passengers would have free access. Furthermore, tolls would be collected electronically and would vary by the time of day, as with the SR-57 proposal. Construction has reportedly begun on the SR-91 project.

The final project was in Northern California, and involved building a new eighty-five mile toll road, to be called the Midstate Toll Road. The road would begin at the existing Interstate 680 at the southern end of San Francisco Bay and lead to Interstate 80 to the north. This would relieve some of the congestion on the east side of San Francisco Bay, facilitate access to Sacramento, the state capitol, and open a largely agricultural area to development.

Two of these proposals, the SR-125 project and the Midstate Toll Road, are of the "development" type, similar in some ways to the Virginia project. That is, their financial viability depends, at least in part, on the development that is anticipated to occur along the highway right of way. The prospect of rising land values in the vicinity of the highway may be sufficient to induce present owners to donate or sell at reasonable prices the land required for the right of way, thus reducing the cost of the project. In addition, the anticipated population growth resulting from development will be a primary source of the traffic volumes (and toll collections) required to make the project profitable.

During the decades of rapid economic and population growth in California, it seemed inevitable that development would quickly follow any highway construction. In today's economic climate, that inevitability is considerably diminished. That renders these projects somewhat more speculative than would have been the case a few years ago.

The other proposals in California are for the construction of highways designed to relieve congestion in areas that are already developed. The feasibility of these proposals as purely private ventures is open to serious question. In a developed area, land is commonly held in relatively small parcels, rather than in a few large blocks, as is often the case before development. This makes assembling the land for a new highway right of way through the mechanism of voluntary sale an exceedingly difficult and expensive task.

Thus a purely private undertaking would probably require special circumstances, such as the availability of an abandoned railroad right of way or the existence of a convenient strip of land that had remained undeveloped for some reason. (The land might be unsuitable for development because of adverse soil conditions or might have been reserved for open space.) It seems unlikely that the purely private assembly of land for a highway right of way in a congested corridor will be possible on more than rare occasions.

In the absence of such special circumstances, acquisition of land for the right of way may well depend on a governmental assistance. The most likely forms of assistance would include the donation of land already in public ownership or the involuntary taking of private land. This is already evident in the California cases. The SR-57 project involves government donation of "air rights" to permit building over a dry river bed (SR-57). The SR-91 project involves government donation of part of an existing public highway right of way. The legislation authorizing the development of private toll roads also specifically authorized Caltrans to take land involuntarily for the construction of private toll roads, but Caltrans has indicated it would do so only as a last resort.

If the land acquisition hurdle can be overcome, a toll road (whether publicly or privately owned) that is intended to relieve congestion might well prove less speculative financially than one depending on future development. Current traffic volumes are readily ascertainable. The portion that will choose to use the toll road to escape congestion is uncertain, depending on a number of factors such as the level of the tolls, the efficiency of the toll collection mechanisms, and the extent to which congestion on other (free access) roads is reduced, thus reducing the incentive to use the new toll road. A combination of careful market and traffic engineering analyses should permit the development of estimates with a reasonable level of confidence.

The governmental risks of the California proposals seem considerably different from those in Virginia. The state invited the proposals, selected the ones that will be permitted to go forward, and granted an exclusive franchise guaranteeing that no competing highways will be built. In at least two of the projects, the government will have participated in the land acquisition process by donating publicly owned land for the right of way.

With these actions, the projects cease to be purely private ventures. They take on much more of the character of public/private partnerships. The government has made a commitment to the success of the project, making it difficult to disavow responsibility in the event of financial problems during construction. The pressure for financial aid to complete a failing project would be much greater than for a purely private venture.

In these circumstances, the risks to the government may increase rapidly because of a "moral hazard" problem. When the private firm facing financial difficulties recognizes that its prospective profits from the project have disappeared, it has little incentive to control costs. An unscrupulous manager may even be tempted to siphon off any remaining resources in the form of inflated salaries or management fees, knowing that the government or the creditors will be left holding the bag.

As has become apparent in other situations, public/private partnerships of this sort require careful management by the public authorities. The interests of the government and its private partners do not always coincide, especially with respect to control over costs. Protecting the public interest requires careful oversight of the private managers.

Arizona proposals

It is reported that the state of Arizona has conducted a competition for privately financed highways, modelled on the California program (Gomez-Ibanez and Meyer, 1993). It appears, however, that the program has not yet reached the stage of selecting proposals for further development, and none of the projects is yet under construction.

CONCLUSION

The history of highway construction in the United States is relatively brief, concentrated in the period since 1920. It has been financed overwhelmingly by the federal, state and local governments, with the construction process being managed by agencies of state, county and city governments. Heretofore, the role of the private sector was limited to carrying out construction projects under contract to, and with close supervision by, those governments.

In recent years, as the growth in demand for highway capacity has outstripped the resources available for public highway construction, interest has turned to the development of privately financed highways. In the US context, the opportunity for purely private ventures appears quite limited, and will exist primarily in situations where the prospect of future development both eases the land acquisition problem and can help finance the project. Where this situation is found, a privately financed highway (with no government involvement in land acquisition or guarantees of the debts of the private venture) is a reasonable solution, provided that appropriate regulatory mechanisms are employed to preclude excessive monopoly rents.

Before encouraging such construction, however, the affected areas should examine carefully the likely consequences. Of special concern is the need to finance rapid expansion in other elements of public infrastructure and in needed public services that will accompany development.

In other circumstances, such as highways to relieve congestion on existing routes, a purely private venture seems likely to encounter insurmountable obstacles, particularly in acquiring land for the right of way. Governmental assistance, in the form of donation of public land or the involuntary taking of the needed land from private owners, may be required if the project is to proceed. This involvement alters the relationship between government and the private firm, considerably increasing the risk to the government.

Having explicitly committed itself to the project in partnership with the private firm, the government should take appropriate safeguards to avoid finding itself faced with the unanticipated cost of completing a project for which the costs proved too great for the private partners. The first of these safeguards should be the establishment of effective mechanisms for continuous oversight of the performance of the private managers and for rapid intervention if problems come to light.

NOTES

1. These data are drawn primarily from material supplied by the partnership.

2. This is the author's primary source of data for the discussion of developments in California and Arizona.

BIBLIOGRAPHY

GOMEZ-IBANEZ, Jose A. and John R. MEYER (1993), *Going Private: The International Experience with Transport Privatization*, The Brookings Institution, Washington, DC.

HAZARD, John L. (1977), *Transportation: Management, Economics, Policy*, Cornell Maritime Press, Cambridge, Maryland.

Chapter Nine

**SHARING AND MANAGING RISK
IN THE ACQUISITION OF MAJOR WEAPONS SYSTEMS
FROM PRIVATELY OWNED INDUSTRIAL FIRMS:
AN OVERVIEW OF UNITED STATES EXPERIENCE**

by

Harry S. Havens
Former Assistant Comptroller General
United States General Accounting Office

INTRODUCTION

This chapter provides a brief summary of the experience of the US Government in acquiring major weapons systems from privately owned industrial firms. The objective of the chapter is to identify the risks that are present in this process and the measures that have been taken to manage and control those risks, in the hope that lessons learned from the US weapons acquisition process can be generalized to a broader set of relationships between democratic governments and private sector firms.

To provide a basis for drawing such conclusions, the chapter discusses the environment in which major weapons are acquired in the United States, some of the problems that the US government has experienced in purchasing weapons, and the various contractual arrangements it has tried in seeking to equip its military forces with effective airplanes, tanks, ships, etc. at reasonable cost.

The chapter is concerned primarily with the process by which these weapons are acquired, not the decision to acquire them. Thus the often debated question of whether or not the United States needed to build nuclear-powered aircraft carriers or long-range supersonic bombers is not examined. The paper also does not address the purchase of items such as food, clothing, non-combat vehicles, and other items which might be presumed to have a non-military equivalent, although some of the same problems (as well as some different problems) have been seen in that part of the procurement process. Finally, although for much of its history the United States made extensive use of government-operated manufacturing facilities (arsenals, shipyards, etc.) for the production of military weapons, the paper does not discuss their use because of the relatively minor and declining role that these facilities have played in recent decades in the production of the major weapons systems that are the focus of the chapter.

THE DEFENSE CONTRACTING ENVIRONMENT

To understand the problems of buying modern weapons of war, it is essential to recognize the unique nature of the environment in which those weapons are acquired. There is no "market" as economists are accustomed to finding. There is a single buyer, the government, for a highly specialized item, to be acquired in small quantities from a very small number of possible vendors. Consider, for example, the purchase of a nuclear-powered aircraft carrier. It is generally considered that there is only one shipyard in the United States with the capability of building such a ship. This creates the situation of a monopolist (the shipyard) facing a monopsonist (the government). Economic theory provides little basis for suggesting the likely outcome of such a relationship.

The situation is further complicated by the fact that the two parties to the transaction have a symbiotic relationship in that each is very dependent on the other. The shipyard's existence depends on the continued production of ships for the government. In recent decades, US shipyards have been unable to compete with lower cost shipyards in other countries for the production of commercial shipping. Thus if the government contracts cease, the shipyard will probably go out of business. But the US government has been unwilling to accept the possible loss of its only domestic source of an essential weapon, so it cannot afford to adopt a negotiating posture that risks driving the shipyard out of business.

This is an extreme, but not unique example of the relationship that is found throughout the defense industrial establishment. The most important of the contractors are heavily, if not totally, dependent on government purchases for their business livelihood. The producers of military aircraft, for example, make almost no effort to compete in the production of commercial aircraft. The principal exception is McDonnell Douglas. That firm, however, despite its past success in the production of commercial airliners, is having increasing difficulty in that field in the face of intense competition from Boeing and Airbus. Boeing, once one of the major producers of military aircraft, now does relatively little defense aircraft business. (Boeing is still active in the production of missiles and helicopters.) Thus, in many areas, the government finds itself dependent for the development of any particular weapon on one, two, or possibly three business firms with the technical, engineering, and manufacturing capability to produce that weapon.

THE WEAPONS PROCUREMENT PROCESS

In theory, the weapons procurement process is relatively straightforward. The military services define an operational requirement based on the responsibilities that are assigned to them and the estimated military threat posed by possible adversaries. In principle, the operational requirement is stated in terms of the ability to carry out a particular mission. The operational requirement for a new attack fighter, for example, might be stated as the ability to deliver certain munitions with a specified accuracy on a target at a specified distance from the starting point within a certain time after launch and against specified defensive weapons. Such a statement of operational requirements might be based on knowledge that a possible adversary was developing a defensive weapon that appeared likely to reduce greatly the survival rate of existing attack fighters.

When the operational requirement has been developed and approved by the civilian hierarchy of the Department of Defense (DOD) and preliminary approval has been granted by Congress, the military services invite proposals from contractors for ways of meeting that requirement. Based on these proposals, which include preliminary designs and estimates of the cost to develop and produce the fighter, one or more contractors is selected. If a single contractor is selected, the contractor submits a design for government approval. After agreeing on any needed changes, the contractor develops a detailed design for the system and, when that has been approved, produces a prototype for testing, perhaps revealing the need for further design changes. At some point the design is agreed and the fighter goes into production. More recently, a different approach has been used, in which two contractors are selected to develop prototypes. The final decision on contractor selection is then based on a competitive "fly-off" between the two aircraft, rather than on the design proposal.

Reality, however, is much less straightforward than this theoretical description suggests. The complexities begin with the determination of operational requirements. The military services usually assume, with some justification, that a particular weapon system has a limited period of effectiveness, after which the weapons of potential adversaries will render it obsolete. Knowing that it will probably take a number of years to design, develop, and produce the successor weapon, the military service is likely to begin looking for that successor long before the threat it will face can be specified with precision. In these circumstances, the military service will always seek the maximum possible performance of any new weapon, an understandable search since many years may pass between "generations" of weapons and lives may depend on seemingly small differences in performance.

The military services, however, have little capacity to design in detail the weapons they wish to purchase and may have little direct knowledge of technological advances that might yield significant improvements in performance. For this knowledge, they are heavily dependent on the research and design talent of the defense industrial firms. Thus it is quite common to find the military leaning on the knowledge of the industrial firms in developing the operational requirements--the same industrial firms that will then seek the contracts to produce the weapons to meet those requirements. This has certain advantages for the government, in that it obtains access to skills otherwise unavailable to it. But it often means that government actually has delegated to a contractor some of the most fundamental decisions affecting the design and thus the cost of the weapon.

If the new weapon system is a new model of an existing weapon, such as the upgrade of a fighter, the government's choices are further constrained. Usually, there is only one potential source, the maker of the original weapon, and no competition.

IMBALANCE OF EXPERTISE

The limited technical knowledge of the military services is only one element of the imbalance between the government and the defense industrial firms. There is also a vast difference in the background and experience of the two parties to the negotiations.

The leaders of the project teams from the industrial firm are usually individuals who have spent their entire careers in these endeavors. Thus, in negotiating the design of the weapon and the terms of the contracts for producing it, the contractor team brings a high level of technical and managerial expertise. If additional expertise is needed, the contractor team can call on the entire resources of the company, such as its research and development staff, to provide additional information in response to questions or concerns raised by the government team.

The government teams, on the other hand, are usually led by military officers who have spent most of their careers preparing for the command of combat forces--the most promising avenue for professional advancement in the military. The US military services believe that control by officers with operational experience is vital in assuring that weapons will meet the essential needs of the operating forces. The normal pattern is for officers to "rotate" into a procurement assignment, remain there for two or three years, and then return to an operational assignment. A weapons acquisition cycle--from the initial design stage to the completion of production--may last twelve to fifteen years or even longer. Thus the leadership of the government team (and many of its members) may change four to six times or more over the course of the program, with possible serious damage to the continuity needed for effective management.

The US military personnel serving in this role commonly have little procurement experience and the likelihood of rotating to the operating forces after no more than two or three years in procurement activities gives them little opportunity to acquire the needed expertise. The common pattern has been for officers to serve no more than two or three assignments in procurement during the course of a career, so there is little opportunity to build expertise through repetitive experiences. It is recognized that these officers need technical (engineering) knowledge to perform the procurement activity although, even in this regard, there is no effort to match the technical expertise of the contractor team. A more serious deficiency, however, may be in the skills needed to manage the business aspects of the procurement function, an area in which most military officers have little experience and little or no training, and in which they are far surpassed by the managerial skills of the contractor team.

The career civil servants who are involved in the weapons procurement process often are considerably more experienced than their military counterparts although they, too, have usually had relatively little formal training in business management and only rarely have any extensive experience actually working in the private sector. Moreover, they serve primarily in a supporting role and are rarely, if ever, given overall responsibility for a major procurement program.

Political appointees in the civilian hierarchy of DOD often have considerable experience in private industry and, in theory, could compensate for the lack of such experience on the part of the military officers leading the project teams. To a degree, they have done so, being responsible for most of the efforts to reform the procurement system over the past three decades. For the most part, however, these officials spend their time on policy issues, rather than on the specifics of individual procurement actions. Moreover, their tenure is too brief (averaging about two years) to have an enduring effect.

In recent years there has been considerable concern expressed about the imbalance of expertise between the government and the defense contractors. Several studies have concluded that there should be a more professional approach to the problem, including the development of a strong cadre of procurement specialists among the ranks of the military services. Some progress has been made in this regard, but it would be premature to reach any conclusions about its success or about the degree to which it will improve the efficiency of the procurement process (Fox, 1988).

GOVERNMENT'S OBJECTIVES

The unusual, non-market environment in which defense procurement occurs has led the participants in the process to behave in ways that are not typical of economic actors found in more market-oriented situations. The behavior of the participants--and the motivations and incentives which cause that behavior--are a central factor in the defense contracting process because the resulting actions have often added considerably to the risks that are inherent in buying technologically advanced weapons.

In principle, the government seeks to acquire effective weapons, to be delivered when they are needed, at reasonable cost. In fact, however, the government's objectives are much more complex than this. As the previous discussion of operational requirements demonstrates, the determination of what the government needs is often based on what the defense industry says is possible rather than on a careful analysis of missions and threats. Furthermore, unlike the self-interested buyer in the theoretical model of a market economy, the government is not indifferent to the economic fate of the seller and has consistently avoided using its monopsony position in ways that would threaten to drive major suppliers out of business. It remains to be seen whether or not this posture will change in the context of declining DOD budgets.

INCENTIVES FOR MILITARY PROCUREMENT

Officers

The complexity extends not just to government's stated and unstated policies, but to the behavior of its agents, as well. The military officers who lead most weapons procurement teams face a number of conflicting goals. As individuals, they seek to advance in their chosen profession. This is most likely to occur through success in "command" assignments, not in procurement. Thus when they find themselves in a procurement assignment, there is a strong incentive simply to avoid the appearance of failure and to avoid disclosing problems.

There are other incentives for this behavior. The military services quite understandably want every possible advantage in combat. When military officers learn of a possible advance in weaponry, they want to have it. This often translates into the wish to develop a new weapon system. The military services have learned through experience that the best way to gain approval for a new system from the civilian hierarchy of DOD and then from the Congress is to be highly optimistic about the likely performance of the proposed new weapon, about its cost, and about the speed with which it can be developed and produced.

Once initial approval for a new weapon has been granted, the best strategy for assuring the program's continuation is to postpone acknowledging any problems for as long as possible and to remain optimistic about solving any problems that come to light. Experience has also demonstrated that once a system is in the advanced stages of development, particularly when actual production has commenced, the chances of cancellation because of rising costs, delayed delivery, or diminished performance are rather slight. (Even when performance is considerably less than promised, the system is almost always superior in some respect to the previous generation of weapons and thus remains desirable.) Thus there is a strong temptation to hide the problems until they can be solved or until the program is sufficiently far advanced that termination is not a feasible action.

Another complexity in motivation arises from the relative brevity of military careers. US military officers typically retire after only 20-35 years of service, at an age (the early forties to mid-fifties) when people in private industry are reaching their peak earning years. The military retirement system is relatively generous but not sufficient to permit most retired officers to maintain their previous standard of living. Many undertake second careers in the defense industrial firms. Such retired officers remain in close contact with colleagues who remain on active duty. Thus, out of friendship and respect and because of concern for their own future employment, some officers in the procurement system may be less aggressive in their negotiations with defense contractors than would otherwise be expected (Stubbing, 1986).

There are strict laws and regulations to prevent blatant conflict of interest in the relations between government personnel (both military and civilian) and contractors. (Some have suggested that these "ethics" rules are so rigid as to create a serious impediment to the recruitment of able people into the government's procurement activities.) No set of rules, however, can prevent the more subtle changes in attitude that are likely to occur as a military officer finds himself in contact with former peers and superiors who are in the defense industries, or as he approaches the end of his military career and begins to explore the options for the remaining years of his professional life.

Contractor incentives

The defense contractors themselves also exhibit behavior that contrasts with what is usually assumed in the competitive market economic model. Profit is clearly a goal but the desire for profits does not translate into the behaviors that would normally be expected of an entrepreneur. The theoretical profit-maximizing firm seeks to increase profit by increasing sales and achieving the highest possible profit on each sale. Prices are usually subject to some competitive constraint, so the desire for profit provides a strong incentive to control and reduce costs.

Most defense firms, however, face no meaningful competitive constraints on their prices. They know from experience that, once a contract has been awarded, the government will tolerate substantial increases in the price, provided that those increases are a reflection of rising costs incurred by the contractor, so cost becomes a secondary consideration for the firm, as well. For the defense firm, economic success is much less dependent on the immediate profits from an individual contract than from the maintenance of a volume of work sufficient to cover its costs, including the cost of capital. Its goal, therefore, is to continue the production of each system as long as possible and to achieve a continuing flow of new contracts to replace those coming to an end.

Assuring the continued flow of new weapons contracts requires the firm to satisfy at least two conditions. First, it must maintain a strong research, design and engineering capability. This allows the firm to continue generating ideas for weapons that can enter the requirements determination process, leading to new contracts for successor weapons systems. Second, it must produce weapons that the military services consistently like to have and use. The failure to meet cost goals on a contract rarely prevents a firm from obtaining a successor contract. Failure to meet performance goals is a more serious matter. However, if the system is perceived as being an improvement over its predecessor, the failure to achieve some promised aspect of performance will be tolerated and will not affect the contractor's stature or its ability to obtain subsequent contracts.

Political considerations

The procurement process is further complicated by the fact that it has unavoidable political implications. The decision to acquire a weapons system means employment in the locations where the contractor will be producing that weapon. Local employment opportunities are a matter of great concern to elected officials. In 1986, for example, one newspaper noted that defense contracts provided employment for 175 000 workers in the state of Massachusetts and indirectly supported the jobs of another 260,000 workers, for a total of one of every seven jobs in the state (*Boston Globe*, 1986).

With so many jobs (and votes) perceived as being at stake, Senators and Representatives often intervene on behalf of a contractor or subcontractor from their region with the justification that doing so promotes the interests of their constituents. Some of these elected officials also hold important positions in Congress overseeing the defense budget, so that their views carry considerable weight with the Defense Department. Sometimes this has influenced the selection of a contractor but more often it has appeared to cause the continuation of a contract after cost or performance considerations or changing military requirements might otherwise have dictated its termination.

Contractors, aware of these political forces, have a strong incentive to spread the work under a large contract over many geographical locations (primarily through the use of subcontractors) and to assure that elected officials are made aware of the work (and resulting jobs) being performed in their constituencies. Whether or not this adds to the cost of a program, it clearly adds to the political support for continuing that program.

TYPES OF RISK

In the unique politico-economic environment in which defense procurement occurs, there is a wide variety of risks. Most of these risks are found in other economic activities, as well, but some of them assume a special importance in the defense contracting business. As will be seen at various points in this discussion, the motivations of the participants in the defense contracting process adds considerably to the risks by stimulating actions which increase the risks and by discouraging actions which might serve to limit those risks.

Technological risk

Most historians have judged that the Second World War was won by the side with the quantitative advantage in weaponry, not by technological superiority. In only a few areas, such as the development of radar by British scientists and of the atomic bomb in the United States, did the Allies have a significant technological advantage. In almost every area, however, the Allies had an enormous numerical advantage.

Despite that experience, in recent decades the US military establishment has come increasingly to rely on technological superiority, on having weapons that outperform the counterpart weapons of any potential adversary. This is accomplished by incorporating the latest technological advances. Existing technology is assumed to be available to the adversary, so technological superiority can be achieved only by requiring each new weapons system to incorporate further advances in the state of the art.

This approach has led to some remarkably effective weapons but it is accompanied by major risks. An idea that looked promising in the laboratory may not work in the real world or may be impossible to produce efficiently in a real factory. This makes it inherently difficult to predict the costs of moving from an idea that looked good in the laboratory to the development of a prototype and then to the production of a weapon that will be effective in combat. How these costs should be shared between the government and the contractor has been the subject of continuing controversy.

Technological risk is rarely a matter of the system working or not working. Much more common is a situation in which the system works, but not as well as had been hoped or promised. The airplane may fly, but be overweight or lack some promised characteristic such as range or maneuverability. Or the airframe may be fully satisfactory but some of the electronic components may be less effective than expected. In these situations, the first question is whether or not the problems can be corrected. The military services and their contractors display an almost unwavering optimism on these questions because, as noted earlier, each has a strong interest in the continuation of the program. The question of who pays for the corrections is typically negotiated and, historically, these costs have usually been absorbed by the government.

The military service's wish to incorporate the latest technological advances creates a closely related problem of design instability. Throughout the development process, and often continuing until the end of the production run on a weapons system, design changes occur frequently. Some are requested by the military service; others are proposed by the contractor. Many of these "change orders" are of little consequence as individual items, but cumulatively the associated costs can be quite large.

Historically, the services have demonstrated a willingness to approve change orders without careful analysis of the likely cost implications. The reasons vary, but commonly relate to the motivations discussed earlier, such as the wish to incorporate the latest idea, the wish to move ahead as rapidly as possible (thus discouraging anyone who suggests delaying a decision in order to perform a careful analysis), and the imbalance of expertise and other factors that cause an undue deference to the contractor.

The question of which party to the contract should absorb the costs associated with change orders is a frequent source of conflict. If the government requested or formally approved the change, the government is almost always liable for the costs. Often, however, the responsibility is less clear cut, leading to an extended controversy. Over the past several decades, the record is rather clear. Most of the time, the government will cover most of the costs, whether or not it approved the change.

Manufacturing risk

Once the basic design of a weapon has been agreed, prototypes are commonly built and tested and the question of technical feasibility of the approved design has usually been settled. At this point the weapon may be approved for production. But substantial risks remain. The first risk concerns the feasibility of routinely manufacturing the weapon. Prototypes are usually constructed with a high proportion of skilled hand labor, so that the ability to produce a working prototype does not necessarily translate into the ability to build the weapon on a routine basis at the required level of quality and reliability using the tools and skills regularly available in the factory.

Problems in this regard can usually be overcome, but at higher costs. The question of who finances these costs is often an issue in the production stages. Again, however, the historical record is clear. While there may be considerable acrimony before the issue is resolved, once the contractor has incurred the costs, virtually all of those costs will be reimbursed by the government.

In the commercial world, such as among the automobile makers, it has become increasingly common for the design team to include industrial and manufacturing engineers. The objective is to minimize manufacturing risk from the outset. It also provides a good basis for estimating final costs and for making design changes to keep costs competitive with those of other producers. There is little evidence to date of this practice taking hold in the weapons acquisition process.

Coupled with the risk associated with uncertainty about manufacturing processes is the design instability noted previously. As time passes in the production phase, the military service is likely to discover new ideas that it wishes to incorporate in the finished product or will accede to changes suggested by the contractor. Such changes almost invariably add to the cost of the product and someone--almost always the government--must finance those costs.

Adding to the risks in the production stage is uncertainty about the quantity of units to be produced and the rate at which they will be acquired. At the start of production, the military service will commonly have a target number of the weapons that it hopes to acquire, a proposed schedule for acquiring them, and an estimate of the annual funding required to support that program.

The military service, for example, may propose to acquire a specific number of fighter aircraft over a specific period of time. The initial cost estimates, in the form of projected annual funding requirements, will be premised on this quantity and rate of production.

In the US budget system, however, those funds are normally provided on an annual basis through the enactment of appropriations by the Congress. These appropriations and the accompanying guidance on how the funds are intended to be used are quite detailed. DOD has only limited authority to shift funds from one weapons program to another. Thus, if the annual budget for the procurement of fighter aircraft is reduced, fewer aircraft can be purchased in that year, and the program must either be reduced in total quantity or "stretched out" over a longer period. (All parties to the contract, including the Congress, usually prefer stretching the procurement out, rather than reducing the number to be bought.) The manufacturer, however, must distribute his fixed overhead costs over this smaller annual production rate, so the unit cost goes up.

The resulting cost increases must be allocated between the firm and the government, with the government usually absorbing all of them. Even if the government eventually buys fewer aircraft, if it stretches that production run over a longer period of time, it may actually spend more in total than if it had bought the originally planned quantity over a shorter number of years. One observer cites a study that concluded that a reduction of 66 in the number of F-14A aircraft, coupled with an extension of the time during which they would be produced, increased the total program cost by 38 percent (Fox, 1988).

An extreme example of uncertainty about volume is found in the unusual case in which a system is terminated far short of the anticipated quantity. The manufacturer may have invested large amounts in specialized tooling in expectation of recovering those sunk costs over a long production run, only to find himself with a factory full of essentially worthless equipment. Thus premature termination is usually a contingency that is addressed in the contract, with the government usually assuming responsibility for covering the costs incurred by the contractor up to the date of termination.

Subcontractor risk

Individual US defense firms rarely produce all of the components of a modern weapon system for which they are the contractor. In fact, the prime contractor may be chiefly a coordinator and assembler of components supplied by other firms (subcontractors). The performance of these subcontractors with respect to quality, timeliness, and cost are often critical to the performance of the prime contractor and are another source of substantial risk in the manufacturing phase of weapons production.

In some cases the government has a separate contract with a different firm for the production of specialized components, which it then supplies to the prime contractor for insertion in the finished product. For example, the Navy may contract with a shipyard for the construction of a ship and with another firm for the development and production of the weapons control computer systems that must be installed in the ship at a particular point in the construction process. This creates a further complexity in the contracting arrangement. The government is almost always responsible for cost increases resulting from delays in the delivery of such "government furnished equipment."

Economic policy risk

It is not uncommon for the weapons system procurement cycle to take fifteen years or more from the initial requirements determination to the completion of production. The economic environment may change dramatically several times during the course of that cycle. Contracts negotiated at one time may be unrealistically rigid a year or two later. A sudden surge in the rate of inflation, for example, may interject a major increase in wage rates and in prices for raw materials and component parts. A firm anticipating a "reasonable" profit on a contract may suddenly face huge losses unless the contract prices are adjusted. Similarly, firms that finance their working capital requirements from external sources are susceptible to rapid shifts in interest rates while those who obtain components and raw materials abroad (an increasingly common situation) face the risk of adverse shifts in foreign exchange rates.

These risks are commonly covered in procurement contracts, particularly following the chaotic economic conditions of the 1970s and 1980s.[1] In a purely cost-based contract, the problem (along with many of the other risks) is handled automatically; as costs go up, so does the price to the government. However, if the contract for a major system has a target price, ceiling price, or supposedly fixed price, it is quite normal to see provisions included to adjust that price to compensate for inflation in excess of some anticipated rate.

Political risk

As noted earlier, political considerations often act to protect weapons procurement programs and the contractors who are supplying the weapons. Political forces are not always benign, however, and can sometimes work against the interests of those involved in the procurement process. The budget process, for example, is inherently political in nature and budget allocations are subject to change in response to a variety of forces ranging from concern about the aggregate budget deficit to perceptions of a diminished or non-existent threat from the former Soviet Union. As noted earlier, reduced budget allocations can create major (and very costly) disruptions in programs.

Political forces can impinge in other ways, as well. In making the choice between two systems being proposed by different contractors, each of which could probably satisfy the operational requirement, the decision may be driven in considerable measure by the relative strength of the political forces supporting the two proponents. The loser in such a competition may face dire consequences. In the past, DOD appears often to have sought to compensate the loser by arranging for it to receive other contracts, but that is now much more difficult in a period of declining defense budgets. Recently, for example, Grumman Aviation, a long time producer of Navy combat aircraft, lost in the competition for a new Navy attack fighter. It has since announced that it was withdrawing from further competition in that field and closing its factory on Long Island.

CONTRACTING APPROACHES AND FAILURES

The complexity of the defense contracting environment, the diversity of the risks associated with that industry, and a sense from time to time that the defense firms were not entirely trustworthy in their business relations with government have led the US government to a variety of approaches to resolving the question of which party to the contract should bear the risks. Each new "reform" grew out of a perception that the previous approach had failed to achieve the government's underlying goal of acquiring effective weapons when they are needed at reasonable cost. None of the approaches yet tried has resolved adequately the issue of which party should bear which of the risks associated with production in this highly specialized arena. In the final analysis, each approach left the government reimbursing virtually all of whatever cost increases were incurred by the contractor, regardless of the original terms of the contract.

Following is a brief discussion of those approaches, with an assessment of why they failed. There are innumerable variations, so the discussion that follows groups the contracting approaches into "families," with illustrative examples, to simplify the assessment.

Cost-plus contracts

The most common method by which the government has purchased major weapons systems from privately owned industrial firms is through contracts under which the contractor is reimbursed for the costs it incurs, plus a margin of profit. During the Second World War, when the overriding goals were to maximize the volume of weapons that could be produced and the speed with which they could be made available, the usual contract was on the basis of costs, with the profit margin commonly computed as a percentage of costs. Procedures were established to recapture "excess" profits after the fact through the re-negotiation of contracts (which could be invoked unilaterally by the government). This, together with patriotism, the fear of exposure as a "war profiteer," and the extremely high marginal tax rates in effect during the war, was assumed to be sufficient to control the worst of the profiteering. As a general matter, however, costs were not a matter of serious concern.

These contracting arrangements created a strong incentive to maximize production but no incentive at all to control costs. Indeed, payment on the basis of costs plus a percentage of costs as profit creates a strong perverse incentive to inflate costs, since any increase in costs adds to profits.

It was justifiable, perhaps, for the government to ignore costs during wartime, when the need to maximize military potential in the interests of an early victory outweighed all other considerations. However, the same basic contracting method remained in place long after the exigencies of war had passed. The perverse incentives, and the abuses that resulted, were reasonably apparent by the 1960s. A number of alternative contracting arrangements have been tried in recent decades, in an attempt to find a satisfactory solution to those problems.

Fixed-price contracts

In reaction to the problems observed in cost-plus contracts, there have been several attempts to use fixed-price contracts. In its simplest form, a fixed-price contract requires the contractor to agree to deliver a specified quantity of an item on a specified schedule for a specified price. In theory, if the contractor can produce the item for a lower cost, he keeps the difference as profit; if costs exceed the specified price, the company incurs a loss. This was presumed to create a strong incentive to control costs and--when combined with an assumption of competition among potential contractors--to lead to reduced procurement costs for the government. Unfortunately, this has not been the result.

The first large scale attempt to use fixed price contracts for major defense systems occurred in the 1960s, under the leadership of Defense Secretary MacNamara, in a process called "Total Package Procurement" (TPP). One well-informed observer describes this experience as follows:

TPP required simultaneous bidding, on a fixed-price basis, for both the first (development) and second (production) stages as a means of preventing a winning contractor (for the first stage) from facing little or no competition for the second stage. It was applied on such systems as the Lockheed C-5A cargo plane, the General Dynamics F-111 fighter aircraft, and the Grumman F-14A fighter aircraft. All of these had large cost overruns and TPP was judged to be ineffective for two reasons: (1) DOD introduced or allowed numerous changes in the programs, thereby obscuring any incentives for cost control and accountability for cost growth; and (2) DOD was either unwilling or unable to enforce the fixed-price contracts. Military services, reluctant to incur delays by shifting to a new contractor, did not want to enforce provisions of the TPP technique for fixed-price contracts. In 1966, Secretary MacNamara abandoned the TPP concept.

(Fox, 1988)

The military services were not alone in their reluctance to enforce the fixed-price contracts under the TPP concept, with their potential for driving contractors into bankruptcy. The Lockheed case is instructive. The company clearly underestimated the difficulties of designing and building the C-5A.[2] Moreover, as the losses mounted on the C-5A contract, the company was also encountering financial difficulties in its effort to develop a new commercial airliner, the L-1011 (Lockheed's last attempt to compete in the commercial airliner market). A strong belief grew that, left to its own devices, Lockheed would likely collapse, unable to deliver the C-5As for which it had contracted and leaving a large work force unemployed.

To avoid this outcome, the government guaranteed a large loan to Lockheed, to carry it over its short-term cash problems, and re-negotiated the C-5A contract to reimburse Lockheed for most of the losses it had incurred. This experience made it clear to both contractors and government officials that fixed-price contracts could not (or at least would not) be enforced if the losses to the contractor were great enough to risk bankrupting an important defense firm. It was evident that such fixed-price contracts were inappropriate in high-risk situations.

Later experience with fixed price contracts

After the disastrous experience with the C-5A and other systems under the Total Package Procurement concept, weapons acquisition practices generally moved back toward cost-based contracts, particularly for the more risky design and development phases of the procurement cycle. In developing the Airborne Warning and Control System (AWACS), for example, the Air Force used a cost-plus-incentive-fee contract for the development phase, shifting to a fixed-ceiling-price contract for the production phase (US General Accounting Office, 1971b). The primary areas of risk in this case were viewed as being the development of the new radar system, which was to be carried on an existing air frame, that of the Boeing 707 commercial jet liner. It is noteworthy that the contract included specific provisions to control design changes and to compensate the contractor for unanticipated inflation. Each had been the source of problems in the Total Package Procurement cases.

Nevertheless, there remained considerable attachment to the concept of the fixed-price contract, because of its presumed creation of strong incentives to control costs. This was particularly true of the Navy, which continued to negotiate fixed-price contracts despite repetitive failures to achieve the anticipated benefits. About a year before the Air Force negotiated the AWACS procurement, but long after the problems with fixed-price contracts had become apparent, the Navy negotiated a Total Package Procurement contract with Lockheed for the design, development and production of the S-3A, a carrier based antisubmarine aircraft (US General Accounting Office, 1971a).

In recognition of the problems of Total Package Procurement, the Navy did return to its previous practice of contracting separately for the design and construction of new ships. However, it continued to require fixed-price contracts. One observer concluded that this was a "political" judgment reflecting the view that by fostering the illusion that program costs could be predicted and controlled, it was easier to gain approval of a program. In the 1970s, this approach was used for the construction of the SSN-688 class of attack submarines by the Electric Boat division of the General Dynamics corporation. Huge cost increases accumulated, and General Dynamics sought to recover those costs from the government. It succeeded. As one observer noted, "In the end, General Dynamics was compensated for cost overruns, forgiven for delays in delivery, and rewarded with follow-on contracts" (Goodman, 1988).

Despite this experience, the Navy continued its fixed-price contracting practices and consistently resisted pressure to change from the civilian hierarchy of the Defense Department. In the 1980s, for example, the Navy negotiated a number of fixed-price incentive contracts, in which a "target price" is agreed with the contractor. If the cost exceeds the target price, the excess is to be absorbed by the government and the contractor in specified shares. Unfortunately, it rarely works out in this clean fashion. Design changes and various sources of delay often cause costs to rise. If these changes to the original plan were required or allowed by the government, the contractor has a reasonable basis for requesting an adjustment to the target price. The Navy has consistently allowed enough of these adjustments to avoid unacceptable losses to the contractor. Thus a supposedly fixed-price contract loses most of its "fixed" character.

Recently, the General Accounting Office reported that in January 1987, the Navy had awarded an $863 million, fixed-price incentive contract for the design and construction of the first AOE 6 class supply ship, designed to support aircraft carrier task forces, with options for three more ships. By February 1991, the contractor had submitted more than $300 million in claims against the Navy for cost increases stemming from an optimistically low bid, concurrent development and construction, inadequate Navy and contractor management attention, and failure to achieve expected shipyard productivity. The lead ship has yet to be fully tested at sea, where operational problems may first arise. Thus, the final costs, delivery dates, and extent to which the ships under construction will meet expectations are still unknown (US General Accounting Office, 1993c).

In 1989, the Navy awarded Electric Boat/General Dynamics a contract to construct the first ship of the next generation of attack submarines, the SSN-21, to be named the Seawolf. The original target cost was $718 million. By the end of 1992, the estimated cost had risen to about $1,103 million, and further increases are anticipated (US General Accounting office, 1993a). These experiences have led the Defense Department to impose regulations prohibiting the use of fixed-price contracts in the early stages of development of a weapons system (Acting Under Secretary of Defense, 1991).

Cost plus incentive fee

It is now commonly recognized that fixed price contracts are inappropriate and, as a practical matter, unenforceable in the context of high risk major weapons systems development efforts. Realistically, there is no obvious alternative to a contract in which the business firm is to be reimbursed for its costs. However, the adverse incentives of the World War II-style cost-plus-percentage-of cost contracts are equally well recognized. This has led to various attempts to develop cost-based contracts that avoid the adverse incentives and substitute more appropriate ones. Thus it is quite common to find defense procurement contracts which are fundamentally of the cost-reimbursement type, but with special features to reward contractor performance that exceeds specified norms. Provisions may be included in the contract to increase the contractor fee (profit) if a stage in the procurement process is completed ahead of schedule, if the system performs above expectations, or if costs are less than estimated.

While incentive systems such as these have important theoretical advantages, they are very difficult to implement effectively. To have their intended effect, the standards against which the contractor is to be judged must be challenging, yet achievable. If the standards are too lax, the contractor may receive a reward for what is actually mediocre performance. If the standards are too demanding, the contractor may conclude that attempting to exceed them is not worth the effort. The various incentives also must be carefully balanced. For example, if the incentive structure is inappropriately weighted in favor of system performance, it may lead the contractor to sacrifice cost and schedule goals in order to gain the reward for system performance. Finally, it is difficult to establish some standards, especially those related to system performance, so as to capture the real program goals in an objectively determinable fashion.

Considerable knowledge and negotiating skill is needed to develop a contract embodying incentives that are both effective and equitable. The contractor will naturally seek a structure of incentives that will maximize its profits. The government team needs to counter this bias, but without imposing standards so demanding or imbalanced as to be self-defeating. This is one of the areas in which the imbalance of expertise and business experience between the contracting firm and the government contracting officials can have particularly unfortunate results for the government.

BLACK PROGRAMS

Some observers have argued that one of the serious defects of government procurement is the excessive reliance on detailed controls to protect the government's interests.[3] Several examples are often cited as being particularly counter-productive. These include contractual requirements that the supplier comply with voluminous technical specifications, forcing the use of custom manufactured components rather than commercially available items, adding significantly to the cost of the system. Government contracts also require the maintenance of cost accounting systems and records that are different from and much more elaborate than those that are usually maintained by firms in "normal" commercial activities. There is evidence to support the view that some firms decline to undertake government contracts because of the burdensome nature of these requirements, thus further limiting the possible range of competition for meeting the government's procurement needs (Department of Defense, 1993).

It has been suggested that these burdensome technical and administrative requirements not only add to costs, but are unnecessary to protect the government's interests. To support this argument, reference is usually made to the government's "black" or secret programs, where it is said that the controls are much less strict and the oversight less obtrusive. The examples usually cited are the development of the famous U-2 of the 1950s and its successor, the SR-71, high-altitude, long-range reconnaissance aircraft produced at the "skunk works" of Lockheed Aircraft. The available information certainly supports the view that these systems were quite successful technically, and the U-2, at least, was reportedly completed at less than the budgeted cost (Gregory, 1989).

For most "black" programs, too little is known to reach any conclusions about the consistency of success or to make any general observations about the overall consequences of relaxed government controls in this area of procurement. Enough is known, however, to register some reservations about the enthusiasm expressed by the proponents of this type of "deregulation." The B-2 "Stealth" bomber, for example, was developed initially as a "black" program. The cost of that system has grown astronomically and doubts have been expressed about its ability to perform as promised. From an initial plan to acquire 132 of the bombers, the program has shrunk to 20, which are now estimated by the Air Force to cost a total of $45.3 billion, including related military construction costs (US General Accounting Office, 1993b).

Without much more extensive and systematic information concerning the experience of procurement in "black" programs, it would be inappropriate to draw any conclusions about the role of reduced government controls in facilitating whatever successes may have occurred. The apparent success of the U-2 and SR-71 programs, for example, may reflect an entirely different factor that is not easily replicated and which cannot be assumed to exist. Both systems, after all, were developed under the leadership of the same unusually brilliant and dedicated designer.

There can be little doubt that excessive bureaucratic controls and procedures can be a significant impediment to efficient production of needed weapons systems. They can add to costs directly, reduce potential competition among suppliers, and constrain managerial flexibility and production efficiency. The difficulty lies in drawing the line between what is necessary and what is excessive. Detailed technical specifications, for example, are a response to the experience of contractors substituting substandard or defective components in an effort to reduce costs and increase profits. No doubt the specification process has sometimes gone too far, but it is clearly a natural response to a real problem.

In an attempt to attack this problem from a different direction, DOD has recently given much greater emphasis to buying commercially available items wherever possible, rather than items designed for unique use by the military services.[4] The presumption is that an item being sold in the commercial market place is subject to the quality and price tests of that market. If the government buys the same item, it is presumed to be reasonable to pay the market price without detailed examination of the supplier's costs or production processes. This presumption is undoubtedly reasonable when the government is buying common use items such as pencils and typewriters. Unfortunately, it provides little help in connection with the acquisition of major weapons systems which, by their very nature, are custom designed and built in relatively small numbers and for which there is no meaningful commercial market test for quality and price.

SURVEILLANCE OF CONTRACTOR PERFORMANCE

In the theoretical world of the purely private sector, the buyer chooses among those offering a product, agrees to buy it from the supplier at a specified price, and the supplier delivers it. In this model, the buyer has no interest in how the product is manufactured, only in the delivery of the agreed product at the agreed time and price.

In reality, of course, there are many deviations from this model, even in the private sector. When a person contracts with a builder for the construction of a house, for example, it is quite common for the customer to spend considerable time at the building site observing the construction process to assure that it is according to plan. In more expensive construction endeavors, such as an expensive custom-built home, an apartment building or an office building, it is usual for the customer to hire an agent, such as an architect, to assure that the construction does not depart from the plans or to adjust the plans from time to time to accommodate the customer's wishes.

Other examples of departures from the theoretical model can be found in manufacturing. When a company producing automobiles or commercial airplanes buys critical components from another firm, the buying firm may insist on observing the supplier's production processes to assure itself that the supplier can meet its obligations for quality and delivery times.

In the weapons procurement process, the government's oversight of contractor operations resembles in some ways the model of the buyer of a new office building overseeing the activities of a builder. For each major weapons system, the government commonly establishes a "program office," headed by a senior military officer, which is actively involved in the design of the system and continues to be involved throughout the production process. Any changes in the design must be approved by this office and, through this office, by other levels of government. The program office also plays a key role in negotiating each of the potentially numerous contracts (for design, development, initial production and follow-on production) that must be established during the life of the program and for approving change orders and other adjustments to the contract.

The program office is commonly located in the headquarters of the military service that is acquiring the system. In addition, the government has "plant representatives" who are located in the manufacturing facilities of the contractor. These personnel are responsible for observing the activities of the contractor, reporting problems, and acting as a channel of communications between the contractor and the government.

There is a continuing flow of information from the contractor and the government's plant representatives to the program office and from the program office to others in the DOD hierarchy concerned about the progress of the contract. On major contracts, formal reports are submitted on a monthly or quarterly basis. These formal reports focus on the progress of the work (the completion of specified elements of the contract, problems encountered in completing the work, etc.) and on costs incurred by the contractor. In addition, on any major contract, there is continuing informal communications on a daily or weekly basis among the contractor, the plant representative, and the program office. These informal contacts serve to elaborate on information contained in the formal reports and to give early warning of problems as they arise.

On contracts covering an extended period of time, arrangements are usually included to make "progress payments" to the contractor as work on the contract proceeds. These payments are commonly based on the costs incurred to date by the contractor, with a modest percentage withheld until completion of the contract or of specified stages of the contract. The cost reports submitted by the contractor are the primary basis for making these payments. As noted earlier, the government requires that its contractors employ a cost accounting system that is more detailed than those used by most commercial activities. These systems underlie the cost reports that are submitted by the contractors.

Because of the prevalence of cost-based contracts in military procurement, there is an extensive auditing system that is also an important part of the contractor surveillance network. The Defense Contract Audit Agency (DCAA), with about 6 000 auditors, has the primary responsibility for assessing compliance with weapons system procurement contracts.

DCAA routinely scrutinizes the reported costs incurred by defense contractors to assure that the cost accounting system complies with government standards, that costs are allocated to the correct contract, that improper costs are not reimbursed, and that amounts paid to subcontractors are reasonably in line with amounts estimated at the time the contract was negotiated. DCAA audits routinely reveal problems in all these areas. DCAA's reports, however, are only advisory. Those managing the contract are responsible for obtaining corrective action. All too often, the program office fails to do so because of its predominant concern about the performance of the weapon rather than its cost.

The General Accounting Office (GAO), an agency in the legislative branch of government, also devotes considerable resources to overseeing DOD procurement activities. These audits and investigations are primarily for the purpose of providing information for use by the Congress in its policy making processes, such as by testing the reliability of information supplied to the Congress by DOD and by providing reliable current data about the cost, schedule, and performance of weapons systems in development. In addition, however, GAO performs some detailed contract audits, primarily to assess the adequacy of the work being done by DCAA. As with DCAA, however, GAO reports are only advisory; GAO has no power to enforce its recommendations.

Performance testing

Formal reports, on-site supervision and auditing, while necessary, are not enough to assure that the contractor has developed an effective weapons system. The system must be tested to determine if it performs as intended. The testing process usually begins in the early stages of development with laboratory tests of newly designed components to see if it is technically possible to achieve the desired result.

At some stage in the development of a weapon, the contractor must produce a prototype of the completed system which is then subject to extensive tests. Perhaps the most critical of these are the "operational tests," in which the system is operated by military personnel (not the experts who designed it) and is operated in the field in simulated battle conditions (rather than in the clean and safe environment of the factory or laboratory).

Important weaknesses are sometimes revealed in the operational testing stage. A few years ago, for example, the Army was trying to develop a new anti-aircraft gun to accompany rapidly maneuvering armored formations. When that system, called the Division Air Defense system, or DIVAD, was subjected to operational tests, it was found to be ineffective against the anticipated threat and the program was terminated. More recently, when the Bradley Fighting Vehicle (a lightly armored vehicle for transporting infantry) was subjected to live-fire operational tests, it was found that the armor was not sufficient to defeat the armor-piercing weapons that it was likely to encounter. The system continued in production, but the revealed weakness has required significant changes in the way in which the vehicle will be employed.

Few complex systems perform precisely as promised in the design stage. Thus extensive operational testing is, in principle, a critically important step in the procurement process. For the testing process to achieve its intended purpose, the tests must be designed and conducted with care and the results must be examined closely for the revelation of any flaws. Operational tests, in particular, require special care. To provide reasonable assurance of combat effectiveness, the tests must simulate, as realistically as possible, the threats against which the system will be deployed, the circumstances in which it will be used, and the military personnel who will be operating it. Of equal importance, the results must be reported objectively.

Unfortunately, those conducting the tests do not always adhere to these standards. For example, in the early operational tests of the DIVAD, the standard of realistically simulating the threat was violated by requiring the test target to fly in a straight line, rather than maneuvering to avoid the antiaircraft fire, as one would expect in actual combat. The standard of objective reporting was violated by reporting as a "hit" any projectile that came within about 15 meters of the target, even though such "near misses" would actually have caused little or no damage (Stubbing, 1986). Thus the tests were pronounced as being successful and the development process continued. Later tests revealed the actual defects of the system and, eventually, it was terminated but only after much more money had been spent in a futile attempt to build an effective weapon.

There are a number of reasons why the military services and the contractors resist extensive testing. The process of testing, discovering the weaknesses, adjusting the design to overcome those weaknesses, and then testing again can be a lengthy one. The military services and the contractor, impatient to proceed with producing and fielding the new weapon system, often prefer to forego the tests or, more commonly, to begin production while the tests are being conducted. This decision to permit "concurrency" of design, test, and production has been heavily criticized by many who have examined the defense procurement system. If serious problems are revealed after production is under way, correcting the problems is usually much more difficult and expensive, and sometimes it is impossible, creating permanent limitations on the effectiveness of the system, as with the Bradley Fighting Vehicle.

Resistance to realistic testing also stems from concern that the test results, if publicly disclosed, may threaten the continuation of a program, as they clearly would have done in the case of the DIVAD. Program proponents, including both the contractor and those in the military service who have become committed to the program, are invariably optimistic that the system can be made to work effectively. If weaknesses are revealed by the objective reporting of realistic tests, it may make it more difficult for the program's supporters to convince the DOD civilian hierarchy and the Congress of the program's worth, particularly in an environment of increasingly scarce budget resources.

Because of the importance of testing prototypes before approval is given to production of a system, there is increasing support for the "fly before you buy" approach to procurement. In this approach, the design and development of a system is fully separated from the production of that system. Sometimes this concept is taken a step further, to the development of competing designs intended to meet a stated military requirement, with only one of the two (or more) designs being chosen for further development and eventual production.

In the recent program to develop the next generation of Air Force fighter aircraft, for example, two separate design teams (each representing a consortium of contractors and subcontractors) were required to go through the design and early development stages in parallel, to the point of building a prototype aircraft. The two prototypes were then flown in a competitive performance test. While both designs apparently satisfied the basic requirements, the Air Force found that certain performance differences were sufficient to allow it to choose one design over the other. That team will continue to develop its design and presumably will eventually produce it, while the other team was dropped.

The approach of "fly before you buy" has clear advantages in terms of producing effective weapons systems. However, it has clear costs, as well. One of those costs is the delayed delivery of the system. As noted earlier, the testing process can add considerable time--as much as several years in some cases--to the procurement process, particularly if it reveals the need for design changes. In the meantime, the military services must make do with existing weapons. In the event of a military emergency, the new weapon--even if not fully tested--may be enough of an improvement over those currently available to make a difference in battle. In addition, while the weapon is being tested, the factory in which it is to be manufactured may be standing idle. If the period of idleness is lengthy, the skilled work force required to produce the system may disperse and it may prove difficult to reassemble the workers when approval for production is eventually granted.

The competitive testing of alternative prototypes raises a different problem. Who pays for the cost of the two (or more) designs and prototypes? In the Air Force example cited previously, the government agreed to reimburse both teams for the costs they incurred up to a specified limit in designing and constructing the competing prototype. Both teams reportedly exceeded the limits by a considerable margin, with the excess financed by the companies supporting the team. The winning team has some prospect of recouping this investment from the profits on future contracts to develop the system. The losing team, however, can only hope to do so through the profits from other contracts. It remains to be seen whether or not contractors will be willing to participate in such a competition in the future unless assured that all their costs will be reimbursed.

CAN THE PROBLEMS BE SOLVED?

In the decades since the end of the Second World War, the US government has tried a number of different approaches in its search for ways of obtaining from US industrial firms effective weapons incorporating the latest technological advances, and doing so with reasonable speed and at a reasonable cost.

The effort to obtain technologically advanced weapons appears to have been largely successful. In most areas of weaponry, the systems available to US forces are superior to those of any potential adversary, although there are some notable exceptions. (The US M-16 rifle, for example, is widely regarded as being inferior to the much simpler and more reliable Russian AK-47. It is also believed by some that Russian and Israeli air-to-air missiles are superior to their US counterparts.) The US procurement system has been much less successful, however, in terms of the speed with which new ideas are translated into weapons available to the military services and the cost of doing so. Of the various approaches that have been tried, none has really overcome these problems.[5]

The fact that so many different forms of contractual relationship between the government and the contractor have been tried without solving the cost and timeliness problems suggests that the solution does not lie in further "reforms" in this area. The US General Accounting Office, for example, is convinced that the problem grows out of the culture in which weapons acquisition decisions are made. This culture, defined as the "collective patterns of behavior exhibited by the numerous participants in the acquisition process and the incentives for that behavior," has evolved as the acquisition process has become a vehicle for meeting the diverse needs of participants through the steady initiation and sustaining of weapon programs.

> *These needs, as translated into weapon systems, transcend the filling of voids in military capability at minimal cost; they involve the definition of roles and missions, the justifications of budget levels and shares, service reputations, organizational influence, the industrial base, jobs and careers.*
>
> *Individually, participants act rationally, for they see their needs as aligned with the national interests. However, collectively, these needs create an environment that encourages "selling" program, along with undue optimism, parochialism, and other compromises of good judgment.*
>
> (US General Accounting Office, 1992)

Correcting the problems will require fundamental change in that culture.

So long as the military services continue to demand complex, highly sophisticated weapons incorporating the latest technological advances, the design and development of those weapons will remain a high risk endeavor, for which the costs and the time to achieve the desired effectiveness in the weapon will remain uncertain. In these circumstances, it is inevitable that contractors will undertake this development effort only if they are highly confident that their costs will be recovered either explicitly (through cost-based contracts) or implicitly (through after-the-fact reimbursement of cost overruns on fixed-price contracts).

Similarly, so long as the military services continue to request or approve changes in the design of weapons, in the quantity to be bought, and the rate at which they will be purchased, well into the production stage of the procurement process, that phase, too, will be subject to uncertain costs, with similar results. Unless these uncertainties can be greatly reduced, it is folly to believe that costs can be controlled through the character of the contract document. Contractors will, in fact, be reimbursed for their costs, regardless of the form of the contract.

The search for more effective ways to control costs, therefore, should not center on tinkering with the form of the contract, but on reducing or controlling the sources of risk, where that is possible, and on changing other aspects of the relationship between the government and the contractor. To a considerable degree, this is two ways of saying the same thing because the government's own behavior creates many of the risks for which the government must later pay the bill:

-- the overwhelming desire of the military services for the most advanced weapons possible creates much of the technological risk in the development stage;

-- concurrency, or the decision to proceed with production before completion of testing, leads to the need for expensive design changes in the production stage;

-- the acceptance or request for innumerable changes throughout the design and production stages creates instability and adds substantially to costs;

-- unanticipated changes in funding, and resulting changes in production rates and quantities, adds further to costs.

Until these sources of risk can be brought under control, there is little likelihood of avoiding the massive cost overruns and lengthy delays in the weapons development cycle that have characterized the defense procurement process in the past. Controlling these factors, however, will require a different view of the relationship between government and defense contractors and different behavior by those on the government side.

It has often been said that the relationship should be seen as a "partnership," implying that the two parties to the contract share common goals and objectives. This is a fallacy. No doubt both parties are patriotic and each is surely committed to its view of the national interest. Beyond this point, the goals and objectives diverge. The contractor's interest lies in assuring sufficient work to support a skilled and highly paid work force with sufficient profits to compensate for its invested capital. The government's interest should lie in acquiring the most effective weapons when they are needed at reasonable cost. These interests can lead in very different directions with regard to scheduling and cost control. It seems evident that in the past the contractor's interests have carried substantially more weight than the government's.

Inadequate concern for the government's true interests reflects, in significant degree, the fact that those responsible for protecting the government's interests are often amateurs in managing a very complex business relationship. They lack both the knowledge and the experience of their counterparts from the contracting firm, placing them at a marked disadvantage in the negotiating process. In addition, however, they face severe constraints in their ability to negotiate, imposed by the parochial interests of the military service to which they belong (and to which they must look for future career advancement) and by the often narrow, short-term political interests of their civilian superiors in the Defense Department and in the Congress.

As others have suggested, one step that is clearly needed is the movement toward greater professionalism in the government's procurement work force. Accomplishing this will require greater specialization and substantial investment in developing the skills required for effective performance of this function on the part of both the military officers and the civil servants who will be responsible for acquiring major weapons. In principal, this part of the challenge can be defined clearly, although meeting that challenge will be difficult in a DOD environment that, historically, has resisted such changes.

Other aspects of the problem will be even more difficult. For example, major improvements in the efficiency of the procurement process will require that ways be found to insulate procurement officials who must make difficult decisions. They will need to be protected from the political pressures that--in the past--have encouraged, or even forced them to engage in such costly practices as "stretch-outs," required by unanticipated fluctuations in annual funding levels, and the continuation of production of systems that are not needed, justified solely by the desire to avoid laying off workers. Finding answers in this area will require going to the heart of what it means to "manage" the affairs of government in a system of democratic pluralism.

GENERALIZING FROM THE US EXPERIENCE

The US government has tried in numerous ways to assure an equitable sharing of risk with defense industrial firms and to create other incentives to control costs. None of these efforts has been truly successful. This experience may be instructive in considering how to manage risk in other government/private sector endeavors.

It is possible that the impediments to risk sharing and cost control discussed in this paper are uniquely associated with the US weapons procurement process, but that seems unlikely. The general reluctance of democratic governments to accept the demise of major economic entities and the willingness in many countries to provide large subsidies to prevent that outcome suggests that some of these considerations are virtually universal. Thus the appearance of risk sharing between government and a private firm may prove to be illusory in circumstances other than the US weapons procurement process.

In the US experience, a considerable element of risk came from efforts to employ untested technologies. In other situations that may be a less significant source of risk, although counterparts can often be found. (Unanticipated soil or geologic conditions or the need to overcome unexpected environmental problems, for example, can cause dramatic increases in construction costs.) But technology is not the only source of risk in the US experience and often has not been the most important.

A firm may lose control of the costs of a project for a variety of reasons. A sudden acceleration of inflation or an adverse shift in exchange rates may render previous cost estimates unrealistic. A firm may also lose control because of managerial carelessness or mistakes or the lack of reliable financial systems to track costs. Whatever the source of the cost growth, it may be particularly difficult to enforce a fixed price contract (or other rigid risk sharing arrangement) if the firm has an especially strong bargaining position vis-a-vis the government.

In some cases, this strong position might reflect special political influence but that need not be the case. It might also result from the firm being the largest (or the only one) of its type in the country. This could lead to a perception that the firm was a vital national asset, warranting protection comparable to that of a major US defense firm.

A firm's bargaining position may also reflect the nature of the project on which it is working. If a project is of sufficient public importance, such as the completion of a vital link in a nation's transportation network, it is quite likely that a serious miscalculation of the risks will generate great pressure for the government to absorb the additional costs. The private "partner," for example, may choose to cease work and withdraw from the project rather than continue to absorb growing losses-- particularly if those losses threaten the financial viability of the firm. Shifting to another contractor in the event of such a default, in addition to delaying the completion of the project, may not solve the cost problem. Any successor firm, aware of the problems of its predecessor, will demand a more satisfactory financial arrangement.

This discussion is intended to suggest that it is very difficult to establish a truly arms-length business relationship between a government and a firm in the private sector. It is especially difficult to do so on a large project of major public significance and visibility. On such a project, the government is not just another customer and it is unlikely to be indifferent to the economic fate of its supplier or partner. Under these circumstances, wise policy would include considerable skepticism about the extent to which risk has, in fact, been shifted to the private firm, whatever the literal terms of the contract or other agreement.

Thus, drawing on the US experience, it can be very naive to rely on the use of fixed-price contracts or other rigid arrangements to allocate risk and to provide incentives to control costs. If too much risk is shifted to the contractor, it may be self-defeating. Such contracts seem appropriate in a limited set of circumstances in which careful analysis demonstrates that

-- the project relies on proven technology and appropriate tests (soil samples, geologic surveys, etc.) have been performed to preclude unanticipated technical problems of major proportions;

-- the work to be done is well-defined and not subject to change in scope or schedule, the source of much of the cost growth in US weapons programs; and

-- any economic policy risks are well-understood and can be readily handled within the resources of the business firm, including the use of hedging mechanisms, if warranted.

In the absence of a high degree of confidence on each of these points, a more flexible risk sharing arrangement is probably preferable, in that it avoids the illusion that the risk has been shifted.

The greater the government's exposure to risk (either explicit or implied) the greater the need for government oversight of the project and of the contractor's performance. It would always seem wise to maintain some degree of oversight of any project in which there is government involvement or in which there is some other strong public interest. In some circumstances the needed oversight may be quite modest. Even on purely "private" construction projects in the US, for example, it is customary to perform inspections of compliance with health and safety regulations. If government resources are involved, even in what is believed to be a relatively risk-free project, periodic review is usually warranted to assure effective performance by the contractor and to provide early warning in the event of serious technical or managerial problems that might necessitate intervention.

In other situations, more intensive oversight may be needed. For example, if the government faces significant risk of being required to cover cost growth, it would be wise to maintain careful scrutiny of contractor costs, both to assure that any costs allocated to the project are proper and to assure that the contractor is managing and controlling the costs. Furthermore, in a publicly financed construction project, protecting the public interest often will require on-site observation and appropriate testing to assure that the work is being performed in accordance with the agreed specifications.

Effectively employing private sector firms in the execution of major public sector projects is not a simple matter. Success requires that the relationship be wisely managed. A further lesson from the US experience is the importance of a strong government team, both in negotiating the arrangements and in overseeing the implementation of the project. The members of the team need to be held accountable for the successful and efficient completion of the project while being insulated from the conflicting pressures seen among participants in the US weapons procurement process. Continuity of leadership is also important to strengthen accountability and to build a sense of professional responsibility for the outcome of the project. Finally, the team should contain the professional skills needed to manage the relationship with the contractor. These usually include substantive knowledge (such as strong technical or engineering experience, if appropriate for the particular project), managerial training and experience, and negotiating talent.

It is often appropriate and frequently essential to involve private sector firms in the execution of major public sector projects. For the public/private relationship to contribute to the efficient provision of public services, however, that relationship must be wisely and actively managed by the government. Regardless of the form of the contract or other agreement with the private firm, a government may expose itself to considerable financial risk and to the possible failure of the project if it assumes otherwise.

NOTES

1. It is possible for a business firm to hedge against some of these risks, such as fluctuation in exchange rates, but the cost of doing so will be reflected in the contract price.

2. In addition to being the largest airplane ever built at the time, the C-5 incorporated a number of other innovations, such as cargo doors at both ends of the fuselage, and was intended to be capable of landing on primitive runways. These added considerably to the design challenge and to the eventual cost of the airplane.

3. Gregory (1989) is particularly strident on this point.

4. The previously cited DOD Acquisition Law Advisory Panel was organized for the purpose of identifying legal and regulatory changes that would facilitate the use of commercially available items. Its report contains an extensive list of suggested revisions.

5. A possible exception may be found in the "black" programs, with their reduced bureaucratic constraints. Too little is known about the outcomes of these programs, however, to reach any firm conclusions.

BIBLIOGRAPHY

Acting Under Secretary of Defense (Acquisition) (1991), Memorandum, April 15.

Boston Globe (1986), "Defense Spending Spurs the State Economy," August 17. Cited in FOX (1988), *The Defense Management Challenge: Weapons Acquisition*, Harvard Business School Press, Boston..

Department of Defense (1993), *Streamlining Defense Acquisition Laws*, Report of the Acquisition Law Advisory Panel, January.

FOX, J. Ronald (1988), *The Defense Management Challenge: Weapons Acquisition*, Harvard Business School Press, Boston.

GOODMAN, Sherri Wasserman, "Legal Dilemmas in the Weapons Acquisition Process: The Procurement of the SSN-688 Attack Submarine," 6 *Yale Law and Policy Review* 393, 1988.

GREGORY, William H. (1989), *The Defense Procurement Mess*, Lexington Books, Lexington, Massachusetts.

STUBBING, Richard A. (1986), *The Defense Game*, Harper and Row, New York.

US General Accounting Office (1971a), *Contractual Features and Related Matters in the S-3A Aircraft Program*, B-163058, March 29.

US General Accounting Office (1971b), *Contractual Features and Related Matters in the AWACS Aircraft Program*, B-163058, June 30.

US General Accounting Office (1992), *Weapons Acquisition: A Rare Opportunity for Lasting Change*, GAO/NSIAD-93-15, December.

US General Accounting Office (1993a), *Navy Ships: Problems Continue to Plague the Seawolf Submarine Program*, GAO/NSIAD-93-171, August.

US General Accounting Office (1993b), *B-2 Bomber, Comparison of Operational Capabilities and Support Costs for 15 Versus 20 Aircraft*, GAO/NSIAD-93-209, August.

US General Accounting Office (1993c), *Navy Contract: AOE-6 Shipbuilding Claims Settled but More Delays and Cost Growth Likely*, GAO/NSIAD-93-298, September.

MAIN SALES OUTLETS OF OECD PUBLICATIONS
PRINCIPAUX POINTS DE VENTE DES PUBLICATIONS DE L'OCDE

ARGENTINA – ARGENTINE
Carlos Hirsch S.R.L.
Galería Güemes, Florida 165, 4° Piso
1333 Buenos Aires   Tel. (1) 331.1787 y 331.2391
                            Telefax: (1) 331.1787

AUSTRALIA – AUSTRALIE
D.A. Information Services
648 Whitehorse Road, P.O.B 163
Mitcham, Victoria 3132   Tel. (03) 873.4411
                                  Telefax: (03) 873.5679

AUSTRIA – AUTRICHE
Gerold & Co.
Graben 31
Wien I   Tel. (0222) 533.50.14

BELGIUM – BELGIQUE
Jean De Lannoy
Avenue du Roi 202
B-1060 Bruxelles   Tel. (02) 538.51.69/538.08.41
                          Telefax: (02) 538.08.41

CANADA
Renouf Publishing Company Ltd.
1294 Algoma Road
Ottawa, ON K1B 3W8   Tel. (613) 741.4333
                                Telefax: (613) 741.5439
Stores:
61 Sparks Street
Ottawa, ON K1P 5R1   Tel. (613) 238.8985
211 Yonge Street
Toronto, ON M5B 1M4   Tel. (416) 363.3171
                                Telefax: (416)363.59.63

Les Éditions La Liberté Inc.
3020 Chemin Sainte-Foy
Sainte-Foy, PQ G1X 3V6   Tel. (418) 658.3763
                                  Telefax: (418) 658.3763

Federal Publications Inc.
165 University Avenue, Suite 701
Toronto, ON M5H 3B8   Tel. (416) 860.1611
                                Telefax: (416) 860.1608

Les Publications Fédérales
1185 Université
Montréal, QC H3B 3A7   Tel. (514) 954.1633
                                Telefax : (514) 954.1635

CHINA – CHINE
China National Publications Import
Export Corporation (CNPIEC)
16 Gongti E. Road, Chaoyang District
P.O. Box 88 or 50
Beijing 100704 PR   Tel. (01) 506.6688
                          Telefax: (01) 506.3101

DENMARK – DANEMARK
Munksgaard Book and Subscription Service
35, Nørre Søgade, P.O. Box 2148
DK-1016 København K   Tel. (33) 12.85.70
                                Telefax: (33) 12.93.87

FINLAND – FINLANDE
Akateeminen Kirjakauppa
Keskuskatu 1, P.O. Box 128
00100 Helsinki

Subscription Services/Agence d'abonnements :
P.O. Box 23
00371 Helsinki   Tel. (358 0) 12141
                      Telefax: (358 0) 121.4450

FRANCE
OECD/OCDE
Mail Orders/Commandes par correspondance:
2, rue André-Pascal
75775 Paris Cedex 16   Tel. (33-1) 45.24.82.00
                                Telefax: (33-1) 49.10.42.76
                                Telex: 640048 OCDE
Orders via Minitel, France only/
Commandes par Minitel, France exclusivement :
36 15 OCDE
OECD Bookshop/Librairie de l'OCDE :
33, rue Octave-Feuillet
75016 Paris   Tel. (33-1) 45.24.81.67
                      (33-1) 45.24.81.81
Documentation Française
29, quai Voltaire
75007 Paris   Tel. 40.15.70.00
Gibert Jeune (Droit-Économie)
6, place Saint-Michel
75006 Paris   Tel. 43.25.91.19
Librairie du Commerce International
10, avenue d'Iéna
75016 Paris   Tel. 40.73.34.60
Librairie Dunod
Université Paris-Dauphine
Place du Maréchal de Lattre de Tassigny
75016 Paris   Tel. (1) 44.05.40.13
Librairie Lavoisier
11, rue Lavoisier
75008 Paris   Tel. 42.65.39.95
Librairie L.G.D.J. - Montchrestien
20, rue Soufflot
75005 Paris   Tel. 46.33.89.85
Librairie des Sciences Politiques
30, rue Saint-Guillaume
75007 Paris   Tel. 45.48.36.02
P.U.F.
49, boulevard Saint-Michel
75005 Paris   Tel. 43.25.83.40
Librairie de l'Université
12a, rue Nazareth
13100 Aix-en-Provence   Tel. (16) 42.26.18.08
Documentation Française
165, rue Garibaldi
69003 Lyon   Tel. (16) 78.63.32.23
Librairie Decitre
29, place Bellecour
69002 Lyon   Tel. (16) 72.40.54.54

GERMANY – ALLEMAGNE
OECD Publications and Information Centre
August-Bebel-Allee 6
D-53175 Bonn   Tel. (0228) 959.120
                      Telefax: (0228) 959.12.17

GREECE – GRÈCE
Librairie Kauffmann
Mavrokordatou 9
106 78 Athens   Tel. (01) 32.55.321
                        Telefax: (01) 36.33.967

HONG-KONG
Swindon Book Co. Ltd.
13-15 Lock Road
Kowloon, Hong Kong   Tel. 366.80.31
                                Telefax: 739.49.75

HUNGARY – HONGRIE
Euro Info Service
Margitsziget, Európa Ház
1138 Budapest   Tel. (1) 111.62.16
                        Telefax : (1) 111.60.61

ICELAND – ISLANDE
Mál Mog Menning
Laugavegi 18, Pósthólf 392
121 Reykjavik   Tel. 162.35.23

INDIA – INDE
Oxford Book and Stationery Co.
Scindia House
New Delhi 110001   Tel.(11) 331.5896/5308
                            Telefax: (11) 332.5993
17 Park Street
Calcutta 700016   Tel. 240832

INDONESIA – INDONÉSIE
Pdii-Lipi
P.O. Box 269/JKSMG/88
Jakarta 12790   Tel. 583467
                        Telex: 62 875

ISRAEL
Praedicta
5 Shatner Street
P.O. Box 34030
Jerusalem 91430   Tel. (2) 52.84.90/1/2
                            Telefax: (2) 52.84.93
R.O.Y.
P.O. Box 13056
Tel Aviv 61130   Tél. (3) 49.61.08
                          Telefax (3) 544.60.39

ITALY – ITALIE
Libreria Commissionaria Sansoni
Via Duca di Calabria 1/1
50125 Firenze   Tel. (055) 64.54.15
                        Telefax: (055) 64.12.57
Via Bartolini 29
20155 Milano   Tel. (02) 36.50.83
Editrice e Libreria Herder
Piazza Montecitorio 120
00186 Roma   Tel. 679.46.28
                      Telefax: 678.47.51
Libreria Hoepli
Via Hoepli 5
20121 Milano   Tel. (02) 86.54.46
                        Telefax: (02) 805.28.86
Libreria Scientifica
Dott. Lucio de Biasio 'Aeiou'
Via Coronelli, 6
20146 Milano   Tel. (02) 48.95.45.52
                        Telefax: (02) 48.95.45.48

JAPAN – JAPON
OECD Publications and Information Centre
Landic Akasaka Building
2-3-4 Akasaka, Minato-ku
Tokyo 107   Tel. (81.3) 3586.2016
                    Telefax: (81.3) 3584.7929

KOREA – CORÉE
Kyobo Book Centre Co. Ltd.
P.O. Box 1658, Kwang Hwa Moon
Seoul   Tel. 730.78.91
              Telefax: 735.00.30

MALAYSIA – MALAISIE
Co-operative Bookshop Ltd.
University of Malaya
P.O. Box 1127, Jalan Pantai Baru
59700 Kuala Lumpur
Malaysia   Tel. 756.5000/756.5425
                  Telefax: 757.3661

MEXICO – MEXIQUE
Revistas y Periodicos Internacionales S.A. de C.V.
Florencia 57 - 1004
Mexico, D.F. 06600   Tel. 207.81.00
                                Telefax : 208.39.79

NETHERLANDS – PAYS-BAS
SDU Uitgeverij Plantijnstraat
Externe Fondsen
Postbus 20014
2500 EA's-Gravenhage   Tel. (070) 37.89.880
Voor bestellingen: Telefax: (070) 34.75.778

**NEW ZEALAND
NOUVELLE-ZÉLANDE**
Legislation Services
P.O. Box 12418
Thorndon, Wellington   Tel. (04) 496.5652
   Telefax: (04) 496.5698

NORWAY – NORVÈGE
Narvesen Info Center – NIC
Bertrand Narvesens vei 2
P.O. Box 6125 Etterstad
0602 Oslo 6   Tel. (022) 57.33.00
   Telefax: (022) 68.19.01

PAKISTAN
Mirza Book Agency
65 Shahrah Quaid-E-Azam
Lahore 54000   Tel. (42) 353.601
   Telefax: (42) 231.730

PHILIPPINE – PHILIPPINES
International Book Center
5th Floor, Filipinas Life Bldg.
Ayala Avenue
Metro Manila   Tel. 81.96.76
   Telex 23312 RHP PH

PORTUGAL
Livraria Portugal
Rua do Carmo 70-74
Apart. 2681
1200 Lisboa   Tel.: (01) 347.49.82/5
   Telefax: (01) 347.02.64

SINGAPORE – SINGAPOUR
Gower Asia Pacific Pte Ltd.
Golden Wheel Building
41, Kallang Pudding Road, No. 04-03
Singapore 1334   Tel. 741.5166
   Telefax: 742.9356

SPAIN – ESPAGNE
Mundi-Prensa Libros S.A.
Castelló 37, Apartado 1223
Madrid 28001   Tel. (91) 431.33.99
   Telefax: (91) 575.39.98

Libreria Internacional AEDOS
Consejo de Ciento 391
08009 – Barcelona   Tel. (93) 488.30.09
   Telefax: (93) 487.76.59

Llibreria de la Generalitat
Palau Moja
Rambla dels Estudis, 118
08002 – Barcelona
   (Subscripcions) Tel. (93) 318.80.12
   (Publicacions) Tel. (93) 302.67.23
   Telefax: (93) 412.18.54

SRI LANKA
Centre for Policy Research
c/o Colombo Agencies Ltd.
No. 300-304, Galle Road
Colombo 3   Tel. (1) 574240, 573551-2
   Telefax: (1) 575394, 510711

SWEDEN – SUÈDE
Fritzes Information Center
Box 16356
Regeringsgatan 12
106 47 Stockholm   Tel. (08) 690.90.90
   Telefax: (08) 20.50.21

Subscription Agency/Agence d'abonnements :
Wennergren-Williams Info AB
P.O. Box 1305
171 25 Solna   Tel. (08) 705.97.50
   Téléfax : (08) 27.00.71

SWITZERLAND – SUISSE
Maditec S.A. (Books and Periodicals - Livres
et périodiques)
Chemin des Palettes 4
Case postale 266
1020 Renens   Tel. (021) 635.08.65
   Telefax: (021) 635.07.80

Librairie Payot S.A.
4, place Pépinet
CP 3212
1002 Lausanne   Tel. (021) 341.33.48
   Telefax: (021) 341.33.45

Librairie Unilivres
6, rue de Candolle
1205 Genève   Tel. (022) 320.26.23
   Telefax: (022) 329.73.18

Subscription Agency/Agence d'abonnements :
Dynapresse Marketing S.A.
38 avenue Vibert
1227 Carouge   Tel.: (022) 308.07.89
   Telefax : (022) 308.07.99

See also – Voir aussi :
OECD Publications and Information Centre
August-Bebel-Allee 6
D-53175 Bonn (Germany)   Tel. (0228) 959.120
   Telefax: (0228) 959.12.17

TAIWAN – FORMOSE
Good Faith Worldwide Int'l. Co. Ltd.
9th Floor, No. 118, Sec. 2
Chung Hsiao E. Road
Taipei   Tel. (02) 391.7396/391.7397
   Telefax: (02) 394.9176

THAILAND – THAÏLANDE
Suksit Siam Co. Ltd.
113, 115 Fuang Nakhon Rd.
Opp. Wat Rajbopith
Bangkok 10200   Tel. (662) 225.9531/2
   Telefax: (662) 222.5188

TURKEY – TURQUIE
Kültür Yayinlari Is-Türk Ltd. Sti.
Atatürk Bulvari No. 191/Kat 13
Kavaklidere/Ankara   Tel. 428.11.40 Ext. 2458
Dolmabahce Cad. No. 29
Besiktas/Istanbul   Tel. 260.71.88
   Telex: 43482B

UNITED KINGDOM – ROYAUME-UNI
HMSO
Gen. enquiries   Tel. (071) 873 0011
Postal orders only:
P.O. Box 276, London SW8 5DT
Personal Callers HMSO Bookshop
49 High Holborn, London WC1V 6HB
   Telefax: (071) 873 8200
Branches at: Belfast, Birmingham, Bristol, Edinburgh, Manchester

UNITED STATES – ÉTATS-UNIS
OECD Publications and Information Centre
2001 L Street N.W., Suite 700
Washington, D.C. 20036-4910   Tel. (202) 785.6323
   Telefax: (202) 785.0350

VENEZUELA
Libreria del Este
Avda F. Miranda 52, Aptdo. 60337
Edificio Galipán
Caracas 106   Tel. 951.1705/951.2307/951.1297
   Telegram: Libreste Caracas

Subscription to OECD periodicals may also be placed through main subscription agencies.

Les abonnements aux publications périodiques de l'OCDE peuvent être souscrits auprès des principales agences d'abonnement.

Orders and inquiries from countries where Distributors have not yet been appointed should be sent to: OECD Publications Service, 2 rue André-Pascal, 75775 Paris Cedex 16, France.

Les commandes provenant de pays où l'OCDE n'a pas encore désigné de distributeur peuvent être adressées à : OCDE, Service des Publications, 2, rue André-Pascal, 75775 Paris Cedex 16, France.

11-1994

OECD PUBLICATIONS, 2 rue André-Pascal, 75775 PARIS CEDEX 16
PRINTED IN FRANCE
(42 94 56 1) ISBN 92-64-14306-8 - No. 47621 1994
ISSN 1023-0726